INTERIOR
DESIGN IN
PRACTICE

INTERIOR DESIGN IN PRACTICE

Case Studies of Successful Business Models

Terri L. Maurer, FASID, and Katie Weeks

WILEY

John Wiley & Sons, Inc.

Published by John Wiley & Sons, Inc., Hoboken, New Jersey
Published simultaneously in Canada

For general information about our other products and services, please contact our Customer Care Department within the United States at (800) 762-2974, outside the United States at (317) 572-3993 or fax (317) 572-4002.

Wiley also publishes its books in a variety of electronic formats. Some content that appears in print may not be available in electronic books. For more information about Wiley products, visit our web site at www.wiley.com.

Library of Congress Cataloging-in-Publication Data:

Maurer, Terri L.
  The business of interior design : case studies of practice / by Terri L. Maurer and Katie Weeks.
     p.   cm.
  ISBN 978-0-470-19053-1 (pbk. : alk. paper)
  1. Interior decoration–Practice–United States–Case studies.   2. Interior decoration firms–United States–Management–Case studies.   I. Weeks, Katie. II. Title.   III. Title: Case studies of practice.
  NK2116.2.M38 2009
  747.068–dc22

                                                                      2009011954

Printed in the United States of America

10 9 8 7 6 5 4 3 2 1

Contents

Preface   *ix*

Part I: Starting an Interior Design Business   *1*

Chapter 1: The Beginning   *3*

Why Do You Want to Have Your Own Business?   *3*

Will You Make the Cut?   *4*

Do You Have What It Takes?   *5*

The ABCs of Planning   *6*

    Business Planning vs. Strategic Planning: Johnson Consulting Services   *6*

    Thinking Ahead: Peterson-Arce Design Group   *8*

    Thinking Strategically: Carson Guest Interior Design Services Inc.   *9*

Financial Planning   *10*

    Sound Structure: Daroff Design Inc. + DDI Architects PC   *11*

Establishing Fees: Deciding What You Are Worth   *13*

Protecting Your Business: Insurance and Contracts   *18*

    Preparing for Risk: Buying Insurance   *18*

    Complete Contracts = Profitable Projects   *20*

Setting Up Shop   *23*

    Location, Location, Location   *23*

Looking Back for Those Moving Forward   *25*

    Advice in Hindsight: If I Were Starting a Firm Today   *26*

Chapter 2:   Structure and Support   29

    Building the Team   29
        Finding Their Motivation: Rabaut Design Associates   31
    Help Wanted: Finding Team Members   32
        Getting Started: Studio 2030   33
    Making the Cut   35
    Tips for Avoiding Costly Hiring Mistakes   35
    Going It Alone: Sole Practitioners   36
        Flying Solo: Patterson House Design Group   36
    In Process: Design Team Structure and Project Management   38
        Process Makes Perfect: Soucie Horner Ltd.   39
        Step-by-Step: Chute Gerdeman Retail   41
    Come Together: Working with Collaborators and Consultants   43
        LEEDing the Way: Ecoworks Studio   45
    Supply and Demand: Vendors and Suppliers   46
        Love the One You're With: Bullock Associates Design Consultants Inc.   46
        Love the One You're With, Part Two: Renwall Interiors Limited   47
        A Two-Way Street: Coopertech Signs & Graphics   48
    Clients and Customers   50
        Know Your Client   50
        Constant Communication: Duffy Design Group   51
        Keeping It Personal: Adesso Design Inc.   53
        Decoding the Design Process: Steven Miller Design Studio   54
        Building Long-Term Relationships: SJvD Design   55

Chapter 3:   Communications and Technology for a Modern Practice   59

    Who Are You? Creating the Brand   59
    What Is a Brand?   60
        A Decade of Design: JJ Falk Design LLC   63
        Repositioning, Rebranding, Reinventing: Pallädeo   67
    To Market, To Market: Marketing and Public Relations   71
    Being a Professional: Networking and Professional Organizations   74
    Integrating Technology   76
        The Wired Practice   76
        The Communications Business: Domus Design Group   78
    Log On   81
        Going Global, Going Mobile: Retail Clarity Consulting   81

Using the Web to Market Your Firm: Resolve Digital	*83*
Marketing through the Web: Merlino Design Partnership Inc.	*85*
Plugged In: Slifer Designs	*87*
Being a Professional: Ethics	*91*
Ethics in Business: The Designers Furniture Gallery	*91*
Being a Professional: Licensing and Certification	*93*

Part II: Sustaining and Growing Your Business

		99

Chapter 4: Taking Your Business to the Next Level

	101
Deciding When to Grow	*101*
Deciding How to Grow	*102*
On Her Own, but Not Alone: Mosaic Design Studio	*103*
Jumping Right In: Catlin Design Inc.	*105*
A Deeper Look at More Complicated Means of Growth	*107*
Deciding to Franchise	*107*
Picking a Franchise	*108*
Evaluating a Franchise Package: Questions to Ask	*109*
A Franchise in Practice: Designs of the Interior	*109*
Let's Make a Dealership	*111*
Finding the Right Mix: Elements IV Interiors	*111*
Ownership Transition: Contract Office Group	*114*
Residential Roots: Barbara Goodman Designs	*115*
A + B = C: Mergers and Acquisitions	*117*
Buying In: Larry Wilson Design Associates	*117*
Preparing for an Acquisition	*119*
A Successful Future: Sustaining Growth	*121*
Suite Success: Cole Martinez Curtis and Associates	*121*
Riding the Tide: Mancini Duffy	*123*
Open to the Possibilities: Wilson Associates	*125*
Parting Shot: A Sixty-Second Guide to Managing Growth over the Long Haul	*127*

Chapter 5: Transitioning from Small to Midsize and Large Firms

	129
Sprint to the Start: Diane Boyer Interiors	*129*
Getting It Down on Paper	*131*
Team in Training	*134*
Hire and Seek: Creative Business Interiors	*134*

Personnel Management Issues: Looking Outside for Internal Help   *136*

Creating Policies and Guidelines   *137*

Bringing in Benefits   *139*

Monitoring Growth and Progress   *140*

     Success in Seattle: EHS Design   *140*

     Added Responsibility: Sechrist Design Associates Inc.   *142*

Part III: The End Game   *149*

Chapter 6:   Planning for the Future   *151*

     Learning from Experience: KSA Interiors   *151*

Thinking Ahead   *154*

     The Value of Planning   *154*

Next in Line: Succession Planning   *159*

     An Action Plan for Succession   *159*

     Setting Goals: Facilities Connection   *161*

     Successful Succession: TRIO Design Group and David-Michael Design Inc.   *167*

     Conclusion   *171*

     Appendix A: ASID Sample Interior Design Services Agreements   *173*

     Appendix B: ASID Code of Ethics and Professional Conduct   *213*

     Notes   *217*

     Bibliography   *219*

     Index   *223*

Preface

From the slew of interior design magazines populating local newsstands to the twenty-four-hour schedules of cable television channels like HGTV and Fine Living, design is big business. A research publication completed in 2004 by the American Society of Interior Designers (ASID) revealed that there were 11,000 small interior design firms, and another 21,000 practicing as sole practitioners. Together, these two groups made up two-thirds of the interior design businesses operating in the United States. They're not just design fanatics, either: They're trained professionals. ASID's research further revealed that 95 percent of the designers surveyed hold college degrees, with 75 percent of them coming from a four- or five-year interior design program. Clearly, this expanding group of interior design professionals is highly educated in its chosen field.

So how do you stand out from the crowd? Consider the classroom to be a starting point. When it comes to curriculum, the basics of an interior design education are leveling out across the country, thanks in part to the influence of professional organizations like the Council for Interior Design Accreditation (CIDA, formerly FIDER, the Foundation for Interior Design Education Research) and National Council for Interior Design Qualifications (NCIDQ). But even with this background, most interior designers are missing one critical area of education: business acumen. For those who enter the profession assuming that they will become gainfully employed by a design firm and remain a paid employee for the duration of their career, the limited business courses included in a typical college curriculum for interior design may meet their needs. But for those with an entrepreneurial bent and an interest in one day either owning their own company or rising high in the managerial ranks of a larger practice, the business education incorporated into many of today's design programs is sorely lacking. A general business course in economics or marketing does not provide the background information required to open or support a stable business that will succeed in the marketplace over time.

Interior designers who want to run a successful practice often find themselves impeded by a lack of knowledge of how to begin the process of launching a business, as well as how to then grow the venture and take it to a higher level. *Interior Design in Practice: Case Studies of Successful Business Models* aims to help meet this need. Armed with a broad selection of business topics focused on planning, starting, and sustaining an interior design business, designers can begin thinking about how they can start a business of their own and how to grow that business toward their own vision of success. This is not, however, a textbook of facts and forms. It is, instead, a compilation of useful in-the-field advice, anecdotes, and information. In addition to discussing the basics of starting, operating, and growing a business, *Interior Design in Practice* includes firsthand case studies, examples, and advice from design and business professionals who have worked their way from fledgling startups to successful design firms that span the globe in projects and practice.

A collaborative effort by an experienced designer with nearly three decades of experience in a variety of interior design business models and a successful editor and writer with experience covering architectural and interiors practices of all sizes, this book is meant to assist an interior designer on topics that arise throughout the life of a thriving firm—ranging from the skills and traits that successful entrepreneurs possess, to the planning and development necessary to successfully begin a one-person operation and potentially transition to a variety of larger models. From there, *Interior Design in Practice* looks even further, working its way through the process of building a business with real value, and culminating in end-of-the-road issues like succession planning and selling the business.

There is a wide array of business textbooks on the market as well as a wealth of information online that address the more analytical side of starting or running an interiors practice. In complement to these resources, the from-the-trenches stories and advice encapsulated in the following pages are meant to serve not as hard and fast processes that must be followed to the minute detail, but rather as glimpses into the choices that may be made. The ultimate goal of *Interior Design in Practice* is to connect readers with their peers, an approach that also aligns with ASID's strategic goal of fostering a sense of community among interior design practitioners. This book is meant to live on the desk—not just the reference shelf—of both the budding entrepreneur and the seasoned design practitioner, to be reviewed at one's convenience on-site and at a minimal cost. It is meant as a stepping stone along the journey to success, to be augmented by the growing number of continuing education programs, business textbooks, and websites available to interior designers today.

As coauthors, we hope you find the insights on the forthcoming pages useful and entertaining. We'd be remiss if we did not thank here the contributors and interviewees who shared their trials and tribulations with us unabashedly. We hope you can learn from their experiences and challenges, but more important, from their successes—we certainly have.

Part I:
Starting an Interior Design Business

Chapter 1:
The Beginning

Interior design is a unique profession, one that flourishes on passion and innovation. It is a profession founded on variety, offering projects of all scopes and sizes, from intimate residential spaces to large-scale commercial ventures to the latest hotels and restaurants or state-of-the-art medical facilities, to name but a few. What's more, when interior designers leave for home at the end of the workday, they hardly leave their work at the office, as our everyday environments—our homes, grocery stores, doctor's offices, restaurants—are designed in some way, by someone. Should you seek them, inspiration and possibility abound at every turn.

Included in the realm of possibility are the myriad ways a designer can choose to operate. A professional interior designer may work within a larger firm, operate as a design consultant, or log hours as a retailer, educator, researcher, historian, critic, or journalist, or as a product and manufacturers' representative, among other options. Many interior designers, however, choose at some point to start their own firm. In fact, while large design firms often appear in the headlines, it is small firms with fewer than five employees that make up the bulk of the industry.

Why Do You Want to Have Your Own Business?

As many practicing designers come to learn, it is one thing to be inspired and another to be profitable. To be successful, interior designers must learn to balance unbridled creativity with practicality and professionalism. As exciting as the design field is, it is a competitive industry—and today, as in many industries, business savvy is just as essential as talent.

When it comes to the desire to hang one's own shingle, interior designers are not alone. Many do it. According to the National Foundation for Independent Business (NFIB), small businesses represent over 99 percent of all employers in America, with about 24 million such businesses in the United States alone.[1] With this scope, small business creates 60–80 percent of all new jobs in America.[2] Other interesting statistics:

- Small businesses generate more than 50 percent of the American nonfarm private gross domestic product (GDP).[3]

- The United States has almost 6 million small employers, 90 percent of which employ fewer than 20 people.[4]

- About 6–7 percent of the U.S. population is in the process of starting a business at any given time.[5]

- About 53 percent of new small businesses begin in the home with less than $10,000. Many start with borrowed capital and leased or used equipment. About 3 percent are franchises.[6]

Within this realm, interior design practices are an ever-growing segment. In its 2007 report *The Interior Design Profession: Facts and Figures*, the American Society of Interior Designers (ASID) found that between 2000 and 2005—a mere five years—the number of employed interior designers grew by more than 20,000, and from 2002 to 2006, the total number of interior design firms increased by 450.

In 2002 the U.S. Census Bureau classified interior design as an independent profession for the first time, separate from design in general (which also includes floral design, ceramic design, and graphic design). Under these new classifications, the Bureau of Labor Statistics estimated that in 2004 there were 65,000 interior designers employed in the United States, with about three in ten of those self-employed. However, ASID notes that privately conducted studies raise that overall total as high as 96,000 or even 112,000, depending on how you define a practicing interior designer.

Will You Make the Cut?

Success in business is never automatic, nor is it strictly based on luck—although a little luck never hurts. Success depends primarily on an owner's foresight and organization. Yet even then there are no guarantees.

Starting a small business is always risky, and the chance of success is slim. According to the U.S. Small Business Administration, roughly 50 percent of small businesses fail within the first five years. In his book *Small Business Management,* Michael Ames gives the following reasons for small business failure: lack of experience, insufficient capital or money, poor location, poor inventory management, overinvestment in fixed assets, poor credit arrangements, personal use of business funds, and/or unexpected growth.

Another business writer, Gustav Berle, added two more reasons in *The Do-It-Yourself Business Book*: competition and low sales.

Such odds might, and perhaps should, give the uninitiated pause. Underestimating the difficulty of starting a business is one of the biggest obstacles entrepreneurs face. However, success is achievable for those who are patient and willing to work hard, and who take all the necessary steps. It's true that there are many reasons not to start a business. But for the right person, the advantages of business ownership far outweigh the risks. You will be your own boss. Hard work and long hours directly benefit you, rather than increasing profits for someone else. Earning and growth potential are far greater. A new venture is as exciting as it is risky. Running a business provides endless challenge and opportunities for learning.

Do You Have What It Takes?

Is entrepreneurship for you? Consider the following advice from the U.S. Small Business Association[7]: In business, there are no guarantees. There is simply no way to eliminate all the risks associated with starting a small business—but you can improve your chances of success with good planning, preparation, and insight. Start by evaluating your strengths and weaknesses as a potential owner and manger of a small business. Carefully consider each of the following questions:

- Are you a self-starter? It will be entirely up to you to develop projects, organize your time, and follow through on details.

- How well do you get along with different personalities? Business owners need to develop working relationships with a variety of people, including customers, vendors, staff, bankers, and professionals such as lawyers, accountants, and consultants. Can you deal with a demanding client, an unreliable vendor, or a cranky receptionist if your business interests demand it?

- How good are you at making decisions? Small business owners are required to make decisions constantly—often quickly, independently, and under pressure.

- Do you have the physical and emotional stamina to run a business? Business ownership can be exciting, but it's also a lot of work. Can you face six or seven twelve-hour workdays every week?

- How well do you plan and organize? Research indicates that poor planning is responsible for most business failures. Good organization of financials, inventory, schedules, and production can help you avoid many pitfalls.

- Is your drive strong enough? Running a business can wear you down emotionally. Some business owners burn out quickly from having to carry all the responsibility for the success of their business on their own shoulders. Strong motivation will help you survive slowdowns and periods of burnout.

- How will the business affect your family? The first few years of business startup can be hard on family life. It's important for family members to know what to expect and for you to be able to trust that they will support you during this time. There also may be financial difficulties until the business becomes profitable, which could take months or years. You may have to adjust to a lower standard of living or put family assets at risk in the short term.

The ABCs of Planning

Although advice and anecdotes abound on things to consider when weighing the idea of opening your own interior design practice, there is consensus on the necessity of one aspect: planning. In a very basic overview, the necessary planning can be broken down into three realms: business planning, strategic planning, and financial planning. Financial planning is straightforward in its name, but business planning and strategic planning may be a little more confusing, as their exact definitions vary.

Let's take a moment to focus on business planning. Myriad resources are available for designers today that not only offer in-depth advice on how to structure a business plan but also provide templates to get you started. Typically, a plan at minimum contains an introduction that should entice readers to want to learn more about your specific business. This is often followed by an industry analysis that shows how your venture fits into the competitive landscape, a resume of the founder's (or founders') business accomplishments, and marketing and financial plans.

Strategic planning, by nature, is much more subjective and less formulaic, containing quantifiable, measurable steps specific to an individual firm's success.

Business Planning vs. Strategic Planning: Johnson Consulting Services

Johnson Consulting Services, founded by Jill Johnson in 1988, works with professional services companies, impacting business decisions valued in excess of half a billion dollars. The firm's client base of corporations, government agencies, and nonprofit organizations spans twenty-one states in the United States, as well as Europe and Asia. Bringing strong analytical and comprehensive research skills, objectivity, candor, and integrity to each client's project allows Johnson's firm to play an instrumental role in the clients' organizational and financial success.

There seems to be considerable confusion about business planning, strategic planning, and marketing plans in the business world. It is not uncommon to have all three terms used interchangeably in the course of a discussion. With this in mind, Jill Johnson, founder of Johnson Consulting Services (JCS) in Minneapolis, Minnesota, defines the differences.

Business planning is about the functional areas of business: operations, market analysis, competition,

---

pricing methodologies, and marketing mechanisms to reach customers. **Strategic planning** defines the vision, mission, and organizational values of the company, and develops a plan that will enable the company to move in those specifically defined directions.

The greatest difference between a strategic plan and a business plan is that the strategic plan will include performance indicators in the form of quantifiable measures. These indicators can be used as a scorecard to determine how well the firm is doing in achieving its vision, mission, goals, and objectives.

Business plans are usually prepared by those seeking funding from banks or investors to start their business, but that is not necessarily the best approach. According to Johnson, everyone going into business, whether they seek funding or not, should engage in business planning and research as a means for improving the business's chances of success. Preparing a business plan requires a significant amount of research, for example, into where a business will be located. Will it be in a home office, a storefront, or a showroom? Will there be one location or multiple locations? Potential competitors must also be researched, and target markets must be identified. Financials must be addressed: What is the cost of setting up the business and running it until a revenue stream is created? Cash management must be examined and, in conjunction, decisions made on who will represent the company's support team for banking, legal, and accounting expertise.

A good business plan should be grounded in reality. If a plan's scope is too broad, it extends beyond what is realistic for owners to accomplish and will likely fall by the wayside rather than serve as a guiding document upon which to build a solid business. A business plan should be revisited annually and revised in depth every three years or so to allow owners to reevaluate staffing, skill sets, locations, and financials as they relate to the original plan.

A strategic plan, on the other hand, defines the long-term vision and mission of the firm, identifying its organizational and cultural styles. While "long-term" can mean different things to different business owners, a strategic plan generally has an outlook of three to five years and comprises specific goals and objectives that move the company forward and are further supported by specific strategies and tactics that formulate the day-to-day operation of the business.

Unlike a business plan, a strategic plan incorporates quantifiable measures to allow owners to determine performance and success. Attaching measurable, quantifiable achievements like numerical increases in clients or projects makes it easy to determine whether a firm is successful. Attaching time frames to objectives also allows for easy review to assure elements are on track and on time. A good strategic plan creates a road map toward the organization's vision, providing small, measurable steps and stages to ensure forward motion. For instance, if the plan is to grow the business from a one-person operation to one with multiple designers on staff in numerous locations, strategies might address collaborating with other designers or firms early on to take on larger projects and achieve greater visibility before adding one or two in-house designers at a given point in time. Each strategy may have a number of tactical segments, all of which lead the firm toward that ultimate goal of being a larger entity with multiple locations.

In addition to business and strategic plans, owners should keep several other key factors in mind. First, it is crucial to develop the psychological mindset of a business owner, not just that of a designer. If your education or background has not provided the necessary ownership skills, a company's plan should also include strategies and funding to strengthen this skill set. Second, new business owners must keep reality in mind. While there is nothing to stop a business owner from growing beyond initial expectations, it is advisable to develop a realistic plan that will successfully get a business to one level before expanding to a higher, more challenging level. Third, owners must think long-term and begin planning their exit from the business from the start.

Thinking Ahead: Peterson-Arce Design Group

B. J. Peterson, FASID, is a long-time member of the interior design profession with forty-four years of practice in a number of capacities: staff designer, sole proprietor, showroom owner, retailer, and partner. In 2000, she entered into partnership with Hugo Arce, forming Peterson-Arce Design Group Inc. in the mid-Wilshire area of Los Angeles, with an auxiliary office in Laguna Beach, California. The firm works on high-end residential remodeling and reconstruction projects in Southern California ranging from small to multimillion-dollar budgets. Peterson has been an active member and fellow of the American Society of Interior Designers, serving as president of her local chapter, on the national board of directors, and as national president from 1992 to 1993. In addition, Peterson was chair of the board of trustees for the ASID Foundation from 2007 to 2008.

Although B. J. Peterson has far more industry experience than many designers in practice today, her introduction to the concept of strategic planning and management did not occur until she began serving on ASID's national board of directors in 1989. The Society had recently begun using this business management tool in an effort to move forward in an organized, focused manner. Accordingly, Peterson, along with other board members, was indoctrinated into the strategic planning and management process, including environmental scanning. Before long, she found herself using the planning concept for both her personal and business endeavors.

Looking for a way to ease into semiretirement and eventually complete retirement, Peterson used the strategic planning process to help her design a business model that would meet her needs: a small firm with one partner with whom she could build a valuable asset to sell as she eased into retirement.

Hugo Arce had worked with Peterson for some time at her previous design firm, B. J. Peterson Interior Design, and seemed the ideal partner for her plan. Peterson found that she and Arce shared standards of service and business ethics, focusing on a client's needs-based practice. There was also an age factor—Arce is twenty years younger than Peterson—and a gender-opposite fit. The new partnership not only accorded with Peterson's ideal structure, it also allowed Peterson and Arce to identify and develop the client base they wanted, creating a very targeted base upon which to build the firm's value for an eventual sale.

In May 2000 Peterson-Arce Design Group was born, first located on Melrose Place in Los Angeles and later moving to the Miracle Mile in the city's mid-Wilshire district. The move offered the team an opportunity to open a retail shop, The Home Grown Store, in an area with more affordable rent. The store, opened with a third partner, John Wilson, is another avenue for generating revenue for when Peterson or Arce want to slow down the design practice. On the design firm side, Peterson-Arce has one support person but no plans to add more staff or grow the firm.

From the firm's start, strategic planning and management has been the rule of order. Because of Peterson's extensive experience with the strategic planning process, Peterson-Arce Design Group generally does not bring in an outside facilitator to help with its planning; accordingly, Peterson is the partner most responsible for the planning process.

Each January or February the partners meet at Peterson's beach house in Laguna Beach to plan for the coming year. Occasionally, their office administrator or an outside facilitator is included, but usually it is just the two partners. The planning session lasts one day, with a few shorter, follow-up meetings that last a couple of hours each held back at the office in L.A. to firm up details. Once a plan is developed, it is reviewed every other month to be sure the firm remains on track. Reviews usually take place during regularly scheduled office meetings. "What is really important is keeping the plan active and not filed away in a drawer somewhere," says Peterson. "It's not the planning that is problematic as much as the implementation."

The typical Peterson-Arce plan includes the firm's vision and mission statements; specific, prioritized goals and objectives; and measurable strategies and tactics through which the firm will achieve its goals for the year. Seldom do Peterson and Arce change course in any major way once the plan is in place, but they understand the need to be ready to make quick changes when big issues—such as changes in the economy or rapidly rising gasoline prices—come along. Peterson believes that it is difficult to plan more than three years out, feeling that "anything beyond gets dicey." Occasionally, a few issues, like Peterson's retirement transition, might be planned out further in advance, but most of the focus remains on the current year as well as a year or two out.

As she learned to do through her experience with ASID's planning processes, Peterson frontloads the firm's process with environmental scanning of outside influences that may impact the firm. She reads business publications throughout the year, identifying issues that may affect the planning process and the firm's future. The most significant change she has noticed in the firm since implementing strategic planning is this long-term perspective. "We're not so focused on day-to-day issues and operations, but rather focused on the big picture and working toward it," she says. "We planned to have an administrative support person to pick up that end of the business so we could focus and work toward the big-picture goals, and the types of clients and projects we wanted to be developing." The biggest issue to be faced in the future is identifying a junior partner who, over time and with studious planning, will be positioned to buy out Peterson's stake in the firm as she moves into retirement. That planning, of course, is already underway.

Thinking Strategically: Carson Guest Interior Design Services Inc.

Rita Carson Guest, FASID, founder and president of nationally recognized and award-winning Carson Guest Interior Design Services Inc., established her firm in Atlanta in 1984. Since then she has grown from a solo practitioner to managing sixteen employees, with Guest serving as director of design for all projects, which include law offices, corporate offices, institutional, and special residential projects. Guest was the first interior designer registered in the state of Georgia, and also holds interior design licenses in Alabama, Florida, and Washington, D.C. In addition, she was the first interior designer appointed to the Georgia State Board of Architects, a position she held for ten years, and has served in ASID leadership at the national level, holding positions on the national board of directors and serving as national president from 2007 to 2008.

Like other interior designers who have served in leadership positions with the American Society of Interior Designers, Rita Carson Guest was indoctrinated into the strategic planning and management process during her time in service to the organization. For Guest, it was during her 1992–93 term on ASID's national board of directors that she realized this process could be used to help focus her own firm on planned, measured growth and success.

Prior to the move toward strategic planning and management, the firm had employed business consultants to assist with organization and planning for growth. Thanks to her ASID leadership, however, Guest's experience in strategic planning and management positioned her to facilitate and manage the strategic plans in-house, without the assistance of external business consultants.

In the early 1990s, an office retreat and inaugural strategic planning session was scheduled in New Orleans to get the process started. At the time, Guest felt the process would be an excellent way to bring the entire team in line with the strategic goals of the firm. Since that initial session, every three years the firm holds a daylong, off-site retreat to work on the strategic plan for the following five years.

Everyone in the firm participates in the process. They take advantage of ASID's annual environmental scanning report to assess possible outside influences, and use input from individual staff members as a starting point for the planning session. As the firm's owner, Guest maintains control of the process, and although it is just a one-day session it is not unusual for her to spend up to forty hours on preparation.

Stating that they should probably devote more time to the process and use it more effectively, Guest feels they could do a better job of measuring and evaluating their progress. But as busy as the firm is, its only measures of success are year-end profits and awards won. Given the turbulent economy of late 2008, Guest is considering scheduling another session to create new goals alongside a process to review how they work through a tough economy. "I believe this will take some of the fear out of everyone's concerns about what is coming next," she explains. "We have never laid off one person since I started the firm, and I do not plan to start now."

Guest believes that a strong plan, revised to meet the current environment, is a great way to start. Although Guest and her team seldom have time to review and revise the plan during the year, they have discussed the creation of a more streamlined process for design.

"Our fees are at the top of the market, and we are finding companies that want to hire us if we will match other firm's fees," she says. "Getting people to hire us has always been easy based on our reputation, but getting them to pay top dollar is more difficult."

To keep the firm in line with its goals, the company's vision and mission statements, along with its corporate values, were pulled from the strategic plan and framed for display in every office and workstation. This serves as a constant reminder to keep the whole team focused on the firm's plan, as well as who they are and where they are going. Has Guest seen success in the switch to strategic planning? "Yes," she says, "by focusing our efforts on excellent design and excellent service, and entering design competitions to validate our success." She also notes that the process has been a highly effective way to energize her team and give staff members pride in their contributions to the success of the firm, as well as making the firm a desired place to work and giving it a competitive edge by focusing on law office design.

Financial Planning

Another essential item on any entrepreneur's to-do list is the issue of financial planning. Passion will only get you so far. In the long run, it's finances that will make or break a business. How will you finance your firm? Will you borrow from friends or family to get started? Apply for a loan? Seek out business partners or silent investors? Apply for government assistance programs? Or simply charge it to Visa or Mastercard? Given the bleak picture of the global financial markets in recent years, saving as much as possible before venturing out on your own is highly recommended.

In considering finances, it's important to spend some time thinking about how a firm will be officially structured and how that chosen structure will in turn affect not only the business's profits and debts but also the owner's personal finances. In a sole proprietorship, for example, all profits earned belong to the owner, but so do all losses. In both an S corporation and a limited liability company (LLC), shareholders receive limited liability protection, and profits and losses are taxed on an individual's personal tax return. In many states, however, an LLC must be formed by at least two people, while an S corporation requires just one. If there is more than one owner involved, who will own the firm's real estate? What will happen financially should one partner in a two-person partnership want to leave? A firm's financial arrangements may also have direct impact on other certifications, which in turn may affect project opportunities.

Sound Structure: Daroff Design Inc. + DDI Architects PC

Daroff Design Inc. is a women-owned, full-service architecture and interior design firm headquartered in Philadelphia. Founded in 1973 by president and design principal Karen Daroff, the firm also is affiliated with an architectural partner, DDI Architects PC. Daroff Design Inc. specializes in the design of entertainment facilities, including themed hotels, resort properties, casinos, restaurants, and retail facilities, as well as corporate headquarters and conference and training centers. As a professional designer, Daroff was named Designer of the Year in 1990 by *Interiors* magazine and also has been named one of the Best 50 Women in Business in Pennsylvania by the governor of Pennsylvania.

When award-winning interior designer Karen Daroff first founded her Philadelphia-based interior design practice, Daroff Design Inc., in 1973, the professional landscape was a bit different than it is today. "At that time, architects were not very interested in the practice of interior design," she recalls. "Interior designers were under pressure to rationalize earning fees, while interior decorators were typically not charging fees but earning a profit on the purchase and resale of the furniture, finishes, and equipment they selected for their clients." Additional competition came from product manufacturers and their furniture dealers, who were offering free design services to their retail customers, in direct competition with her professional interior design practice.

In setting up her practice, Daroff focused on the programming, planning, and interior design of major corporate headquarters offices and operational facilities. The business quickly expanded to include large corporate conference and training centers, some of which also had adjacent hotels and restaurants. The practice's work grew even more from these hospitality projects, capitalizing on Daroff's growing passion to design destination hotels and resorts.

She structured the firm as a Subchapter S entity, which would allow her to plan her tax obligations both personally and corporately. Daroff also deliberately sought certification as a Women's Business Enterprise (WBE), which requires that at least 51 percent of the certified business be owned or controlled by one or more women who are American citizens or legal resident aliens; whose principal place of business is in the United States; and whose management and daily operations are controlled by one or more of the women owners. Her first certification was in Philadelphia, which also requires that WBE-certified businesses operate within the City of Philadelphia.

One benefit of such certification is that many government departments and agencies are required to give a certain percentage of their purchasing contracts to women-owned businesses. A similar process accommodates minority-owned businesses (MBE). "My interest in the women-owned business certification process began when Philadelphia's mayor issued an executive order setting aside a certain percentage of all of Philadelphia's governmental projects for companies owned by women and minorities," recalls Daroff.

As a 100 percent women-owned firm, Daroff Design Inc. benefited from local, regional, and national WBE certifications, joining project teams around the country where WBE certification was required or desired. Many of Daroff's national and international corporate clients also began to require project teams to include both WBE and MBE team members and suppliers. "It has been my experience that when these governmental set-asides and/or benchmarks have been in place, our firm and our WBE peers have been invited to participate on more projects that otherwise might have been assigned 100 percent to the major A&E firms," Daroff notes.

But not everyone was happy with Daroff's success. "A few architects began to question my success and wanted to take business away from me by telling clients we were not qualified to do this or that type of project because we could not offer full professional service and could not prepare and sign our client's project's permit documents," she recalls. "They, of course, were not correct in their comments, because from day one I employed talented architects who prepared, signed, and sealed DDI's drawings for building permits. But I realized that we needed to offer licensed architectural and professional services. At that time, many architectural firms had interior design departments. I thought we needed to have an architectural affiliate."

Back then and to this date, Daroff Design Inc. teams and collaborates with third-party architects on many of its corporate and hospitality projects. However, licensing for interior designers has more recently added another legal constraint to the practice of interior design on a national basis. What's more, Pennsylvania has not passed state licensing for interior designers; so, legally, in order to sign and seal permit documents in Pennsylvania (as well as in many other states), the architects functioning as architect-of-record must be majority shareholders in the business and be insured for professional liability.

To address this legal requirement and to provide the full range of service Daroff's clients were requesting, DDI Architects PC was founded as a licensed architectural entity owned by Daroff's husband, Jim Rappoport.

In creating DDI Architects, Daroff was careful not to put Daroff Design Inc.'s WBE certification at risk.

Legally, a non-WBE-certified entity cannot exert undue control over a certified WBE entity—and, similarly, a nonlicensed person or entity cannot exert undue control over a licensed person or entity. With this in mind, Daroff Design Inc. + DDI Architects PC operates as a partnership, with Daroff owning 100 percent of Daroff Design Inc. and Rappoport, a licensed architect, owning 100 percent of DDI Architects. The two entities practice in close collaboration, with each owner careful to collaborate with, while not unduly influencing, the other.

DDI's project management processes integrate teams from both entities in a matrix format that incorporates peer review and quality management across the board. The team from DDI Architects frequently tackles the projects' upfront scope of programming, master planning, code compliance, lease review, test-fit planning, budgeting, and scheduling. Daroff Design Inc.'s interior designers take over during the design activity. Along the way, both entities also oversee consultant relationships, with the architects coordinating with the firm's engineering consultants and the interior designers coordinating lighting designers, specialty consultants, design builders, and FF&E sources.

For instance, while the architects prepare contract documents for a project's fit-out, the interior designers prepare drawings and specifications for FF&E. After these sets of documents are done, Daroff Design Inc.'s quality management team reviews the documents for coordination, Rappoport provides peer review, and programs are tested for master planning, code and ADA review, lease compliance, test fit, and the like. After revisions, Rappoport signs and seals all drawings and specifications. In addition, Rappoport and his senior architects conduct ongoing risk management and professional development seminars for all staff.

Establishing Fees: Deciding What You Are Worth

In calculating your financial obligations and potential profits, it is also important to decide up front how you will charge for your services. Long-term success takes money, so what exactly is your work worth? Unfortunately, there is no magic answer or formula to this question. The topic of billing and fees is ever challenging. Each job and client is different, and so too are the fees associated with work and the billing methods that may be employed. Consider the various billing and fee methods currently in use, as shown in Table 1-1.

Finding the billing method and fee structure that works best for each practice takes time, experimentation, and discussion, not just with current or

---

Table 1-1
Show Me the Money: Billing Methods

- **Design concept fee or consulting fee:** A fee that covers a basic design concept or consultation only.

- **Hourly fee:** Charging an hourly rate, which varies depending on geography and experience, and sometimes simply what the market will bear.

- **Fixed fee:** A single total fee based on an estimated amount of hours related to project size and scope.

- **Per-square-foot fee:** Exactly as it sounds; for example, charging $5 per sq. ft., multiplying that by the total square footage.

- **Per diem fee:** Charging per day.

- **Retainer:** A predetermined fee that reserves a professional's time for a project. The retainer is set to assure commitment of the designer for a specific project or time frame. A retainer can be a separate amount in addition to the design fee or a portion of the project design fee. A retainer, and sometimes the full fee, may be paid in advance of beginning the project.

- **Retail-based models:**
  a. **Merchandise and product services fee:** Determining and negotiating a percentage of the cost of the goods and installation involved in a project. This percentage is multiplied by the budgeted or final costs of the project.
  b. **Cost plus markup:** Charging for the cost of materials plus additional amounts for administration and profit. Percentages covering the purchasing of fixtures, furnishings, and equipment may also be included.

- **Combining a number of the above methods**

---

potential business partners but with other practitioners—and sometimes clients—as well. What an interior designer charges in Manhattan may differ dramatically from the fee scale of a practitioner in Casper, Wyoming; San Antonio, Texas; or Chicago—and while one business's billing methods may differ from a neighboring firm's, understanding the going rate and method of billing of interior design services as a whole within a specific geographic market is essential. Consider the following excerpt from an industry panel entitled "Demystifying Fees," conducted in May 2008 in Brooklyn, New York, during the borough's annual BKLYN Designs trade show. Moderated by Judy Sheridan, principal of Sheridan Interiors Inc., the panel included three New York–based designers: Kathryn Scott, principal of Kathryn Scott Design Studio (which has a secondary office in Shanghai); Susan Huckvale Arann, president of American & International Designs, Inc.; and Kati Curtis, IIDA, ASID, principal of Nirmada Interior Architecture and Design. While these three women practice largely in the same geographical region, their billing processes are as individual as their practices:

Question: What are the basic ways that you, as a designer, charge for your services?

Kathryn Scott: For a long time I've worked on an hourly basis because it is simple and straightforward and gives you flexibility. Often the client is not sure what they want, so hourly billing fares well. I've also done fixed fee, which is usually determined by figuring out how long it takes to do each component of a room. You figure that out by calculating the amount of manpower and adding 20 to 25 percent to it. That is before the design concept. Purchasing would be extra, and I would often add 30 percent on top of that. I've found that to work, but some people are unsure if it is for them.

Susan Huckvale Arann: I charge hourly. I also charge a flat fee, and I check my charges on square foot: If I'm developing a flat fee, I take the square footage and multiply that by $5 per square foot or $8 per square foot to see if it matches what I calculated for the flat fee, just to check [that I'm charging an appropriate amount].

Kati Curtis: My firm does commercial and residential projects, so I don't have a set way of charging. It's based on scope. If I have a very, very clear scope after I meet with a client and have an initial interview, then I will work on a fixed fee. Coming up with that fixed fee is easy, because I have a master task list and spreadsheet to figure out how many hours are involved and who will do what, and then I add on for revisions. If the scope is not clearly defined, we work on an hourly basis.

Q: Are you charging hourly when you're out shopping with clients?

KC: Absolutely, and then 50 percent [of the designer discount] on top of that. We call that a specification fee.

SA: I call it a purchasing fee or specification fee, and my specification fee is 38 percent.

I started at 30 percent for a while and then moved up to 35 percent. Then I went to a seminar years ago that encouraged everyone to increase their fees by 3 percent, and at the end of the year it makes a big difference. I very rarely get someone questioning it.

KS: It's important to add that if you have a limited fee, you have to have a limited scope.

Q: When is hourly applied and when is percentage applied? Do you charge hourly in addition to the percentage, or is it an either/or situation?

SA: I always charge hourly and always a percentage. Do I make everyone sign a purchasing agreement with me? I decide on the job. I may add a shopping day fee where I drive them in, take them to lunch, and we shop no more than 5 hours. I lead by my hourly and always add my percentage fee on top of my hourly.

Q: Do you collect a design fee or retainer?

SA: Always. Working hourly, I project the hours. If I do a flat fee of $20,000, I require a retainer of $10,000.

Q: Are your hourly fees lawyerly, where you charge every 15 minutes or every 10 minutes? Where do you draw that cap? What about things like email or correspondence—do you just charge when you're designing?

SA: I don't bill 15-minute increments. When I look at email, which is a big time-consumer, I lock it in at 30-minute increments and I bill out 3.5 hours, 5 hours, etc., which includes everything.

Q: How specific do you get when documenting your time?

SA: The last line in the bill is email and correspondence. I'm very specific on the time when I'm working on programming or the time I'm out in the field, and I do it by day.

Q: How do you handle shopping for a specific item when you don't find anything?

SA: If I'm out shopping and I haven't found anything, the customer does not pay. I also preshop many times.

Q: Are you currently happy with what you're charging?

KC: I'm thinking of increasing my fee because I am a professional. . . . I have been charging fixed fees for residential jobs, and I'm thinking of throwing that out the window. I have a problem with letting people get away with things. I'm finding in a lot of instances that I have to go back with an addition to our original fee, and I hate to do that. I think it causes problems and tension in the relationship, and I'd rather keep it out of the mix. I find that it has always been quite possible to do hourly if you charge enough, and if I charge hourly, then you can call me anytime to work.

SA: I'm thinking of raising my hourly fee, but I'm reluctant. However, with my international clients, I've recently started incorporating a higher fee.

KS: I try to figure out ways my two offices can work together and am always trying to adjust my fees to fit the market.

Q: I'm starting out on my own and it sounds like hourly is the better way to go, but I have no idea how to guesstimate. How long you are going to be working changes. How do you assess the hours you will be working?

KC: I have a master service list and I figure it out from that based on experience. But if you're just starting out, basing it on square footage may help. If it's going to take you this long per square foot, and this much time for presentations and estimate, then test it against $5 per square foot or $8 per square foot.

Q: How do you charge for a design fee?

KS: You have to figure out how much time it will take. A living room can mean many different things, and even two living rooms can be different amounts of work and the scopes can be different. You try to figure out how long it will take you.

I'm told that sometimes a fee can be more profitable than doing hourly, especially if you have a reputation where you can get a premium fee. I've heard of some people charging anywhere from $15,000 to $25,000 for a design fee, and the hourly not being equal to that. It's hard to say. It depends on the client. It depends on the project. Some clients are wonderful to work with. You show them something, they like it, and you go the next day. Other people may have to go over it again and again and they're not sure, and then they don't like it. These are very different experiences.

KC: I find, especially with residential clients, the scope grows and changes and becomes many different things. If I start with a design fee and the client understands what it is for, we work from there. I hope I'm offering them additional solutions . . . but I think I shortchange the client and myself when I do that, so I started charging hourly.

Q: Do you tailor your financial arrangements for each client?

KS: It always has to be different. I have two contracts that I use. One is more residential, and one is more commercial. The one that is more commercial is for bigger jobs and it's quite long, about seventeen pages. If it's residential, I don't put all of that on there because it may not be necessary. It was ASID's template, but altered. I was hoping that all I would have to do is just change the name and the date, but it doesn't work like that. You have to adjust it to what the client's needs are, taking things out, adding things in. It's never just changing a name.

SA: My contract changes. If it is a referral, I have a paper that goes out ahead of time explaining how we work and listing what we do, along with our fees. I send that out when I specifically know where the client came from. The contract changes if I am doing retail or if I want something that is a little bit less defined. I would be afraid of anything over three pages and I try not to go past two if I can, as I think it's intimidating. I have a difficult time with clients when it is longer. I make sure it specifies the design fee, purchasing fee, and compensation.

KC: Our standard contract is based on a mix of IIDA and ASID agreements. It's always different. What I've been doing is clearly outlining in the scope of services what we're going to do so the client understands what they are paying for when they get that bill. We bill monthly or biweekly, which is shocking to some clients. If you outline it, they understand it and don't just think I am going to come in and give them furniture. They see that it takes time.

However, I have to rewrite the scope every single time I send out a proposal. I like Susan's idea of sending that out in the beginning to say this is what we do, particularly with residential clients. I think TV shows are killing us. People think I'm going to come in and in two hours my entire workforce will transform the space. When they see the breakdown, they see it is much more involved, and they will pay for it.

Q: Assuming that the way you charge now is the result of an evolutionary process, what would say was the one important thing you've learned?

KS: When I took on my first client in my own business, I had no business sense at all. I just wanted to design and didn't think about it. My first client was very sharp and would not pay both the commission and the hourly fee, saying I had to choose one or the other and he would rather pay the commission fee. I didn't know any better, so I agreed to the commission. . . . I learned that flexibility is good because a client often changes their mind. If you have a fixed fee and then have to say this is extra because it is not in your scope, clients are not happy about that, which is why I charged hourly for so many years. If it is hourly, they know what they are getting and they don't abuse it. The client who was only on a commission was abusing my time.

KC: With a background at the architectural firm, going out on my own I had no idea outside of my project management experience at the bigger firm. Coming to panels like this, I realize I can be charging a lot more. My first project was an entire house. It was a great experience but I felt guilty about getting an hourly rate that I had considered higher than I thought I would obtain. Then I got more involved in ASID and IIDA, and I started learning that I could charge a lot more. I was worth it and really began looking at it as a business entity. How much is my overhead? How much is my insurance? How much is my software? When you look at it from a business standpoint, you need to charge those fees by the hour.

SA: My most important person was my accountant. One day he walked in and gave me my end-of-the-year information and said I had to evaluate the fact that unless I took a paycheck every week, I should reconsider staying in business. He said look at all the money that is coming in and whom you are paying and what you are investing in—and you are not taking a paycheck. That made me go back and figure out what it was costing me every day to open and close my doors. The first check I would write would be my check. There are still times when I don't take a check every week, but I make sure I pay myself before reinvesting in the business.

Protecting Your Business: Insurance and Contracts

Risk is inherent to any business venture. Protecting both business and personal assets from risk is crucial for any entrepreneur with dreams of long-term success. Two paths to risk management for your design firm are solid business contracts and insurance.

Contracts are legally binding documents between two or more individuals or entities and are enforceable in court. Depending on how a design firm operates and the types of projects it works on, contracts may be entered into with clients, other professional consultants, vendors, contractors, or installers.

Risk of loss for business owners comes from a wide range of incidents: fire, flood, or earthquake damage to your place of business; injury to visitors at your studio or showroom; or damage to a client's property by your employees. These are but a few of the unforeseen events that could incur devastating financial losses.

Preparing for Risk: Buying Insurance

Jeremy Welsh

Jeremy Welsh is vice president of The Insurance Exchange Inc., a privately held, independent insurance agency operating in the Washington, D.C., area.

Since its founding more than forty years ago, the firm has grown to be one of the largest and most sophisticated agencies in the mid-Atlantic region, serving customers with professionalism, integrity, and innovation. The firm offers employee benefits, property and casualty insurance, and retirement products to businesses throughout the United States and around the world.

Few things in life are as rewarding as launching and running your own business. There are also risks inherent in running a business, some of which can be mitigated by the right insurance plan. Design professionals have significant exposure to losses, and a professionally designed insurance program will limit exposure to loss and help ensure the viability of the company.

Listed below are the most common insurance coverages that designers should consider:

- Property and Liability: crucial to any business
- Professional Liability: strongly recommended
- Workers' Compensation: mandated if you have employees
- Business Auto and Umbrella: strongly recommended

- Employee Benefits: recommended if you have employees

- Key Person and Buy-Sell Agreements: strongly recommended in many circumstances

Property insurance protects a company's assets against losses from a wide array of events, such as fire, smoke, wind and hail, vandalism, and theft. The two major types of coverage are building and contents.

The need to purchase building coverage will depend on whether you own the building you are occupying or are required to insure it as part of your lease agreement. Building coverage can also provide protection for your interest in any improvements made to the building on your behalf.

Contents coverage provides coverage for your furnishings, office equipment, tools, computers, accounts receivable, and valuable papers and records. Design firms also need to be sure their policy covers any client's property on their premises, such as undelivered furniture, accessories, or fabrics, as well as items they may have temporarily removed from the client's premises. Another coverage usually included with property insurance is the loss of business income. The income from your business is what keeps you in business. By making sure that income stream continues, your business can continue even if the income is disrupted.

When purchasing *property coverage*, be sure that your building and contents are covered on a replacement cost basis. This means that the policy will pay to replace the property with no deduction for depreciation.

General liability insurance is crucial coverage for any business. It protects your business against costs arising from claims of injury or damage caused to others by you or your employees. It also protects your company if someone is injured as a result of using your product or service. When you consider that the legal expenses and settlement (or judgment) expenses from a single lawsuit could drive your business into bankruptcy, you'll see why this kind of insurance is considered a "must-have."

Professional liability insurance is a separate liability coverage that is strongly recommended to all design firms. Designers are considered professionals, and problems with their work are not covered by a general liability policy. Claims can be brought against you for a number of reasons, including advice given to clients on proper décor for a building; changes or modifications in design plans; errors in materials used; improper spatial designs; failure to obtain client's written consent to design or materials change; and more. Whether valid or not, a claim for professional errors or omissions could result in an expensive court action, not to mention the possibility of a large judgment if an award is rendered against you.

Workers' compensation coverage is required if you have employees. This is a state-mandated coverage that provides cash benefits and medical care if an employee becomes injured or disabled due to an injury or illness related to their job. It is required in all fifty states. Owners can choose to exclude themselves to reduce costs.

Two other coverage types to consider are *business auto* and *umbrella*. Business auto insurance is required if vehicles are owned by the business, but liability also exists when employees use their personal vehicles while on company business. Personal auto insurance is the primary insurance in this case, but it does not protect the business owner if their business is sued. When an employee causes an accident, the injured person will, more than likely, look to the company to pay damages. Hired and nonowned coverage will protect the business in this circumstance.

Umbrella coverage is an additional layer of liability coverage that picks up where your business auto liability, general liability, or other liability coverage stops. Umbrella insurance is an inexpensive way to provide extra coverage against catastrophic bodily injury and/or property damage.

It's tempting to just ignore employee benefits insurance, but good employees are the key to the success of your business operation. Providing employee benefits such as medical, dental, and disability benefits will not only help keep your employees healthy, but will help keep them content. Think about how much money and time you spend finding and training new employees. Retaining the good employees you already have makes good financial sense.

Some business owners stop here. But there are other types of insurance that wise business owners will also want to purchase as protection against incurring the kinds of losses that can close their doors.

If you are a business owner, you should also carry some kind of disability insurance. Disability insurance pays an insured person an income when that person is unable to work because of an accident or illness. There are various kinds of disability insurance available that are tailored to the needs of business owners.

If your business is dependent on the expertise or knowledge of particular people in your company, you should also consider key-person insurance. This type of plan helps to compensate a business for financial losses due to the death or long-term disability of a key person. The insurance provides additional funds to the business until the key person can be replaced, or until he or she returns to work.

If you are a member of a partnership, you may also want to carry buy-sell insurance. If one of the partners dies or becomes disabled, this kind of insurance provides the surviving partner or partners with the money to buy the deceased or disabled partner's share of the business.

Being a successful businessperson means being able to anticipate events and plan for the future. Business insurance is one way of ensuring that you are in control of your future rather than being controlled by it.

Complete Contracts = Profitable Projects

Debra Browne, ASID; Principal, Harrison Browne Interior Design Ltd.

Debra Browne, ASID, is the principal of Harrison Browne Interior Design Ltd. in Aspen, Colorado. The firm works on residential and commercial projects ranging from small condominium remodels or retail projects to multimillion-dollar residences and national retail chains. Firm capabilities include a specialization in interior construction consulting, new construction, remodels, space planning, material specification, custom furniture design, and home furnishing and fabrics. Browne, who holds a bachelor of interior design from the Interior Design Institute of Denver, is a frequent industry speaker at events like NeoCon® World's Trade Fair and ASID's 'Interiors' conference, where she often presents on design business practices.

A complete contract is the most important tool in a professional interior designer's business. It is so incredibly important that we, as a profession, set a standard and create an expectation in our clients that they will be signing a contract, that it always have the same basic information, and that it look like a previous contract that they had with another firm.

This contract sets us apart from those who are not educated, experienced, or professional.

Consider this scenario: The job is huge, the client loaded. It is a dream job. You rush to get the initial presentation together. You spend oodles of time you would never spend on a smaller job. You think that the clients will pay your fees and that this will be a sensational project to have photographed. You are breathless with excitement.

Hey, wait a minute! Take a deep breath of professionalism. In 2004, I spoke at NeoCon in Atlanta and Chicago with a presentation titled "If I Have to Eat It, At Least Can't It Taste Good?" In the sessions, we shared war stories, practiced skills relating to anticipating problems, and discussed how to avoid pitfalls other designers had encountered. After practicing skills and working through scenarios, the conclusion was a short discussion about contracts. Participants were interested in what constitutes a complete contract and asked for a copy of my contract, and this became the seed of inspiration for another presentation at NeoCon in June 2008, entitled "Complete Contracts Ensure Profitable Projects."

Consider this real-life experience: A dear friend, a very successful designer in Denver, had clients come to her to quickly furnish a second home in downtown. Due to her enthusiasm and the clients' quick turnaround—they were only in town from Dallas for one week—they wanted the home furnished within a few weeks. It was a new build, and the designer felt comfortable, as she knew the builder personally.

The designer and client shopped the local design center and bought as much of the project off of the floor as possible, with the designer paying the showrooms directly as they went along, for fear of losing the products to another buyer and due to the short time frame for the project. The clients left at the end of the week and gave my friend a check for the entire amount, including the design fees.

One short week later, with orders in process, my friend's banker called and informed her that the check did not clear. Indeed, the builder also got a phone call. After calling her attorney, my friend was informed that the products were not in the hands of the clients until delivery, so she was still liable for the orders and products and could not sue. In the end, my friend was able to have the showrooms credit her for items that had not left the floor; however, she did have to "eat" the product that was already on order, for a net loss of $40,000. She had to take out a second mortgage on her home to pay the vendors. A contract prior to the whole shopping trip would have helped.

The contract is the first impression the client has of your business. How does it look? Has an attorney reviewed it? Has it kept you out of trouble? Do you style it to each client? Do you ask for a retainer?

Contracts vary by project and by clients' needs. My research has found three wonderful books that discuss and present sample contracts that are easy to work with and understand. If you feel your contract needs some TLC, I have found the following books most helpful:

1. *The Interior Design Business Handbook*, by Mary V. Knackstedt. It includes a sample copy of the ASID standard for an agreement.

2. A *Guide to Business Principles and Practices for Interior Designers*, by Harry Seigel, CPA, with Alan M. Seigel, Esq. It is very easy to read and understand.

3. *Business and Legal Forms for Interior Designers*, by Tad Crawford and Eva Doman Bruck. It has a

complete CD of a wide range of business forms that you can tailor to your needs by filling in the blanks.

So What Constitutes a Complete Contract?

1. Who's Who: The Identity of the Parties

One general recommendation: When residential projects involve both a husband and wife, both should sign.

2. Where: Description of the Project

Harry Siegel suggests that the reference to "your home at . . ." is too vague, as a client could possibly say the project was not completed, unless the specific room is identified. At Harrison Browne, we do complete residences for the most part, and thus state "your Home at [the address]." If you are a small firm, the room or areas of the job site you are specifically responsible for are critical to the contract.

3. What Do You Want to Do: Specific Services You Will Provide

I use my contract as an educational tool, as it lists "all or some" of the following services that may be provided, which really enables us to review the process with the client. The client is exposed to all of the elements of the job, and it opens the conversation to discuss which phases our firm will handle in the case of a huge design team. To clarify the items we will do is enormously important, as we have had several clients want us to do specific parts of a home without providing the interior architectural services.

Under no circumstances should the contract appear to provide services you are not licensed to perform. You can discuss third-party consultant services at this time, or add them in the form of an addendum. We usually have the client pay directly to the structural engineer and some of the subcontractors, as we have found that this can be the area of most liability to our firm. Do you want to provide the electrician, plumber, or contractors? Do you want to take the liability for the project if the plumbing fails or the electrical work starts a fire? As a remodeling firm, we have taken on this scope of work, as it is more profitable overall for the firm to oversee the complete job. With proper insurance policies in effect, the liability is covered.

4. How Do You Want to Do It: Specification and Purchasing, Budget, and Schedule

Your contract should clearly state requirements of purchasing for the project. The terms of payment should also be specified, and sales tax, delivery costs, and installation changes should be discussed. Written approval of point of sale (P.O.S.) should be standard.

Create a strong paper trail. We have the clients sign tags on the fabrics, the back of the stain samples, the drawings, and the proposals. It is critical to communicate clearly all of your design intent, along with the costs involved. A firm I knew had a standard practice to up-charge reimbursable expenses by 15 percent for bookkeeping costs, but this was not clearly stated in the contract. The client sued for hidden costs and won. At Harrison Browne, we charge for reimbursable expenses, and it is clearly stated in our contract.

5. Who Is Responsible: The Extent to Which You Will Be Responsible for Supervising the Job

If you are charging hourly, does the client understand that each job site visit will be billed? Does the client want your review on a weekly or an as-needed basis? As our firm deals in second homes, we are often the client's eyes on the project. This is also the place to inform the client of their responsibilities. We had a client tell us he would not pay us because his home "would not be ready for the season" when his dining room chairs were not there in time for July 4. We went back to our contract, which stated the approvals needed from him in a timely matter in order for us to perform. His wife had not decided on the chairs until June 1, and with a twelve-week lead time he would not have his chairs by July 4. We were able to borrow chairs from a vendor for the time the client would be in town. The client later apologized.

6. Show Me the Money: Compensation Arrangements

How are you charging for your time? How are you charging for the product? Fixed fee, percentage of costs, hourly rate, or combination? This should be documented and easily understood by the client. State how the billing is to be done and include a payment schedule. A retainer should be standard and is usually applied at the conclusion of the job.

7. The Fine Print: Your Safety Net

Include all the complete details: Reimbursement of out-of-pocket expenses. Ownership of all design documents produced. Disclaimers of designer's responsibilities. Price increases. Photography rights. Third-party services contracted. Consultant's terms. Termination. Nonpayment. Litigation.

No two designers or projects are alike, and each contract must be tailored for the individual project.

Finally, in order to have a complete contract, it obviously must be signed. In the spring of 2008 I had a client tell me we didn't need a contract. "Ask the contractor," he said. "I have been good and have paid all my bills on time." I replied that I did not work without a contract, which we sent and he signed. As it turned out, he ended up being a very difficult client and I ended up terminating our relationship. Because the contract stated, "This contract may be terminated by either party in writing," all monies owed to me were paid.

As we work together to raise the level of our business practices, the general public will see us as professionals, worthy of the payment we have contracted to receive. Be sure to include the basics, tailor your contract to your client, and negotiate win-win situations. Sell yourself and your talents. Make your professional business your finest project. (See Appendix A: ASID Document ID123, Residential Interior Design Services Agreement.)

Setting Up Shop

While many practitioners launch their businesses out of their own homes, the entity eventually may require more space than a spare bedroom or home office can provide. Opening up a new office, however, requires legwork beyond signing a lease and handing over the keys, and a significant amount of preplanning can help avoid obstacles in the long run.

Location, Location, Location

Charles C. Carpenter

Charles C. Carpenter, CFM, CFMJ, has worked in facility management since 1995. A graduate of the University of Texas, he is completing a master's degree at Texas State University, where he has earned a graduate certificate in professional ethics. His research thesis is entitled "The Effects of the Built Environment on Occupational Stress." Carpenter has presented at conferences in North America and Europe and written articles on a variety of topics, mostly related to facilities and the built environment. He is a member of the International Facility Management Association (IFMA), the U.S. Green Building Council's Texas–Balcones Chapter, and the Association of Contingency Planners.

There are a lot of considerations about where to locate an office. The decision to work from a residence ultimately requires a balancing of priorities. While working from home may be cheaper on paper, an interior designer may find it more beneficial to set up an outside office. A home office may add expenses such as commuting to clients or a larger home and mortgage payment, as well as the inconvenience of temporary staff working from your home or distractions from family, neighbors, and pets. A home office may also compromise your privacy, safety, and security.

Once the decision is made to set up an office, interior designers will have to educate themselves about the different options available. It may be possible to lease space within the offices of another firm, such as an architect. Another option may be to partner with a friend or colleague to open an office; however, the splitting of expenses or the insolvency of the other party may strain relationships or, worse, leave you liable for the other person's expenses.

The hardest part of setting up an office may be picking the physical location. There are many items to balance in finding the best fit. Some things to consider when picking your location include:

- Cost of Travel. You will have to consider both the cost to travel from your home to the office and from the office to your clients. A location near mass transit stations may be more valuable, as the physical demands of carting samples a few extra blocks to the subway may increase your dry cleaning bill more than your rent savings.

- Proximity. You will have to decide how near you will want to be to showrooms and vendors. Supply and demand could inflate the cost of real estate the closer you get to popular areas for interior designers.

- Convenience. You will want to consider the ease of finding your office. Will it be easy for clients to locate you? Is ample free parking available? An office building may face a major thoroughfare but have an address of an obscure side street, making it difficult to find.

- Perception. The part of town where you locate may have an influence on your clientele. If you are soliciting business from outside your area, potential clients may be turned off when they see a physical address in Pflugerville, Texas, versus one a block away in Austin, Texas.

Location aside, you will have to make a decision on the type of building to occupy. Commercial space is typically referred to as office, retail, industrial, or mixed-use, with designers typically opting for office space. These spaces are marketed at different prices as well. While industrial space is often quoted at cost per square foot per month, office space is typically priced at cost per square foot per year. Thus, a 400-sq.-ft. office suite at $24/sq. ft. will cost $800 per month ($2/sq. ft. per month × 400 sq. ft.). The costs of these buildings do not stop with the rent. The operating expenses will be dictated by the lease terms, with an estimated payment often due with the rent. Different types of buildings also come with different levels of services to be provided by the property manager. Unless you want to be your own facility manager, selecting a building where the property manager will arrange for all supplies, services, and repairs should free up time to service your clients or take on new ones.

The appearance of a building may be the most important factor in selecting space, as clients may be turned off by a shabby location. The building may also deliver customers, meaning a carefully selected suite might lead to walk-in customers who frequent other tenants. Selecting a suite next to a plastic surgeon instead of a podiatrist might generate the type of foot traffic that engages interior designers. If your expertise lies with sustainability, selecting a green building may be a necessity.

The next issue designers will encounter is the type of lease and the lease language. There are different types of leases, but the most common are the *gross* or *full-service*, where the lease payment includes all expenses, and the *triple-net*, where the lease payment only includes rent, building insurance, and property taxes, with the operating expenses calculated separately. Lease language that is satisfactory for your needs is crucial. Some aspects of a lease to consider:

- Rent Calculation. Will the payment be based on rentable or usable square footage? In older buildings a greater percentage of square footage may be lost to building columns or HVAC equipment; however, that unusable space,

30 percent or more, could show up in your monthly lease payment. Equally important is whether the annual percentage that your rent could increase is written into the lease.

- Holdover/Renewal/Right of Refusal. Does the lease provide the opportunity to renew your lease? If not, the sweat equity put into outfitting your office space could be lost to someone else. Likewise, do you have the right of refusal if the space next door becomes available?

- Subleasing/Exit Strategy. Do you have the right to sublease your space if you move or grow beyond its size? Is there an exit strategy available in case you can no longer occupy the space?

- Tenant Improvement Allowance. Leases typically offer funds to the tenant to be used for building out the space. These funds are far from free and are amortized over the term of the lease. Tenants need to be aware of the conditions of the tenant improvement allowance: there may be specific expenses for which the funds can be spent, or a timeline for those funds to be used before they are forfeited. Work performed in-house may not qualify for reimbursement. In existing space, one option for an industrious designer could be to take the space as-is to reduce the lease payments, and self-finance improvements on an ongoing basis.

- Capital Improvements. Are capital improvements (e.g., HVAC systems, roofs) spelled out in the lease? In an effort to save money, some building owners will continue to repair antiquated equipment instead of replacing it. Repairs are operating expenses and are passed on to you, the tenant. Also, any improvements that are attached to the building may be considered capital improvements—meaning a light fixture, cabinet, or product samples installed by the tenant may have to remain at the end of the lease unless addressed in the lease ahead of time.

One final area to consider is the operating expenses for a location. The operating expenses are all the day-to-day expenses involved with a building and can include such items as janitorial costs, utilities, security, and landscaping. Operating expenses can easily run more than the cost of the rent, based on the price of real estate. Common-area maintenance refers to the cost of maintaining corridors, elevators, and other items shared by all tenants and is a term often used as part of or in place of operating expenses, depending on the terms of your lease. Operating expenses are typically assigned in proportion to a tenant's square footage in a building, so that a 400-sq.-ft. tenant in a 1,600-sq.-ft. building would pay 25 percent of the operating expenses. Some operating expense issues to consider:

- Managed Expenses. Depending on the lease terms and type of building you lease, the property manager could be responsible for arranging all repairs and services, from changing a lightbulb to inspecting the fire-suppression system. Property managers will mark up these expenses; however, the time saved in locating and paying dozens of vendors may well be worth the 10 percent markup. As with anything, a property manager's markup is negotiable.

- Expense Caps. Is there a predefined amount that operating expenses can increase year-over-year? With a property manager collecting a percentage of expenses, there may be little incentive to shop around for the best deal.

- Usage. It is important to know if utilities and other expenses are based on actual usage. For example, a two-person design firm may split a building with a web-hosting company that uses one thousand times more electricity, only to find out that the electric bill is split fifty-fifty. Expenses that are based on square footage need to have methods for auditing and recalculating to reflect true usage. In the event that a tenant closes an office, it is possible that operating expenses for unused services will continue to be billed.

- True Up. At the end of a fiscal year, the property manager will "true up" the expenses for a building by reconciling the estimated charges with the true expenses for the property. Once this calculation is complete, a tenant could receive an unexpected bill and modified operating expenses from the property manager and will need to set aside funds to cover these charges.

Some of the burden of selecting a location can be lifted by using a broker. Brokers typically work at no apparent cost to the lessee; however, most tenants will find that the broker's commission is included in the total cost per square foot. The broker's fee, typically 3 percent, may be well worth the cost when one considers the time savings and expertise that an experienced broker provides. Brokers can help with negotiations, compare lease rates for similar spaces, review leases for tenant-friendly language, and share knowledge about a potential property manager and building owner. The area where brokers may be most helpful is in referral of business, as brokers are always placing companies in new locations that may need interior design services. Developing a rapport with a broker—or a property manager, for that matter—may promote your work and provide you with new business worth hundreds of times the cost of their services.

Looking Back for Those Moving Forward

As a precursor to some of the more detailed logistics of starting and growing a firm that will be discussed in the chapters ahead, consider the following advice, offered by Mark C. Zweig as he neared retirement.

Advice in Hindsight: If I Were Starting a Firm Today

Mark C. Zweig

Being in "the next phase of my career," that is, semiretirement, gives me plenty of time to reflect. A frequent thought is what I would do if I were starting a new A&E or environmental firm today. Here are some of my thoughts, in no particular order of importance:

1. **I would budget (and spend) about 15 percent of my net service revenue on marketing.** I know that's a lot. But underfunding marketing has slowed down more firms in this business than anything else. I would come roaring out of the starting gate with an in-your-face PR campaign, a CRM (customer relationship management system) that was well populated with prospective clients, and high-frequency direct mail with postcards and personal letters. I'd also have a simple, memorable name and good graphic design that was reflected on every sign, plan, presentation, direct-mail piece, and more.

2. **I would be very slow to add more owners, beyond perhaps one or two key partners.** It's taken me a long time, but I have learned that a lot of folks in this business don't really value ownership. They just want the cash. OK—I'd rather give them what they want. Cash is cheaper than stock that appreciates wildly, and my stock would because I'd have a firm that was growing like mad. Plus, more owners inevitably means more meetings, and I *hate* sitting in internal company meetings. Little is more boring and less productive. In general, the more owners, the more complicated things get, and the slower decision making is.

3. **I would hire for personality and train for skills.** You cannot change most people's behavior. That said, you *can* teach a teachable person how to do something. Think about it. I have had too many people work for me over the years who have had a lot of specific skills, but didn't have the personality

attributes to succeed over the long haul. Conversely, I have been blessed with many great employees who had soft skills and intellect and strength of character to succeed with few of the basic skills to do what we needed them to do. Employees in this group learn quickly and adapt to new situations easily. The others either get run off or quit. You can't grow a firm if you can't keep the right people working in it.

4. **I would be incredibly flexible with my work rules.** Today, everyone has a lot to do, both at home and work. I would go overboard to accommodate the life schedules of my good workers so we could afford to keep the best of them. Of course, nothing comes free. Those who can't work the hours we want them to might make less—but we'd all be happier about it.

5. **I would get a BlackBerry PDA for everyone who wants one and some of those who don't.** I heard a little while back that a study concluded BlackBerry wireless devices pay for themselves in less than one month! I don't doubt this at all. And, as far as I am concerned, every manager must have one. This would not be optional because, without one, certain people will fall behind and be less responsive. I know there are people who don't want to be reachable twenty-four hours a day. They aren't cut out for management and leadership jobs in a high-growth firm.

6. **I would have an open-book firm.** Everyone would know how we are doing and exactly how they would benefit personally from that success. This takes great accounting, and I would be sure to have the systems it takes, along with the qualified accounting person, to implement and maintain the system.

7. **I would charge a lot for my firm's services.** The only strategy that really makes sense for a professional services firm, as far as I can tell, is one of high quality *and* high price. You cannot hire good people, pay them well, market yourself effectively, and invest in your business without the funds coming in to do so. This takes high prices. The only way to get high prices is, first, market

yourself as a quality service firm. Second, be a quality provider. And, third, keep doing these things til you get out of the business! Firms that are trying to be the lowest-cost providers in their market sectors are destined for failure.

8. **I would decide when I am going to get out before I even started.** Everyone in the firm would know that from the start. I would ensure the firm's success after my departure by having good people, great systems, and a well-known brand name that results in work seeking out the firm, instead of vice versa.

No doubt, there are many lessons one could employ if starting over again. But, wait, these things could all be worked into an ongoing firm as well. If these lessons make sense to you, what is to stop YOU from implementing them?

This article originally appeared in *The Zweig Letter*, a publication of ZweigWhite. © ZweigWhite.

Chapter 2:
Structure and Support

I n Chapter 1, we took a look at big-picture issues—business planning, strategic planning, and financial planning—that come along with deciding to launch a new interior design practice. What follows in this chapter, as well as in Chapter 3, are more detailed examinations of the various components that come to comprise those bigger picture ideas, including hiring, building client and industry relationships, branding and marketing, and incorporating technology. First, let's look at structure and support issues.

Building the Team

For some interior designers, what starts as a one-man (or, more often, one-woman) shop often remains just that. In fact, the average interior design firm only has between two and six employees.[1] Of course, even these smaller firms have additional help, and finding the right mix of collaborators for your particular firm is key to long-term success.

As expected, lawyers and accountants are linchpins to a successful practice and should be consulted not only in the business planning stages, but also on an ongoing basis. There are many ways to go about finding both an attorney and an accountant who best fit your business. The Web provides a great starting point, with a multitude of sites that offer advice, forms, and directories. When looking for an attorney, consider visiting sites like Free Advice (www.freeadvice.com), Nolo (www.nolo.com), Law Info (www. lawinfo.com), and Find Law (www.findlaw.com). Other small business sites, such as SCORE (www.score.org) and NFIB (www.nfib.org), offer legal and financial advice on hiring professionals for small businesses. In addition, reach out to your local community and other design professionals for references. Your local bar association, for example, can provide a listing of local attorneys.

Although an attorney or an accountant may not be in-house like a junior designer, it's just as important to screen candidates for the best possible match. Conduct initial phone interviews, followed by in-person meetings, and consider asking about the following factors:

- Can they provide references of past and current clients who have businesses that are a similar size or are in the design industry?

- How do they bill? Do they charge an hourly rate or a fixed fee?

- What services do they provide year-round? What business advice can they offer you that will help you grow your business?

- How do they prefer to conduct business: in person, by phone, or over email? How quickly do they return calls or emails?

- In interviewing accountants, ask whether they are a certified public accountant (CPA), a designation that means they have passed state-administered tests regarding financial education levels.

In conducting interviews, pay attention to body language and interactions. Do they seem eager for your business? Are they able to explain complex legal or financial issues in terms that you can understand? Also, do not underestimate your gut: If something doesn't feel right, the relationship probably will not work out.

Looking at other employees that may be needed, it is important to go back to the concepts of business planning, strategic planning, and financial planning and examine not only the support—clerical staff, perhaps, or an assistant designer—that you will need at the beginning of a practice, but also whom you may need in the near future. Think about what kinds of projects you are looking to take on and what kinds of work, specifically, will be required. What support positions will be required, and what design staffers will be needed? Will assistance be needed on an ongoing basis, or can it be contracted out on a freelance, per-project basis?

There are many hiring questions and issues that arise over the course of a firm's life, and as the firm grows, so too does the list of considerations and potential complications. While we will address growing the firm to a higher operating level and the issues that are associated with such growth in a later chapter, let's first take a look at the basics.

For many firms, large and small alike, the biggest challenge in building a team is the hiring process itself. How, exactly, do you go about finding and hiring new team members? Jim Heilborn, the namesake consultant of Jim Heilborn Associates in Lincoln, California, which offers consulting services regarding sales, operations, human resources, and strategic planning, suggests breaking the hiring process into six key steps:

1. Defining the job and qualifications

2. Attracting applicants for the position

3. Assessing the applicants

4. Extending an offer of employment

5. Starting the employment relationship

6. Looking back and then going forward

Take a moment to think about the exact position that must be filled. What are the basic duties that need to be accomplished, and what skills and training will be necessary to accomplish them? Think not only about the ideal candidate, but also about the company as a whole. How will this person fit into the general mix? What does the firm have to offer them? Will there be room to grow this position and this person?

Finding Their Motivation: Rabaut Design Associates

Founded in 1989 by Jo Rabaut, ASID, IIDA, Rabaut Design Associates in Atlanta has planned and designed more than 30 million square feet of space. The seven-person firm works on a range of commercial projects, including offices, institutional, education, retail, and spa projects, as well as a small amount of residential work.

It's a scene many have seen in the movies: Surrounded by crew on a soundstage, an actor pauses in his dialogue, a look of confusion or frustration spreading across his face. He breaks character, looks off-screen, and asks, "What's my motivation here?"

As clichéd as this anecdote may be on screen, the question—What's my motivation?—plays a crucial role in the hiring process of Rabaut Design Associates. For Jo Rabaut, when hiring for her small, Atlanta-based practice, it is an issue that is considered from both sides of the equation. From the beginning, nearly twenty years ago, Rabaut has sought to keep the practice small, and to do so she takes great care in hiring new employees, preferring to work a little harder or leaner for a short period if the workload may not be there to support a new team member in the long run.

"My reputation and the firm's reputation is really important to me," she explains, citing the industry-wide horror stories of firms that staff up for a big project, but then lay off as soon as the work dries up. "I

feel like that does so much damage to the psyche of the employee, and is also bad PR within the community. For me, it is important to hire someone and look at it as a relationship."

With this in mind, Rabaut also continually checks in with her employees to ensure that the firm is providing motivation to keep them fulfilled, which often goes beyond the dollars and cents of salaries. "Smaller firms aren't nearly as sexy as the bigger firms that have name recognition and a lot of people who are members of the staff but not necessarily an integral part of the development of the firm. Since we are smaller we have to sell it a little differently than a big firm," Rabaut says. Over the past ten to fifteen years, she's seen candidates focus less on money and more on quality of life. "It is one of the biggest changes when people come to interview now. Before, it was 'I love interior design and I want to get ahead. I'll do anything. I just want to get into the firm.' In the past ten to fifteen years, there has been more of a trend where they want a different quality of life, or being top dog in the firm is not the most important thing because they want to spend more time with their dog."

As a smaller firm, Rabaut finds this advantageous. For example, recognizing that many people are looking to get involved in industry organizations but cannot afford the annual dues, Rabaut pays for each employee's dues to one professional organization a year, so long as they are actively involved. Likewise, to support her personal interest in giving back to the community, employees in the firm are allotted four hours a month to do philanthropic work of their choice. Overall, however, Rabaut works closely with employees to find the perks most important to them, whether it is never working overtime, having every Friday off, or going back to school. One employee, for example, took a leave of absence to work with a New York City fashion designer, while another simply wanted a bigger refrigerator for the office.

This back-and-forth discussion starts in the hiring process, where candidates are interviewed with an eye on not just their skills and portfolio, but also on their behavior. "When I talk about the things we offer in the interview, I try to read body language. Does the person perk up or do their eyes glaze over?" she says. "Does the person talk too much, or is she listening and engaging in a dialogue?"

Typically, Rabaut has found her most successful candidates through word of mouth, with local reps being especially helpful. She has yet to successfully work with an external recruiter, especially during a soft economy when candidates are plentiful. Even then, however, resumes that come with some sort of connection—a recommendation from an industry colleague, say—are usually much more promising than a cold call.

Potential candidates are brought in for an initial interview, and along with each resume, Rabaut finds a mini digital portfolio to be helpful. "We get so many resumes, the mini portfolio or at least a couple of images gives you a quick snapshot of where they are at, shows a level of quality, and leaves me with an image," she says. In reviewing these images, however, Rabaut

is cautious. "They could show a pretty picture or a technical set of drawings where all they did was pick up red lines," she explains, so she asks very pointed questions during the interview to ferret out the extent of the candidate's work on each portfolio piece.

Candidates progressing beyond the initial interview are brought in for a second meeting, during which they can tour the office. Rabaut also checks all references, something that twenty years ago she might have done with only one of every twenty candidates. "Some people can really gear up for an interview, but when you live with them day to day, they are nothing like their interview," she says.

As the process continues, Rabaut gives serious candidates the contact information of one or two employees in the firm, suggesting he or she call them with any questions about the firm's policies or culture. For example, she says, if someone tells you that you will never work overtime, and in reality the firm is working every weekend, it is important to know that up front.

After a candidate comes on board, this open dialogue continues. New employees are brought in on a three-month probationary period. "Sometimes this is a chance for people to say they want to do more of this or less of that," Rabaut says, adding that this probationary period also gives her some flexibility from a managerial standpoint. "Sometimes, someone may come in wanting a bigger salary than I am willing to give them. I can then say to them, "I will hire you at this range, and after the three-month period we will review to see if we can get you to where you want.""

Help Wanted: Finding Team Members

When it comes to seeking candidates there are many potential avenues, from traditional means like word of mouth and newspaper classified ads to more contemporary approaches such as social networking sites and online job hubs like Monster.com. Consider these options:

- In-house referrals from employees, dealers, and vendors
- Local interior design programs and schools

- Newspapers and trade journals (both online and in print)
- Professional associations and networks (which often have their own job boards)
- Larger Internet job boards such as Monster.com, HotJobs.com, or CareerFinder.com
- Job fairs
- Open houses

Getting Started: Studio 2030

Minneapolis, Minnesota–based Studio 2030 was created on the conviction that environmental and economic objects are not mutually exclusive, and that the ideals of sustainability—resource conservation, energy efficiency, pollution prevention—are fully compatible with design excellence and work that is highly original, high performance, and sublimely beautiful. The firm is run by partners Rachelle Schoessler Lynn, ASID, CID, LEED AP, and David Loehr, AIA, AICP, LEED AP. Schoessler Lynn serves on the interior design licensing board for the state of Minnesota, previously chaired the National Sustainable Design Council for ASID, currently serves on the ASID board of directors, and is an adjunct faculty member at the University of Minnesota. Loehr holds an architecture license in twenty-nine states, and in twenty-one years of practice has led the design of urban mixed-use projects throughout the United States and internationally.

While finding and hiring the best candidates is a challenge for all business owners, it is especially tricky when starting a new firm. "Having your own business allows you to be much more hands-on in the design process, but it also means that when you are hiring your staff, you have to think about different things. You have to think about the talent or perspective that others can bring to enhance the talents you have, but as a small firm you also have to think about the financial and technical perspectives," explains Rachelle Schoessler Lynn.

The four-person firm was founded on Earth Day 2007 by Schoessler Lynn and David Loehr. Both came from larger firms, having spent a number of years at practices ranging from 160 to 800 employees. While these large entities give principals more flexibility, at least financially, in hiring decisions, when it came to structuring Studio 2030 Schoessler Lynn and Loehr sought a smaller venture that would allow them to be more invested in the design process. The firm's smaller size also influenced their approach to hiring.

As a small firm, Studio 2030 is cautious and practical about adding full-time employees. "I've learned that there are a lot of creative, talented people in our business, and it has always worked out best if I wait for the right person to come around, rather than hire just because I need the help," Schoessler Lynn says. With this in mind, candidates are interviewed throughout the year regardless of whether a specific position is open. However, the ultimate decision to hire is based on current workload, with an eye on whether there is enough future work to sustain a full-time employee. If the long-term support is not there, the firm outsources work. "If we are writing really detailed specifications, we may not need that talent in the studio all day, every day, so we outsource it," Schoessler Lynn explains. The firm also actively partners with other firms to take on larger projects.

In interviewing candidates, the founding partners require employees with complementary and varied skill sets. "We try to find people with a broad perspective, people that can spend part of their day understanding building code issues, another part looking at schematic design ideas, and perhaps another part researching the sustainable components of a project. They have to be multitalented," Schoessler Lynn explains. This multitasking need makes crafting a set job description difficult, and

Studio 2030 was in business for more than a year before it devised set descriptions for its first two employees. Even then, the definitions of each position were kept purposefully loose.

"It took us a while to get the descriptions written and distributed," Schoessler Lynn says. "They are still somewhat traditional from the standpoint of defining the role of a designer within the firm, but there is some language that talks about willingness to do what needs to be done. It also lists the contributions expected at each person's level."

When it comes to attracting potential employees, new firms may not have the reputation of bigger or more established entities, but Studio2030 benefits from its founders' long-standing reputations. "Our involvement in the industry, whether it is at a university, with ASID, or giving a lecture, has been one of the greatest recruitment tools. Being present in the community and being out there to share our knowledge has been a real benefit in both recruiting and retention," Schoessler Lynn says. "It doesn't cost anything other than time. When we have a position, we are not spending money by putting ads in the newspaper. Word spreads and we always have people contacting us." In fact, the firm has not advertised open positions, as resumes frequently come in from the Web, attendees of Schoessler Lynn or Loehr's speaking engagements, and local designers and industry colleagues. Schoessler Lynn also draws from her teaching experiences at local universities. The firm's first two full-time employees, for instance, are past students. J Chesnut, an ARE candidate, was Schoessler Lynn's teaching assistant at the University of Minnesota, and Megan Hoye, an interior design graduate pursuing an undergraduate degree in architecture, was a student intern for Schoessler Lynn at a previous firm.

The firm also benefits from a dedication to sustainable design. "We receive resumes weekly from people all over the country," notes Schoessler Lynn. "There are so many people that want to work for a firm that practices sustainable design." The firm's focus on sustainability also impacts its interviewing and vetting process, as it is one thing to have a personal interest in sustainability and another to have the skills and work experiences to support that interest. In interviewing candidates, Studio 2030 requests a resumé and portfolio sampling but leaves the portfolio contents to the discretion of the candidate. Like many in the hiring seat, Schoessler Lynn and Loehr take care to dig into a candidate's past work to discern their direct contributions. "We once had a candidate who had a beautiful portfolio and seemed to have some really creative ideas and approaches to problem solving. This candidate worked for a well-respected studio in Minneapolis and everything seemed perfect, except the candidate could not explain any of their ideas," Schoessler Lynn recalls. "It led us to think that maybe this person was misrepresenting themselves. The candidate has worked on the projects presented, but we came to believe that their contribution was less than we had hoped."

The firm does not require potential employees to be LEED accredited, but they must show a true commitment to sustainable design. "We ask to see project work and experience that speaks to their level of sustainable knowledge and experience. We ask them what they read or how they continue to deepen their knowledge of sustainable design. We ask about how they have created opportunities to integrate sustainable design thinking. Those that just have an interest but have not done any of the above are not suitable for our company."

The firm also continues to support interest in sustainability, which benefits both employees and the firm's continued stature as a practice devoted to the cause. Once hired, employees of Studio 2030 are strongly encouraged to pursue LEED accreditation and are offered incentives including membership in the U.S. Green Building Council and the local USGBC chapter, as well as membership in Emerging Green Builders if they are eligible. The firm also pays LEED AP examination fees upon exam passage.

Making the Cut

Once a selection of candidates is in hand, the process is just beginning. Narrowing down a field of potential employees can be nerve-wracking for both the employer and the interviewees.

As much as hiring is part of a successful firm's life cycle, often so too is turnover. In fact, turnover is a natural part of every business, and as contradictory as it may sound, it may often be a part of growth. Turnover occurs for a wide range of reasons, from response to a change in corporate strategy or direction to a disappearing profit margin and tightening market, as many firms came to find during the subprime mortgage crisis and turbulent global economy of 2008. Turnover can also result from mis-hires and personality conflicts. While there is no scientific formula to guarantee that the final choice will be a successful relationship, there are a number of tips that may help avoid disasters.

Tips to Avoid Costly Hiring Mistakes

Joan Lloyd

Joan Lloyd has a solid track record of excellent results. Her firm, Joan Lloyd & Associates, specializes in leadership development, organizational change, and team building. Services include executive coaching, 360-degree feedback processes, customized leadership and presentation skills training, team assessment and team building, and retreat facilitation. Joan also provides consulting skills training for HR professionals.

Why is it that most organizations spend so little time and resources helping managers hire the right people? I would argue that hiring is one of the key activities that can make or break a company. This isn't rocket science, folks. Look around. The companies that invest in getting it right on the front end tend to be financially successful, have less turnover, and have a better reputation overall than their closest competitors.

Help your managers avoid some common hiring traps that can trip up the most seasoned managers:

- But her skills were so perfect!

Hiring someone who isn't a fit for the culture will take you down a slippery slope. You will spend more time doing damage control than President Clinton's press secretary. While the end results may look good, the energy it will take to repair relationships and untangle political snafus is going to drain you dry. And firing someone who doesn't fit the culture is a lot tougher to document and act on than firing someone for an absenteeism problem.

- Halos can be blinding.

We like people who are like us. They seem so smart, so comfortable, so *right*. The problem is that they aren't always the best people to fill a job. Instead, seek out the person who fits the job requirements. "Well, of course," you say. Yet this is the most common mistake managers make.

Unfortunately, this mistake colors the manager's judgment long past the hiring day. The manager tends to look at his or her new employee through rose-colored glasses and often isn't objective about the employee's performance. Sometimes these managers are so protective of their hiring choice, they can't see problems until it's too late.

- Don't settle for a pulse.

Staffing shortages make it tempting to settle for less. Yet, if managers lower their standards, they might have hell to pay for years, with an underperforming employee and resentful coworkers. An employee like this can become the black hole of the department, requiring fellow employees to train and even to cover for him or her. Instead, consider some creative solutions with the employees you already have, such as job sharing, creative work schedules, job rotations, internships, and job redesign.

Another approach is to try some creative recruiting strategies, such as starting an internship program or partnering with a professor in your field. Try not to settle—if you do, you will probably regret it.

- But I get along with him so well!

After a friendly chat, many people seem likable. That doesn't mean they are acceptable candidates for marrying your daughter or babysitting your children. The point is, being likable isn't enough.

When managers are overly swayed by how much they like a candidate, they instinctively avoid asking difficult, probing questions. These managers end up hiring the person based on personality, and that can spell disaster when it comes to performance results.

- I don't have time to kick his tires.

Buyer's remorse is an ugly thing. You wouldn't buy a forty-year-old house without an inspection, or a used car without looking under the hood. The problem is, by the time we are ready to offer someone a job, we like the person enough to believe everything they say. Sometimes managers are so eager to hire a person, they will even shrug off a reference that is damning with faint praise. (Okay, I admit it. I did this once . . . but only once. I paid for it, dearly.)

- Buy—don't sell.

Some managers are so eager to hire, they do more talking than listening during the interview. They blab on about the great benefits and exciting challenges that await the lucky candidate. The problem is that a smart interviewee can manipulate the conversation and have the manager convinced that he or she is the perfect person for the job by using the manager's words in response to his own questions.

www.JoanLloyd.com © Joan Lloyd & Associates.

Going It Alone: Sole Practitioners

As noted at the beginning of this chapter, many interior designers (in fact, a majority of them) opt to operate on their own as sole practitioners. Deciding to go it alone has its own benefits and challenges.

Flying Solo: Patterson House Design Group

Diana L. Patterson, ASID, a consummate sole practitioner, is typical of the majority of interior designers practicing in the marketplace today—she's going it alone. For more than four decades she has actively worked on residential projects for high-end clients and with builders preparing finish and furnishing specifications for condominium complexes. Patterson has worked tirelessly over the years to bring legal recognition to interior designers in several states.

For the vast majority of her forty-one-year career as an interior design professional, Diana L. Patterson has operated as a solo act.

Her first business, Distinctive Decors, began in 1968, following graduation with a design degree from the University of Tulsa in Oklahoma. The profession appealed to her, and she knew she possessed the talent required for success. Feeling the need to be in control of project design and implementation, and wanting to put her personal style and stamp on each project, Patterson seemed destined to operate as a sole practitioner.

In launching Distinctive Decors, Patterson initially hired an employee to help facilitate job orders, and the duo worked together building the business for the next four years. But when her assistant moved out of the area, Patterson continued on as a sole practitioner, picking up her assistant's share of the workload.

It was important to Patterson that she be able not only to take credit for her own work, but also to take direct responsibility for each project. To Patterson, working for another firm under another designer's name would not afford her the ability to receive the recognition for her own designs. She felt that designing at a retail outlet of some type would call into question her ethics. Would recommending a product or service to a client be based on obligation to her employer or on a manufacturer's quota for sales, rather than being the best solution for the client's needs?

At the beginning of Distinctive Decors, Patterson had the advantage of being married to a CPA/attorney, making the need for outside professional business consultants unnecessary. Patterson's husband, Don, advised her to set the business up as a sole proprietor model. Without employees, her liability would be limited to her own personal decisions regarding design and project management. The costs of incorporation for a fledgling design firm were steep, and with her husband's advice, Patterson agreed it would be an unnecessary expense.

When her husband's career took the family from Tulsa to Mobile, Alabama, in 1976, Patterson marketed aggressively in the Mobile market and found a great deal of work, forcing her to expand Distinctive Decors. Without the extra help, she would have been forced to turn away clients, so she added an office manager, a designer, and an interior design student intern from the University of Alabama.

The firm was up and running, but Patterson was uncomfortable with other designers putting out work under her name, and determined to return to her sole proprietor status as soon as she could manage it. After all, she reasoned, her reputation was at stake, and the additional work required to keep track of her employees' work took up a significant amount of time, taking her attention away from clients she was personally working with.

In the early 1980s, the Patterson family relocated again, settling in New England, where Patterson took a position as director of interior design with a design firm in Connecticut. As a new designer in town, she benefited from the high level of visibility to the market and the steady income that the position provided her. It also afforded her a high degree of autonomy for projects, giving her back some of the personal recognition and responsibility she desired.

Following her husband's career, Patterson's family relocated once again, this time to Dallas in 1986. Again on her own, Patterson changed the name of her firm to Patterson House Design Group, returned to operating as a sole practitioner, and added Texas interior design registration to her list of credentials. When she again pulled up roots in 2001, relocating to Tucson, Arizona, a state with no interior design regulations, she qualified for a contractor's license.

As a sole practitioner, Patterson faces a number of challenges. When operating alone, the designer/owner must wear all of the hats for the business: CEO, office manager, designer, marketing director, receptionist, project manager, bookkeeper, purchasing agent, and myriad others. It can be a challenge to keep up with all of the daily tasks required to keep a design firm running smoothly and operating successfully. Inadequate subcontractors and unreasonable clients can be challenging at times as well.

While she enjoys all of the firm's profits and the "glory" for her design concepts, Patterson also is responsible for any client or project problems. "I want all of my customers to be happy with their projects, and I go to great lengths to be sure that happens, even when it requires a costly solution," she says. Her mission includes emphasizing the importance of safety and welfare for her clients, and creating a comfortable environment based on each client' needs.

As is often the case with small business owners and especially with sole practitioners, marketing is one task that can fall by the wayside. Patterson invests a great deal of both time and money participating in local designer showcases, which serve as an excellent platform for potential customers to view her work. She places small advertisements in a number of consumer magazines, and also writes for a number of newspapers and magazines, an effort that has allowed her to build credibility and present herself to the public as an expert in her field.

Furthering her efforts, Patterson wants to develop an online presence. Her basic website needs to be fine-tuned and improved to be a more successful marketing tool. Patterson also views her membership and participation in ASID as a major marketing tool. She uses her ASID appellation routinely in all marketing efforts and has become involved in leadership of the Arizona South chapter, where she served as chapter president in 2009.

Patterson attributes her decades of success as a sole practitioner to simple perseverance and confidence in herself and her talent as a designer, as well as an acute awareness of the world of design. While practicing as a sole proprietor for over four decades has worked well for Patterson, she confesses that in more recent years she has considered the advantages of taking on a partner. In Tucson she found herself integrating with the younger designers, partnering informally with a couple of them on some projects.

Looking to the future and her own end game, Patterson expects to work another five to ten years as a sole practitioner, then close down the business and retire. Before she does, though, she aims to spend time sharing her experiences and knowledge with those young designers coming up to help them pick up their own careers where she leaves off.

In Process: Design Team Structure and Project Management

Interior design may be a creative profession, but it still requires direction, structure, and consistency—and these three elements grow in importance as a firm's head count blossoms. How will projects progress through the firm? Will you establish specific, set teams or specialty studios, or will employees be grouped on a per-project basis? How often will you communicate with each client, and who will be responsible for initiating and monitoring this contact? Will the firm owners remain involved in day-to-day design decisions, or will their role be more strategic and managerial? Who will be responsible for getting contracts signed, placing orders, and supervising installation and construction?

Once again, the structure of a firm on day one may not be appropriate five or ten years down the line. As such, it is important to frequently monitor in-house processes and practices and adjust accordingly.

Process Makes Perfect: Soucie Horner Ltd.

Soucie Horner Ltd. is a nationally recognized residential interior architecture and design firm led by principals Shea Soucie and Martin Horner. Trained together at the Art Institute of Chicago and École Spéciale d'Architecture in Paris, Soucie attends to the architectural aspects of design while Horner specializes in fabric, furniture, and décor. Taken together, their talents deliver lush, layered living spaces that enhance the pleasures of home. Based in Chicago, Soucie Horner has been commissioned for projects throughout the United States and Mexico. Recently, the firm has been featured in magazines such as *House Beautiful, House & Garden, Gourmet, Shelter, Traditional Home*, and *Robb Report: Luxury Home*.

Like many small business owners, when Shea Soucie and Martin Horner first launched their firm, Soucie Horner, in fall of 2000, the two partners managed the business and its projects more by instinct than by a set system. From the beginning, the Chicago-based practice focused on high-end residential projects and grew consistently, adding two to three employees per year in response to a growing workload.

For the first few years, it worked well. Soucie and Horner were both involved in the design process, with Soucie gravitating toward the architectural aspects of a design, while Horner focused on the furniture, fabric, and decorations. To help run the business, the duo worked with an external business consultant.

About three years later, the firm reached eight to ten employees, which required a slight change in operations with the formal addition of a business manager. "Before that, it was a business you could manage instinctually. Martin and I knew that in terms of revenues, we would be able to manage what we were doing. But once we started gaining properties, bought our office, and began looking five to ten years out, we had to strategize how we were going to work," Soucie recalls. New concerns included the addition of employee benefits and incentives like a bonus program. Soucie and Horner set about strategically planning five to ten years in advance, projecting revenue

streams and calculating how many and what type of employees would be needed to reach those goals.

Reaching twenty employees in 2007, however, proved to be an organizational tipping point. "Martin and I felt like the business was taking a step beyond what we were able to manage on our own," Soucie recalls. Several disconnects had developed among employees. On the managerial side, Soucie and Horner felt a growing distance between the two partners and individual employees as the duo's time stretched thin and they were unable to connect with each employee on the same level. "When you grow your business, you may end up being the only one who was there from the beginning, while you have thirty people who do not understand where you came from or how the business started," says Soucie. "People start going in a million directions. How do you get everyone on the same page? How do you maintain and explain your core values?"

A secondary disconnect was arising among employees as well, as they felt segregated by their duties. At the time, architectural and design components of projects were separate from furnishings and purchasing, with many designers disengaging from a project once it was handed off to another employee.

The consensus was that continuing with the original firm management style—with slight tweaks to handle the bigger entity—could establish control, but it could also result in controlled chaos, something neither principal wanted. The firm needed to grow, not in head count but in structure. "Growth doesn't necessarily mean becoming huge, with sixty to a hundred employees. It can also mean internal growth and strategy and change," says Horner. To grow the firm into a well-oiled machine, a systematic overhaul would be necessary.

Recognizing they were in over their heads, Soucie and Horner brought in a business consultant, Tom Beaton of Next Step LLC, whom they had met at a leadership retreat. In analyzing the business, Beaton began interviewing each employee to find out what could be improved. The consensus was that they had a good business that could continue, but in order to be great, change would be necessary. It would not be easy and would require a significant investment of time and money, Beaton cautioned, and they would need external help to execute it successfully.

Soucie and Horner decided it was worth the investment, and after recruiting an organizational consultant, Kris Lonsway of Lonsway Consulting, to help execute the changes, the firm went through an official reorganization, including the development and institution of a specific project management system. To begin, the firm crafted a mission statement and set of values, incorporating feedback from every employee. These values not only guide the firm as an entity, but also are used as benchmarks for employees during annual reviews.

Soucie and Horner also recognized that every aspect of the business could no longer go through the bottleneck of the two principals. Structurally, the firm formally divided its employees into a specific set of studios. Under the new arrangement, individuals are purposefully integrated by studio throughout the life of a project so as to eliminate the segregation that had previously existed between project phases. Two custom design studios—dubbed Orange and Blue—manage fifteen to twenty clients each. They are set up in a structure reminiscent of Soucie and Horner's first division of labor, each with two studio leaders, one from an architectural/design background and another with more of a focus on furnishings. These leads are not only responsible for dealing with clients but also oversee educating and mentoring associate designers. They also help Soucie and Horner manage the firm as a whole. Under them, each studio has a "functional lead" in more of a processing role. Combined, these four studio leaders operate as a check and balance system with one another.

Rounding out the organization are the Green, Yellow, and Red studios. The Green Studio oversees purchasing, while Yellow is a new venture for the firm, created to handle development work. The Red Studio handles procurement, installation, and follow-up. This is a deliberate separation from what Soucie and Horner had observed in other practices. "In most firms, designers are expected to design, purchase, expedite, install, and manage the process. Designers may be great at design, but they're not necessarily great at business, so we hired experts in operations who oversee getting everything installed on time and undamaged. It allows the designers to focus on keeping the client happy," Soucie explains. Studio Green is also the financial management studio and includes a CPA and an assistant who ensure that projects—and designers—stay on track and on budget.

Soucie and Horner also formalized the process for a project from start to finish. With the institution of a set process, everyone now knows how a project goes through the pipeline and whose roles and responsibilities come into play during specific times. Before, Soucie explains, people were working in more of a vacuum, which made it hard to understand why it was so important to do one step months ahead of time, but now, with the more integrated process, each team member understands how each step impacts the overall process of a project.

As Beaton predicted, the new programs and organization were not accomplished overnight. "It's a hard process," Soucie cautions. "When you get big, everything can no longer go through you. You have to set up something that you can manage." The biggest challenge in rolling out the changes? Finding the right person to help implement the system and then making the time to do it. "We struggle with this on a daily basis. We love to design, but in order to achieve this I spent 60 percent of my time over the last four months doing nothing but organizational stuff. It pulls you away from what you went into the business for, but we knew that it had to be done," Soucie says. "When you decide that you want to keep growing and have a great business, you have to implement a system—otherwise it will end up being a bunch of designers in a room that's chaotic."

Challenges aside, both partners agree it was worth the effort. A more organized and delegated system of management also aids employee retention by instilling a deeper sense of individual ownership, and having set project processes in place helps reduce the amount of time needed to get new employees up to speed. Two years into the reorganization, the firm's evolution has continued. In fact, continual tweaking and reevaluation is a key part of the strategic planning so that the firm remains continually successful.

Step-by-Step: Chute Gerdeman Retail

Based in Columbus, Ohio, Chute Gerdeman Retail is a full-service retail design firm with more than fifty employees that emphasizes the power of design to shape clients' brands and inspire their customers. Founded in 1989 by Elle Chute and Denny Gerdeman, the company has been named to *Design and Display Ideas* magazine's annual Portfolio Awards issue for eleven consecutive years. Its clients include M&M's/Mars, Walt Disney Imagineering, Target, Levi Strauss, Kohl's, Smithsonian, Lowe's, Pepsi-Cola, and Starwood.

Everyone loves a good story, and perhaps nowhere is this more important than in the retail and entertainment sector, which is why Columbus, Ohio–based retail design firm Chute Gerdeman Retail approaches each project through a set methodology that has proven successful for more than twenty years.

As a firm, Chute Gerdeman's overriding goal is not just to give clients beautifully crafted spaces or displays but also to give them a business strategy that offers the best return on investment (or ROI) on design. "Our process is probably different from other firms because we're so focused on the business solution. In retail, the question is, how do we take our client's business and increase it? How do we increase market share and brand awareness in a consumer's mind? It's always about bottom-line results," explains Denny Gerdeman, co-principal with Elle Chute.

With this in mind, Chute Gerdeman's team developed a project methodology for the practice that both allows each project to progress smoothly and helps prevent any last-minute surprises. "We put together the process based on our experiences over the years, and it allows us to keep the project focused, but we also put it together in self-defense, in a way," Gerdeman explains. "We don't want to have clients come back at the eleventh hour and change their minds, which is a fear I think every designer has after spending a lot of time and effort developing an idea, concept, and direction."

Thus, each Chute Gerdeman project progresses through five set phases:

1. Foundation

   This introductory phase is an information-gathering bonanza that unofficially begins in the interviewing stage. "When we are first being interviewed by a client and discussing the project itself, we are interviewing them as well," says Gerdeman. "I try to understand the client and their nuances, their personalities, who they are, how they like to work, and what they are capable of, because at the same time I am also determining who from the CG team will best complement the client's team."

   "Many of our clients are national performers that have large internal staffs; different silos manage different parts of the business, and sometimes the major heads don't have much time to talk to each other," explains Chute. "We become the nexus of information between their groups, and this allows us to get a clear picture of what, in their mind, will define a success." Gerdeman adds: "We learned early on that it is important for us to separate out the issues of the individual players and make sure they all have the opportunity to have their voices heard. Otherwise, someone can wait in the weeds for you and trip you up further down the line."

   Using the information gleaned from the client, Chute Gerdeman then crafts its own internal project team, drawing from the variety of in-house disciplines—from brand strategy, brand communications, and environments design to visual strategy, architecture, and design development.

   Assigning responsibility is key to the methodology's success. To this end, each project team is assigned a trio of senior staff—a program manager, a creative director, and an account executive—that manages the team's progress. "It is a necessity to have a strong project manager," Gerdeman notes. "They're the glue."

During this phase Chute Gerdeman also assesses whether any additional external or secondary research needs to be done in the client's marketplace and, if so, works within the firm's network of specialists to conduct an even deeper dive. "We want to make sure we clearly understand what is defined as the true measure of success," Chute says.

2. Ideation

With plenty of background information in hand, the project moves into the ideation phase, in which the design team begins developing "what if" scenarios along with sketches, imagery, and rough concepts and ideas. Within the firm's Columbus, Ohio, office there are several "war rooms" designated for this phase, where clients are immersed in the developing ideas.

"To me, this is the single most important part of the entire process," Gerdeman says. "This is where we really have the client involved and part of the decision process." From its research in the foundation phase, Chute Gerdeman distills the brand's position and personality into five or six words and phrases; and from these words, the war room is filled with imagery, drawings, sketches, and words or phrases that relate to the brand's position.

Bringing the client into the war room for a hands-on session, Chute Gerdeman presents a range of rough project directions and concepts—everything from a brand "evolution" to a brand "revolution"—that, in effect, take the client's temperature on change. Over the course of four to six hours, the client and CG team work through the concepts to determine which is best for the brand. "People are tired when it is done because they are engaged the entire time, but at the end of this phase, we, as a design team, know the direction to head in, and we also have the client's support on this decision. It prevents us from getting off track," says Gerdeman.

3. Creation

From here, the creation phase begins the process of concept refinement. By the end of this phase,

the client should see exactly what their store will look and feel like. The concept that emerges from the ideation phase is modeled and refined, and digital fly-throughs are often created to help show how the environment will affect a visitor's five senses. What will be the feature of the store or restaurant? Will the cash wrap be in the rear or the front? How should the merchandise displays progress through the store? How will the customer flow through the space, from when they first drive up through the purchasing process?

Sometimes in this phase Chute Gerdeman also will conduct surveys with potential customers to test the concept—especially when it is a new prototype—and then adjust accordingly.

4. Evolution

Evolution is design development—or, as Gerdeman explains, where the rubber meets the road. Here, the firm's detail specialists dig in and construct mockups. In some cases, the mockups may be full-scale versions of the graphics. In others, it may involve creating an entire store to better understand where to place merchandise or which lighting is best.

5. Realization

The final phase is just as it sounds: architectural documents are completed, construction bids are compiled and narrowed down, final artwork is produced. The actual services involved in this phase vary by client, as does the time required to complete the project. And wrapping up the entire process is the actual construction.

"Every client is a little bit different and we always need to modify it to some extent, Gerdeman notes. "But that's the beauty of it. The overall process we have up front using our strategy is very consistent, so that when we get to the execution, we can modify it."

Another benefit is the constant client contact that is required. Clients are encouraged to come to the office as much as possible, and before the project even begins the foundation phase, clients receive a general overview of what is to come to ensure they are comfortable with the level of involvement and time that will be required on their end. "You can't communicate with the client too much," Gerdeman cautions. "If you're not communicating, the client assumes nothing is happening and starts to get nervous."

The set phases also provide built-in stopping points for the team to pause, reflect, and check that the project and its goals are still aligned, and that the budget is in check as well. "You can't overpromise and under deliver, giving a concept that will cost $1 million to build when the client only has $500,000," Gerdeman says. "It is the responsibility of our lead designer and the person in charge of design development to make sure we're within the appropriate boundaries for success."

Come Together: Working with Collaborators and Consultants

Just as no man is an island, no designer does it all alone: it is extremely likely that, at some point, a firm may benefit from expertise or experience that only an external resource can provide. Outside consultants or collaborators can prove especially helpful for smaller design firms who are stretched for time or manpower. There is a long list of potential collaborators: contractors, suppliers, vendors and sales representatives, and consultants may be required, not to mention other design professionals, including architects and specialty designers like lighting designers or landscape architects. These working relationships can take many forms, from one-off consultancies or partnerships that span only one phase of a project to long-term relationships that evolve over the course of several years, projects, and clients.

Consider the experiences of HEDGE Design Collective, a consortium of designers that developed among a handful of designers and architects, many of whom were graduating from Southern California Institute of Architecture (SCI-ARC) in 1995.

"At the time, there didn't seem to be a lot of building going on relative to the grand scheme of things," recalls John Hirsch, a founding member of the Collective and cofounder of Space International, a Los Angeles–based architecture and interior design practice. "There was a group of twelve or fifteen of us that went through graduate school together, and we wanted to continue learning from one another. We decided to try and band together, share resources, and continue to share that collaborative sense of learning. Any work that came about we could share as well."

Setting up space in a corner of one of SCI-ARC's buildings (which was bartered: use of the space in exchange for design work to spruce it up), HEDGE Design Collective began marketing by word of mouth, with members informing their instructors and mentors that the consortium was willing to take any work. "We were willing to be hired guns. Drafters, model makers, whatever it took to get us going, we would take any job they could throw our way," recalls Hirsch.

The work came in all shapes and sizes: model-building projects turned into hand-me-down garage conversions. Hirsch received a commission coming out of school and turned to his fellow HEDGE members for help. Landscape architecture, graphic design, web design, even floral design and clothing design—it all got folded into the interdisciplinary nature of the Collective.

Legally, the Collective did not exist as an established firm, so as work came in, people within the group began partnering up and founding official ventures, morphing the initial work-share idea into an association of independent firms that were loosely related under HEDGE Design Collective. Hirsch, for instance, partnered up with Michael Ferguson, another collective member, to form Space International.

As the individual practices grew and founding members moved out of town or returned to academia, the Collective disbanded as a full entity. Loose connections, however, remain. One former member, for instance, lives in the Bay Area, where Space International recently needed help on some retail projects. Naturally, they turned to their old colleague, who completes the project's drafting work at home and ventures to Los Angeles, Space International's locale, every few weeks for a design charette.

In some cases, as with HEDGE Design Collective, collaborators may be former colleagues or employees, but more of ten, the types of collaborators that interact with a firm over its lifetime are numerous. And given the back-and-forth required for success, finding partners who share similar values with your firm is key. Take a moment to revisit the earlier case studies on hiring. Just as a mis-hire can prove costly, so too can mismatched partnerships and collaborations be a drain on finances and resources.

As you would do when deciding whether to hire a new employee, take a moment to think about the exact expertise or advice you are seeking. What will each party be responsible for bringing to the project? What kind of interaction will be expected, and how will the relationship be monitored? Will the collaboration take part during one specific phase of a project, or will it be multiphased? Is there enough work to merit hiring someone on a permanent basis, or will collaborating with an independent consultant suffice?

After determining the type of consultant needed, ask around for references. Similar to preparing a job description and collecting resumes, create a request for proposal (RFP), collect proposals and bids, and narrow the candidates. And, much like extending an offer of employment, prepare a contract that specifically delineates the relationship, including each participant's responsibilities and expectations, and what will define success.

Managing an outside consultant is much like managing an employee: communication is key, so it is also important to define how you will stay in touch. Will you trade daily emails? Weekly phone calls? Have bi-weekly in-person meetings? The earlier this is addressed, the better.

LEEDing the Way: Ecoworks Studio

Carlie Bullock-Jones, ASID, LEED AP, is a sustainable design consultant with Ecoworks Studio in Atlanta, guiding multiple clients, consultants, and design teams through green building initiatives and sustainable strategies specific to their projects. She has collaborated on many award-winning LEED projects and has written, prepared, and presented multiple and various green building topics, including the facilitation of sustainable design (LEED) eco-charettes. She remains current with the industry through her participation in and speaking engagements at many green building conferences, such as the AIA National Convention, EnvironDesign, International Contemporary Furniture Fair (ICFF), and USGBC International Greenbuild Conference and Expo. Bullock-Jones was also a member of the U.S. Green Building Council's former LEED for Commercial Interiors Core Committee and is an active member of the LEED Curriculum Committee as well as the National ASID Sustainable Design Council. In 2004, she received the ASID Georgia Chapter Presidential Citation for Distinguished Service to the Society and Profession. As a frequent speaker on sustainable design issues, Bullock-Jones also serves as a USGBC LEED faculty member and adjunct professor in the College of Architecture, Design and Construction at Auburn University.

As the founder of Ecoworks Studio, LLC, in Atlanta, sustainable design consultant Carlie Bullock-Jones works with designers, architects, contractors, and owners to develop and implement sustainable strategies in both their projects and their practices. Her relationships range from leading in-house workshops or seminars on LEED certification to consulting on projects seeking specific LEED certification and serving as a green point person. "I've received calls from people looking to do their first LEED project who want to do it right the first time. I have received calls because a client is requiring the project be LEED certified and I have been hired from the owner's perspective," she says. "Or I have received calls because a contractor knows the sustainable aspects of their portion of a project but isn't sure about how to coordinate the rest of the team. I also have people call who want to go green but don't necessarily want to get LEED certified."

For some developers, considering sustainability strategies is a competitive necessity as surrounding developments are going green and tenants are requesting it. For some design firms, bringing an external consultant like Bullock-Jones on board frees up resources and time. "I have had firms that have already done LEED projects call and say they have so much going on with schedules and budgets that going green is something they don't have the resources or time to concentrate on full-time. Or they would like to focus on only their portion without having to worry about coordinating all the team members," she says. Her experience also is a benefit. "There may be roadblocks or things that I know are typical of a project that I can foresee and help the team work through, rather than have them not see it coming and stub their toes the first time around," she says.

For Bullock-Jones, when it comes to addressing the sustainable attributes for a specific project, the earlier the communication starts with the entire team, the better. "If you think of all the LEED credits that are available, two-thirds of them are considered design-related, so there is a lot you can address early on—but a small portion of what LEED involves is *not* design- and construction-related, it is location-based," Bullock-Jones says. "If a client calls before they have even selected a site of a building, that is most helpful because we can look at the site and its attributes. Is it near mass transit? Is it in an urban environment that's near a lot of amenities? Many people don't realize the process starts before they get into the actual design."

Entering the relationship, Bullock-Jones prefers to start with an eco-charette, where all team members review the overall goals and what will be needed to achieve them. "The charette is critical for multiple reasons. One, it helps people understand their roles and what they will be responsible for," she says. "It also helps me understand how much I need to be involved, how educated the team already is on going green, and how much direction may be needed. Does the client want to pursue LEED certification, or do they want to aim for a higher designation like LEED Silver, Gold, or Platinum certification? Do they need me to green their specifications, or does the team already have experience with that? It varies with each project, and the eco-charette helps determine the scope of my services." Another benefit of an upfront charette is that it helps rally the troops and build enthusiasm on both sides of the equation. "It's best when everyone comes in with an open mind and realizes that we're all students and can learn from one another," she says.

Integrating consultants within the team throughout the project is key. "Sometimes if the owner has hired me and I have not been introduced early on as an integral team member, it can appear as though I'm there to make their lives difficult and that LEED will simply add one more thing to do," Bullock-Jones says. "That can be a challenge when coming on late without the team understanding why you're involved, and it is why the support of the owner or the client up front is so important."

Keep in mind that the benefits of bringing in an external consultant aren't just one-sided. "As a consultant, I get to meet a lot of amazing people who are working toward the same goal. I also learn something on every project," Bullock-Jones says. "The team member that leaves that first eco-charette and then calls or emails me excited with ideas for the project is what encourages me."

Supply and Demand: Vendors and Suppliers

Assembling a crack team of design professionals able to create elaborate and innovative design solutions is only one part of a successful design project. Identifying and signing on the best team of outside vendors and suppliers to implement the design concept, and turning it into reality, is just as important. Having that perfect implementation team in place before you need them on the job is a crucial process for a successful design firm.

Love the One You're With: Bullock Associates Design Consultants Inc.

Doug Bullock, ARIDO, ASID, self-proclaimed head coach and cheerleader for Bullock Associates Design Consultants Inc., in Toronto, Ontario, has been with the firm since its inception as Jeffrey/Meyrick-Eastick Design Consultants in 1979. By 1985, he was a junior partner in the firm, and two years later, when Tony Meyrick-Eastick left the firm to pursue other opportunities, Bullock became a full partner in Jeffrey/Bullock Design Consultants Inc.

Shortly thereafter he became managing partner. The firm works with corporate clients, with a focus on exceeding client expectations through innovative design solutions.

Bullock Associates Design Consultants Inc. has high standards for itself: a corporate philosophy of exceeding client expectations for its work, and a vision of being known as a leader in innovative design solutions. The firm also promotes design, construction, and operation of buildings that are environmentally responsible, profitable, and healthy for those who occupy them. But this is not all Doug Bullock's firm seeks to achieve.

Highlighted on the company website and repeated on the wall in the lobby of its Toronto offices are the organization's core values. Sandwiched between beliefs about striving to deliver quality interior design services and being ethical is Bullock Associates' belief in "treating all our vendors with respect and fairness." Accordingly, vendors and suppliers are also included in the firm's tenet of treating clients ethically.

These strong corporate standards and cultural values are a manifestation of Bullock's personal passion and enthusiasm for helping people, whether they are clients, vendors, suppliers, employees, or students. It is important to him that his workplace includes diverse personalities and is a fun place to work, and as such, credit is given whenever and wherever it is due to those contributing to a project. The firm creates sixty-second slide shows of projects that include the names of vendors, suppliers, and others involved in the successful completion of projects. These slide shows are sent out to a database of four to five hundred past, present, and potential clients. Bullock also recognizes his vendors and suppliers through email, sending out a news update to the firm's database each year, as well as periodic email notifications of awards the firm has earned, noting all who were involved in the project. What's more, Bullock Associates gives awards to vendors or suppliers who have exhibited excellence in dealing with the firm.

Bullock places high value on vendors and supplier relationships with his firm. These industry firms play an important part in the success of the firm's projects and in its ability to achieve its vision of innovation and philosophy of exceeding client expectations. "We are only as good as the suppliers and vendors we surround ourselves with for each project," Bullock explains.

Few designers, it seems, take the extra steps to incorporate specific requirements and processes into finding the right vendors, suppliers, contractors, or subcontractors with whom to collaborate on projects. However, doing research and interviewing ahead of time to find the best people to work with may go a long way in eliminating frustration and embarrassment when a supplier or contractor is found to be lacking midway through a project. Bullock's firm has gone so far as to establish a process for indentifying new team members to support its projects, and it has developed an International Organization for Standardization (ISO) process through which a vendor can become an "approved vendor" with the firm. The process involves filling out a corporate information form and providing references, which are checked before an in-house committee review and interview. In addition to the basic corporate information supplied by vendors, Bullock also looks for attitude, enthusiasm, professionalism, knowledge, and ethics.

Bullock feels it is extremely important for their supplier and implementation teams to share his firm's corporate culture and ethical standards. "Personalities, culture, and attitude have to be shared," he explains. In developing long-term relationships with the various team members, such as implementation teams and suppliers, Bullock believes that it is done "like all things in life. You be yourself, treat people like you would like to be treated." Bullock's greatest challenge in building project teams, however, is a crux of many relationships, both business and personal: simply finding the ones you like and that like you, too.

Love the One You're With, Part Two: Renwall Interiors Limited

Tony Rainho is the founder and CEO of Renwall Interiors Limited, a privately owned contracting firm located in Toronto, Ontario, and specializing in commercial leasehold improvements. Started in 1984, the firm has built its reputation on professional workmanship, quality performance, and personal service, dealing with customers based on a philosophy of integrity, reliability, fairness, and approachability. Rainho and a team of six employees provide general contractor services, act as project and construction managers, and maintain long-term relationships with clients by providing ongoing services related to maintaining their interior spaces.

"We have been working with interior design practitioners for most of the time we've been in business, nearly twenty years," says Tony Rainho, owner of Renwall Interiors Limited. Rainho believes that his people are part of a team driven by the interiors professionals, and although the company has never marketed directly to interior design firms, approximately 60 percent of its business involves an interior designer. Most of the firm's work comes from its established relationships with building management teams, who in turn hire the designers; or from tenants who bring in their own designers for remodeling or buildouts. Rainho finds that these relationships are usually positive in nature because the design professional sees the big picture. "As a contractor, you can talk to an interiors professional using industry terms," Rainho says, "the benefit being that our involvement is streamlined and allows us to do what we do best on the project."

While Renwall Interiors' services are sold directly to the client, the financial aspects are handled through a tendering process administered by the designer, who also signs off on progress invoicing. The design firm is paid directly by the client as well, not by the contractor, and the designer does not receive a commission from the contractor. The interior designer also acts as the contractor's ally in dealing with the client regarding payment issues, site conditions, and client requests.

Rainho finds that challenges may surface when working with younger, less experienced designers on a project. In some cases, a lack of experience may make a less-experienced designer more reluctant to make quick decisions, which in turn can create costly delays and affect budgets and schedules. Time can also be lost when contractors need to educate junior designers about the construction process as it relates to the issue du jour. For Rainho, an ideal interior design partner is one who is practical and realistic in terms of deadlines and budgets, and has a good understanding of the construction industry. He finds the best arrangements occur when the designer involves the contractor at an early stage of the project, as it allows more opportunity to have input on budgets and schedules.

Renwall Interiors has worked with Doug Bullock and Bullock Associates Design Consultants Inc. in Toronto for more than fifteen years—so long that Rainho can't remember how they first began working together. He suspects that they were working in an office building and Bullock requested a quote on a project for a new tenant. Obtaining the contract and completing the job to Bullock's satisfaction led to more collaboration over the years. At one time, as much as 75 percent of Renwall's work was generated through Bullock projects. They expect to be called on to quote on several projects for Bullock Design each year.

Although the early days of 2009 promised uncertain economic times, Rainho does not believe that vendor-designer relationships should be affected in a negative way, but rather feels the situation should enhance the relationship. Often in turbulent economic times, clients try to forgo a design professional to save money, which puts a larger burden on the contractor. "I find that life becomes much easier when a designer is on board," Rainho offers. "The materials are chosen, usually including associated costs, meaning I don't have to explain costs to the client or lug samples around. Often cost becomes secondary when the materials have been recommended by a designer."

A Two-Way Street: Coopertech Signs & Graphics

Craig Cooper entered the signage industry in 1970 as a shipper/receiver and installation assistant. Briefly leaving the industry to work as a sales representative for several companies, he returned to the sign industry in 1978, using his experience to take a position in sales. His nine years in sales served him well as preparation for beginning his own sign company, Technisigns, in 1987. His sign business thrived for twenty years, until it ultimately morphed into Coopertech Signs & Graphics. Under this new name, Cooper concentrates his efforts on relationships with interior designers and their clients. Cooper finds this approach allows him to combine work with pleasure as he operates his business under the motto "We Perform."

Every relationship is a two-way street (or, in some complex projects, a very crowded highway). Therefore, designers aren't the only ones who may benefit from a working relationship with a vendor—the positives (and negatives) go both ways.

Craig Cooper, owner of Coopertech Signs & Graphics, located in Mississauga, Ontario, has been in the signage business for thirty years, bringing experience in material handling, product availability, and manufacturing to the design project team. In the early days of his business, Cooper did very little work with interior designers. Realizing he really enjoyed this creative side of his business, he turned his marketing efforts in the direction of the interior design community.

Over the years, Cooper has built strong relationships with interior designers—to the point that they now account for approximately 70 percent of his company's business. A sizable portion of the other 30 percent of his firm's revenue is a result of direct sales to end users that come from client referrals from interior designers. An important part of his marketing efforts to reach the interior design community involves networking with designers in local professional associations such as the Association of Registered Interior Designers of Ontario (ARIDO) and ASID. For instance, Cooper has held the industry partner position on the board of directors for ASID's Upstate New York–Canada East chapter for two terms.

Cooper regularly gets projects from word-of-mouth referrals between designers and is quite satisfied with his working designer relationships, as he is considered to be a member of their team. In many cases, designers bring in drawings detailing the signs required, including layouts, dimensions, and required materials. From those detailed drawings, Cooper can create the products that will enhance the final project.

Like many designers, when first becoming involved in a project Cooper wants to know the end result: What are the designer and client's expectations? Possibilities and alternatives are then discussed as potential solutions to the design challenge. Cooper's objective is to assure that all parties are on the same track in fulfilling the design objectives. Often, it is not until near the end of the project—and its budget—that he is brought on board, but Cooper's ability to make recommendations for different materials and price points can help offset this late timing. In addition, his thirty-plus years in the signage business also help him foresee issues that may arise before they become problems.

But in addition to signs and graphics, what are the benefits a close relationship with Cooper offers to designers? Cooper believes he is often a good source of knowledge for new hires at design firms. Seeing many design programs spend little time focusing on his products and their role in a design project, Cooper can educate the new designers about his field and products. He also serves as a resource for signage types that he does not handle personally, and his familiarity with requirements for exterior signage makes him a good source of information. He can also save designers time and money by doing site visits on their behalf before preparing quotes for their signage needs.

Cooper is also on the receiving end of benefits from his relationships with interior designers. Just as he can do site visits to save the designers time, it likewise benefits him to have a designer who does the site visit and works out details with their clients. "I always find it easier to deal with an educated consumer," he notes. There are also a few financial benefits for him in his designer-vendor relationships. Designers usually forward his invoices on to clients for payment, which helps get them paid promptly, But the real benefit for Cooper is that the designers—and their completed projects—serve as "qualifiers" for him. When working on projects for large companies with multiple locations, Cooper has received additional business when managers from a company's home office visit satellite offices where his signage and graphics are used. And as a result of his close industry ties, Cooper finds himself less in a sales position, vying for acceptance of product: designers' clients view him as a solution provider, not a sales representative, allowing him to concentrate on the project. His pricing tends to be budgetary and generally is accepted by the clients, as they know the designer is familiar with his charges and reliability. "When I meet with a designer and their client, the focus is on what, how, and when, not *if* it can be done," he says. "Also, the client tends to give me more information, and trust preexists because the designer includes me as a team member."

As with all relationships, the best benefit everyone involved in some way. Turbulence in the economy makes Cooper's industry relationships even stronger. "In the past few recessions I have been through, designers have relied on me more to assist in site visits, as they are shorthanded. I give suggestions to reduce costs or sign alternatives which still keep the integrity of the design," he says. For instance, there have been situations where he assisted in upscaling existing signage to sharpen up offices, with the ultimate goal of improving client recognition and market share and enhancing client sales. "I become a closer team member during recessions, as time and staff shortages tighten the purse strings."

Clients and Customers

Vendors, suppliers, and other designers or collaborators aren't the only relationships essential to a successful practice. There is, of course, the not-so-small matter of clients and customers.

What clients want in a designer remains an ever-open-ended question, so establishing a connection with each client is key not only to the success of a specific project, but also to the success of a firm. Interior design is, after all, a service industry, and word of mouth goes far. What's more, many clients may have long-term potential. Indeed, many A&D firms are now offering "life-cycle services" or services like ongoing interior and exterior maintenance, updates, and adjustments that last the lifespan of a project.

Know Your Client

ASID, from "Know Your Client: Fundamentals for Effective Relationships"

Knowing the project specifications and scope of work your client wants is important, but the key to a successful project is understanding your client's needs, expectations and what they value most from the working relationship. To find the answers to these questions, ASID conducted multiple surveys of both interior designers and their clients in different specialty areas (e.g., office, healthcare, residential, hospitality). The results provide guidance on the best consulting methods a designer should use with a client. These methods not only secure and guarantee a client's business, but also ensure the client's experiences are positive and develop a long-standing relationship that benefits all parties in the years to come.

Understanding

Communication is critical to pleasing a client. Listening, asking questions and discussing the project goals will demonstrate your ability to understand the project parameters and develop a solution to meet the client's unique needs. Designers must show how the presented project ideas and techniques relate back to the client's objective. If the client is unhappy with your proposed ideas, never impose your solution or aesthetic. Rather, work with them to find out what's not working and develop an alternate plan for the space.

Coordination

Of utmost importance to clients is the ability of the designer to handle all aspects of the project, in particular ordering and being a resource for product and materials. Gain the client's confidence and assure them that you are responsible for integrating all aspects of the design process and will get the job done right. This is a key component to creating a trusting and open relationship with the client.

Experience

Designers may be surprised to find that potential clients are less concerned with referrals and more focused on professionalism. When presenting your credentials and examples of your work, make sure they relate specifically to the client's needs. Don't overemphasize your previous experience, but do demonstrate your expertise and knowledge of the client's business and, if appropriate, the specialty that relates to the client's project.

Budget

Although mentioned least by surveyed clients, it is still important that designers establish a budget with their client and work within it and avoid making costly mistakes. It is not critical to stress that a proposed solution is inexpensive or cheap. Rather, demonstrate that it is the best or most efficient option and will help maximize the client's budget.

Taken together, these guidelines comprise a set of consulting principles to help you effectively work with your clients and bring success to your design practice.

Be knowledgeable about your business and your client's business. Ask questions, share your knowledge, and stay focused on your client's goals.

Offer solutions for the problem in which you have been hired. Put the right team together and provide both yourself and your client with the resources you need to successfully complete the project.

Develop relationships with clients and other potential partners. The most important partner in a project is your client. If you manage their expectations and establish trust, you can almost guarantee repeat business and positive referrals.

Constant Communication: Duffy Design Group

Dennis Duffy, IIDA, founded Boston-based Duffy Design Group in 1987, focusing on residential design projects alongside a small bit of retail, hospitality, and development work. An extension of Duffy's custom furniture design, D SCALE, was founded in 2007. Based on modernistic ideals, D SCALE is Duffy's retail custom furniture store that also features artistic accessories and vintage furnishings and accent pieces.

For Dennis Duffy, founder of Duffy Design Group in Boston, today's clients aren't what they were when he opened his firm in 1987, which may not be a bad thing for the profession. "People have become much more design-focused and aware of what is out there," Duffy notes. "Before, people either didn't focus on design at all or, if they did, they hired someone and said, 'you do it.' I think the era of 'you do it' is gone." In contrast, he says, today's client relationship "is much more collaborative, which is great. You are not working in a vacuum. Instead, you have input that is somewhat informed because clients are aware of more options. The collaboration is better communication."

While not every client is perfect, Duffy works to ensure as smooth a process as possible. In an ideal world, designers would be able to interview potential clients as thoroughly as they are interviewed themselves. "I would love to make them take a Myers-Briggs test or ask for references from three recent business interactions, but we haven't been able to pull that off yet," Duffy says, and he acknowledges that even if this were more frequently done, it is often not possible during economic downturns such as the 1991 and 2008 recessions. To help counteract this, he advocates taking a course in interpersonal psychology to better understand the signals clients may give off.

While he has not taken a formal class on interpersonal relationships, over the years Duffy has developed an awareness of warning signs that may foreshadow a rocky relationship, such as a heightened sense of entitlement or an anger management problem. For Duffy, an ideal client is professional, engaged, informed, and excited. "You want to work with a client who is engaged and contributing to the project, but at the same time, you don't want someone who is looking to go to war with you or looking for conflict."

He begins each relationship by meeting with potential clients several times, both in the firm's offices and in the clients' spaces to get a better sense of their needs and their lifestyles, something that is especially important for his residential clients. "On the residential side, you want to see how they live. You gather visual cues from how they live and, if the client is a couple, how they interact," Duffy explains. "On the commercial projects it is a completely different mindset because there is much less personality involved. It is more about the identity and the function and bringing those two elements together in a three-dimensional architectural envelope."

To help drill down with his residential clients, Duffy assigns them homework. "You can describe your goals in words, but I find that most people have an easier time conveying their goals by picture," he says, noting that clients are asked to sit down with design magazines or a "look book" and, at their leisure, flag images they like. Duffy then discusses their choices, which he considers a key follow-up step. "You can ask a lot of questions and, over time, you learn what questions to ask, what visual cues to watch for, and what things may be implied but not said." (On commercial projects, such homework is already done, as clients usually come with a brand or concept in hand.)

Keeping these initial lines of communication open throughout the life of a project is key for Duffy. In the past, this may have meant meeting with a client weekly for status updates. Now, in the world of email and instant gratification, he makes it a policy to reply to client emails on a same-day basis. If an answer is not available to a specific question that same day, Duffy makes sure the client receives a response to acknowledge the question was received and that its answer is forthcoming. "It is all about service," Duffy notes. "We are offering our talent and experience, but we are also in a service industry, so I try hard to make sure we continually recognize that." For informational inquiries—fact-checking or confirming a delivery date, for example—email suffices as a means of communication, but for more complicated questions Duffy is not phone shy. "Email is not a great form of communication because you cannot understand the nuances or intent," he notes "It is all interpretive."

Constant communication ensures that both designer's and client's expectations remain in line. "Managing expectations is huge, and it is one of the things we as designers have to be really aware of. You don't know that when you first start in the industry," Duffy says. "Clarity in communication is key. What you are expecting to achieve and what the client is expecting to achieve has to be on the same vector."

Duffy's communication with a client doesn't end with the conclusion of a project. Many times, his residential clients have become friends—in fact, most of his client relationships have developed into long-term associations. Although he has no set process in place to turn first-time clients into long-term relationships, Duffy finds it often evolves organically. Near the end of each project, for instance, the firm develops a final punch list, which can, in some instances, lead to future work as clients discover additional wants or needs. The firm also stays in touch with past clients through email blasts, posting firm news on its online blog, and participating in public events like DIFFA's Dining by Design program.

Keeping It Personal: Adesso Design Inc.

Influenced by a father with a PhD in chemistry, Mary Jane Grigsby, FASID, LEED AP, began her career with an undergraduate premedical degree. Although she loved the coursework and research—and the creativity it involved—she ultimately did not care for the field and returned to school for a master's degree in interior design. She opened MJR Interiors in Miami in 1990, working with both residential and commercial clients, and later moved the practice to Boca Raton. In 2000, Grigsby took on a partner, changing the firm name to MJR Design Partnership, and in 2008, she returned to working on her own under the firm name Adesso Design Inc.

Over the course of nearly twenty years in interior design, Mary Jane Grigsby has operated on a number of levels. She launched her first firm, MJR Interiors, in Miami in 1990 with just an office administrator for support. Five years later, Grisgby relocated the firm, which served both residential and commercial clients, to nearby Boca Raton. Five years after that, Grisgby expanded, adding a partner to help with the pressures and time constraints associated with owning and managing a business, and changed the firm's name to MJR Design Partnership. In 2008 she adjusted her business approach again, this time starting her own business, Adesso Designs.

The size of her businesses may have changed over the years, but one thing that has remained constant is Grigsby's focus on customer relationships. In fact, she is adamant that the most important factor in the success of her businesses has been cultivating and maintaining strong relationships with clients. "It is these relationships that are keeping my company above the black line in this bad economy," she noted during the economic crisis in 2008. At MJR Interiors, both Grigsby and her office administrator took responsibility for customer relations, while at MJR Design Partnership, all of the designers were responsible. Although there was no formal training in customer relationship management (CRM), each designer was taught how to answer the telephone, and the firm had rules of conduct for dealing with clients in order to develop and maintain strong relationships.

At Adesso Designs, Grigsby is once again the primary client contact. The firm's structure is such that she operates alone in the office, outsourcing all other functions like drawings, accounting, and design assistance. One of the strong points to this arrangement, she believes, is that all clients receive personal attention from the firm's principal without second- or third-level employees running interference, which in turn makes clients feel important.

Over the years, Grigsby has not used any specialized CRM software or online services for maintaining and tracking customer relationships, relying instead on personal service and lots of personal contact. "As I now outsource all those other tasks, I am free to be the one person in touch with clients," she says. "This arrangement keeps my overhead way down and gives me the time and funds to send flowers or small gifts on appropriate occasions." In addition to project-related communication, Grigsby calls clients from time to time to check on them and their families and sends holiday cards with personal notes throughout the year to stay in touch. Keeping her eye on the future, a key part of those personal phone calls is asking if there is anything she can do for the client, or if they have friends or business colleagues that might benefit from her services.

Providing design services for both residential and commercial customers in corporate and hospitality markets, Grigsby approaches her clients differently. Residential clients—including the snowbirds flocking to Florida in the winter, retirees, and families—require a more personal, hands-on approach, so she works directly with each to understand their challenges, create suitable and aesthetically pleasing solutions, and to reassure them throughout the process. Most contact with her residential clients is done by phone, which Grigsby considers a more personal way to communicate. Commercial clients, on the other hand, generally do not have the same personal connection to their environments and do not require as much in-person communication. Instead, project-related communication is done by email, which provides an efficient way to keep clients who are often on the go updated on progress, schedules, and unexpected challenges. When in-person business meetings are possible in commercial projects, Grigsby finds them much more formal and structured than meetings with a residential client.

Most of Grigsby's long-term, repeat customers come from her residential work, as those projects typically create a personal bond. Commercial work, on the other hand, doesn't always allow for such a bonding experience, and oftentimes the direct contacts on a project are promoted, move to a new department or division, or leave the company. As a result, repeat business with the same organization doesn't necessarily mean working with the same people on multiple projects. However, for Grigsby, keeping customers and getting new clients amounts to the same thing. Ninety percent of her business comes from referrals from existing clients, which creates a cycle. "The new clients become existing clients and refer me to other new clients, and so on," she explains. As a result, developing a successful relationship begins as soon as a contract is signed. Her credo: "There is no substitute for good customer service and continual reassurance that everything being done is understood and client expectations are being met."

Decoding the Design Process: Steven Miller Design Studio

Founded in 1999, Steven Miller Design Studio (SMDS) provides interior design services for both residential and commercial spaces. Originally founded as a one-man practice, the business grew to operate with five employees and, in addition to its original San Francisco studio, opened a second office in New York.

Given that most design across the globe is done for only 10 percent of the world's population, it's not surprising that for the majority of interior designers, a new client means a new introduction not only to the firm, but also to the values and processes of professional interior design as a whole. This makes clear client communication essential.

"It's important to understand that the relationship between client and designer is really what the entire process is about," says Steven Miller, principal and founder of Steve Miller Design Studio. "The more information you can gather from a client, the better you're able to interpret that client's desires."

With this in mind, in 2006 Miller began implementing a set process for communicating with clients before, during, and after a project. Working with Alexis Lerner, a New York–based architectural consultant, Miller developed a binder system that guides clients through a project from start to finish, ensuring that all parties involved are on the same level throughout the project's lifespan.

SMDS's process begins at the contract signing, where clients are deliberately walked through each item on the contract, with time to ask questions about the details. In the past, issues like purchasing have often been misunderstood, and the firm takes care to prevent these miscommunications from happening again. Miller's contract, for example, stipulates that the firm bills for product purchased on a client's behalf at a 33 percent markup on net. Clients, however, have made the assumption that taking products the firm has presented to them and buying them on their own will translate to a 33 percent discount. To counteract this, Miller is careful to explain upfront that the charge is based upon full purchasing services and, in fact, the firm doubles its consultation fees if full purchasing services are not conducted as agreed. "This is precisely why I have adopted a 'read and learn' approach to the contract," Miller explains.

Also at the contract signing, each client receives a 4-inch-thick binder tailored to his or her project. Initially rather empty—in fact, the contract is one of the first true inserts—the binder is divided into specific sections to track what is done and catalogues the phases still to come. It isn't just a guide for the client: by instituting a set process, SMDS is able to maintain consistency between projects in how the firm gathers and archives information.

While each binder's specific sections are modified with each project, they generally all include the following:

1. The signed contract
2. A completed client questionnaire that can be reviewed and updated as needed
3. Specifications, including tear sheets
4. Notes and documents
5. Drawings

"At the onset of a project, it is a great tool for us in explaining the process and clarifying the terms of the contract," explains Miller. "It also helps gather information from them." In this regard, the client questionnaire is especially important. Consider, for example, the insight that may be gleaned from a client's dining habits. Do they dine alone or do they have a family that dines together? Do they watch TV while eating or dine in a more formal setting? In his practice, Miller has come to observe that Californians often have kitchens and great rooms where they dine the majority of the time, reserving the dining room for more formal or special occasions. New York City residents, on the other hand, may never eat in the kitchen, but rather may eat in a separate breakfast or dining room. In another example, Miller cites the influence of family dynamic. A client with children

and pets that will have access to each room may need more durable finishes and no sharp edges. "The answers to these questions not only dictate programmatic concerns such as storage, access, seating, electronics, and lighting, but also define priorities in terms of aesthetics, comfort, and budgeting requirements," Miller explains.

"Every interaction with the client furthers the relationship, and as long as you're listening and open to reading the signs, there's nothing that a client says that can't somehow inform what you're doing," Miller continues. As an example, he recalls a client who was reviewing a color palette and offhandedly remarked that there was an abundance of green. Miller immediately took stock. How should this impact the design of the project as a whole? What color palette was most prominent in the client's home? Should more colorways be brought into the scheme?

How intensely the binder is embraced varies by client, with some bringing it diligently to meetings and others never showing up with it again. In either case, Miller knows he has taken preventive measures toward potential misunderstandings and sees two-sided benefits. "I knew that in developing this, we would have a tool to help them understand the process and help us glean information from clients that in turn help us do our job a lot better." In the end, he notes, if anything, "It's just a means of having a very consistent way of cataloguing things. I think the biggest benefit is that it provides structure to something that at times is very esoteric."

Building Long-Term Relationships: SJvD Design

Based in Long Beach, California, SJvD Design provides interior design and interior construction services for a range of clients in the commercial realm. Having studied both interior design and dance at Florida State University, SJvD Design founder Sybil J. B. van Dijs, ASID, CID, seeks to marry the two worlds in her work, offering functional and practical solutions that fluidly join each room into a choreographed, cohesive whole. Firm successes include a

58,000-sq.-ft. private building of suites in Beverly Hills; more than forty luxury suites, guestrooms, and adjoining pool and outdoor terraces at the Hotel Bel-Air; a 22,000-sq.-ft. private recreation venue in West Los Angeles; and a 56,000-sq.-ft. private residence in Jeddah, Saudi Arabia.

When it comes to the beginning of a client-designer relationship, on paper it may look like clients have the upper hand, as they're the ones interviewing and hiring the designer. In reality, though, designers may benefit from doing their homework as well.

At SJvD Design in Long Beach, California, the client isn't the only one doing research heading into a project. Drawing on personal experience from more than thirteen years as a firm owner, SJvD Design founder and owner Sybil J. B. van Dijs takes care to choose projects—and clients—that are a good fit for her business. The firm researches potential clients as much as possible, visiting their websites, calling those who may have referred the client to the firm, and looking into financials, if possible. Intuition also plays a part. "If you feel in your heart that the client or the project is not a good fit, don't do the job," says van Dijs. "I've gone through it in the past and I'll never do it again. It's not worth the effort in the end."

SJvD Design's ideal client? "Clients that are sensitive to and committed to the impact of design on a project and on its end users. This is critical. We've found that clients who are more sensitive to how design impacts their end users are more willing to be open to the process of design, from programming to installation and all of the phases in between," van Dijs explains.

Recognizing that each new client may also mean a potential long-term relationship, van Dijs looks not only at the task at hand but also at what might be possible in the future. "I look for opportunities for additional work in the framework of a client's corporate structure," van Dijs says. When interviewing for a senior living project, van Dijs not only examined the project itself, but also noted that the client owned sixteen to eighteen additional senior living communities across the country that may need work in the future. "We're always talking about the next thing," van Dijs says. "It's a constant nurturing relationship."

Even if that initial project is a one-time relationship, it may end up turning into something much more expansive as parameters are changed or work is added. "It's a positive thing to get additional work on a project, but it's also a challenge. The scope may change, but the deadline may not," van Dijs says. "We're often asked to do more and we rise to the occasion, but we're also very open about how much we can do when adding scope."

From the beginning of each relationship, communication remains key. Early on in the process, SJvD Design provides clients with a survey, not only to open up the discussion on clients' needs but also to gauge how well the clients know these needs themselves. "It's just to make sure we both understand what their needs are," van Dijs says.

Once hired for a project, the process deepens and client interaction is encouraged. "I feel it's very important to include the client in the process and get their feedback so that they feel like they have ownership in the process. I don't like to shove design down someone's throat," van Dijs says. "It's a collaborative effort." For that senior living project, the client wanted a resort like lobby. The firm worked with a committee of ten community members, interviewing them about their needs, and then presented them with a conceptual package that included a potential color palette and some sketches. For SJvD Design, getting feedback on the design direction early on is crucial. "We try to give them the big picture early on so we can find out if the direction is right. I find our greatest successes with clients have happened when we do that up front, so they're not guessing at what it will look like in the end."

SJvD Design also includes a communication game plan in each proposal. The firm identifies the project timeline, noting when meetings will be held, and over the course of the project provides weekly updates. Clients receive meeting minutes via email, along with project documents that are sent as PDFs. The firm also explains the timeline, identifying each phase. "We bring in sample project books to walk them through the process, so that even before the project begins they understand the steps that are necessary to get to the final design," van Dijs says. The firm will use past project books where the work was similar in size or scope, and includes the design drawings, sketches, preliminary floor plans, and specifications. "What we've found," van Dijs explains, "is that when we walk them through the process, they buy into it immediately because they understand it." While this doesn't eliminate hand-holding throughout the process, it does help reinforce the role of the professional designer. "In more than thirteen years' experience, I've found our greatest success in working with clients comes when they understand our role and what we contribute to a project," van Dijs says. Given the proliferation of home improvement shows with unlimited budgets and quick time frames, this is a key step in managing client expectations. "Clients are exposed to design programs, and their expectations are much higher because of this exposure," adds van Dijs, noting clients are increasingly doing research on their own.

SJvD Design also takes care to survey clients on their experience to find out whether the firm met their expectations and to identify ways in which they could improve or expedite the process. For van Dijs, it continues the open and frequent communication introduced at the start of each relationship. "The greatest success of a project is the continuous flow that blossoms over the course of the work," van Dijs says. "It fuels your passion, which helps work through the good, the bad, and the ugly of a project."

Chapter 3:

Communications and Technology for a Modern Practice

Whereas Chapter 1 focused on planning for an interior design business and the groundwork necessary for success, and Chapter 2 examined various means of structural support within a practice, there are also a number of functional issues that come into play once a firm is up and running. Certainly a modern practice cannot operate in today's business environment without incorporating some sort of technology, from printers and design software programs to file servers and websites. And before we move past the topic of building and maintaining relationships with collaborators, vendors, suppliers, and clients, think for a moment about how a firm, once open for business, markets itself to these external entities. What are the firm's core values, and how does it communicate these ideals not only to the industry as a whole but also to its employees? In this chapter, we take a look at branding and communications, technology, and professional issues like networking and ethics.

Who Are You? Creating the Brand

An important issue that arises for many firms is the question of a brand or firm identity. How will you identify the services you are selling? What sets them apart from your competition? What values does the firm hold at its core, and how will these values be communicated both to outside parties like clients, vendors, suppliers, and colleagues, and also internally to employees?

What Is a Brand?

Romana Mirza, Studio Pinpoint Consulting

Romana Mirza is the founder of Toronto, Ontario–based Studio Pinpoint Consulting. After twenty years on the client side, Mirza founded the studio to provide brand and positioning strategy services and strategic review and counsel to leadership teams. Recognizing that many companies are often forced to adopt messaging and marketing strategies that do not reflect the organization's core values, Mirza developed a methodology that is used exclusively at Studio Pinpoint to build a brand from within, one where the outer expression of the brand matches the core values of the organization. In her career, Mirza has worked with Nienkämper, Bernhardt Design, Gunlocke, the Mansouri Group, and Dunlop Farrow Inc. Architects.

Brand is a relatively new concept in business, one that doesn't yet have a set definition or a standard set of practices or processes. Because of this, there are some common misconceptions about brand. First, because a brand raises product and service awareness, it is sometimes confused with marketing. In reality, a brand begins long before marketing strategies are created, and pervades many aspects of an organization that marketing does not. Second, establishing a brand is sometimes perceived as unnecessary or superfluous to successful business practices. However, a brand isn't a luxury. It is a necessity. It has a ripple effect that not only influences sales figures, but also plays into the way an organization operates on a day-to-day basis. This essay will provide a brief exploration of brand and present an effective approach to the process of building one.

How Can "Brand" Be Defined?

There are a number of useful definitions of brand. A brand may be seen as a story, or a narrative intended to explain who an organization is and what it does.[1] A brand may also be described as the way an organization is perceived by others. In essence, it is the collective response (both positive and negative) from everyone who has experienced its products and services.[2] Alternatively, a brand may be viewed as the emotional response garnered from these products and services, a deep-seated attachment that goes beyond intellect or rational thinking.[3] All three definitions include an indication of the benefits offered by an organization, along with aspects of its work that make it distinct from others in similar industries.

What's Missing?

While of each of these views offers valuable insight into the practice of building a brand, they focus almost exclusively on how an organization and its practices are perceived *by others*. In other words, they rely heavily on *external* perceptions of a brand. It is, of course, essential for an organization to be recognized by others, to garner a strong reaction, to appeal to emotions in addition to intellect, and to convey its story. However, what's lacking in all three of these views is the *authenticity* that comes from an *internal* understanding of an organization. The marketplace is flooded with images, messages, and promotions. In order to truly stand out from the masses, an organization must first have a clear understanding of itself. Building a brand *from within*, as opposed to focusing heavily on external views, establishes a genuine, authentic brand. This not only makes an organization truly unique, but also rings true for all stakeholders, including employees, shareholders, and customers. Authenticity leads to trust, and trust leads to results. In essence, if a brand allows an organization to understand itself first, then others will be more likely to understand and accept it as well.

How Do You Build a Brand from Within?

There are four crucial steps to building a brand from within. First, it is necessary to uncover an organization's values by examining its leadership philosophy. Organizational cultures are formed by leadership style, namely the character, personality, uniqueness, and quirks of the leader or leadership team. An understanding of this helps to uncover the values through which leaders manage, and hence sheds light on how they influence the culture of the organization. For example, a leader might be very inclusive, and nurture a spirit of sharing within their organization. This type of leader might notice subtle signals, such as body language or a lack of communication, and recognize that these issues could create a rift between team members, or difficulties within a project. Alternatively, a leader may prefer a hierarchical approach, focusing more on structure and less on team collaboration. Understanding characteristics of a leader quite often helps to define what a company is on the inside.

Second, it's essential to understand the way members of an organization communicate. This can be accomplished by examining the nature of communication within the organization as well as with customers. Some organizations communicate in a friendly, even jovial manner, while others prefer a more distant and formal approach. It may also be useful to analyze the communication skills and techniques used by a variety of employees. For example, this observation may reveal that empathy and reflection are dominant traits. Noting the communication etiquette that is prevalent within an organization also gives clues to the organization's values. An organization may believe in returning calls and emails within twenty-four hours, or encouraging innovation by allowing for extraneous noise in the workplace. Communication strategies and guidelines are a clear representation of values and beliefs, and examining them will bring an organization one step closer to understanding what it truly stands for.

Third, it's necessary to develop a deep understanding of what an organization has to offer. In some cases, products and services are offered as an improvement on what already exists. In other cases, they are offered as something completely new and innovative. An organization may be motivated to develop products and services due to frustration with existing ones, or it may be driven to create something original. Members of an organization also need to reflect on what they hope customers will say about their products and services. For example, products and services can make customers feel relieved, enthusiastic, safe, comfortable, or inspired. Thinking about issues like these will help to identify the motivations that make an organization what it is.

Finally, it's important to take a step back and record some of these observations and reflections. It's often helpful to lay out the answers to these questions on paper, making particular note of the language used and the concepts that are emphasized. From all of this a personality, or a way of "being," will emerge. It is these patterns and observations that make an organization unique and different from its competition. These are the qualities that will form the foundation of a brand.

Consulting with a professional brand strategist can provide third-party objectivity, and can bring quicker, more accurate results. However, do-it-yourself methods such as the one offered in these four steps are still effective. They still allow for an understanding of an organization's unique identity, and will undoubtedly have a positive effect on the way it presents itself and operates on a daily basis.

How Does the Competition Impact a Brand?

Competition can greatly influence a brand, and it is shocking how little some organizations know about their competitors. A detailed analysis of the competition, in combination with an understanding of what they stand for, will help you to build a brand that is differentiated from others. When researching the competition, it's crucial to examine the operations side of the organizations and how they speak to the world. Both elements will give deeper insights into making one's own brand stronger, as it will become clear precisely how a brand is different or similar to others. Similarities among competitors may serve as a "price of entry" to compete in that particular area of the market, but it is fundamental differences that will set a brand apart. To effectively analyze the competition, follow these four easy steps. If done correctly, analysis like this should present a clear picture of the unique aspects of an organization.

First, choose the most direct competitors. If there aren't any in a particular market, then look to another city or country, even if there are no plans to expand into that area. If there doesn't appear to be any current competition, then try to anticipate potential future competition, and apply these steps to them.

Second, do some research about these competitors and how they operate. Visit competitors' websites to learn about products, services, and areas of focus. A lot may be learned from reading the content, but don't forget to examine visual elements, such as photography (people, nature, etc.) and color schemes (primary, bright, conservative, funky, and so on). These elements give a great deal of information concerning how an organization communicates with customers, in addition to what is important to them. One company may talk about its founder and history, while another may emphasize its customers instead. A view of the visual style will also help to determine a personality, as it may indicate conservativeness, playfulness, seriousness, and so on. A wealth of information is available on the Internet for publicly traded companies, but even privately owned companies often receive media coverage. Unlike actual company websites, third-party sources of information can reveal how *others* perceive these competitors. All of this will give a more complete picture of the similarities and differences between competitors.

Third, it's useful to take note of factual details, such as price, selection, distribution, service delivery, and the like. In the case of service-based organizations, it's necessary to examine their methodology, customer base, and geographic reach.

Finally, analyze the language used, including key terms and catch phrases, such as, "fastest," "best quality," "luxury," "softest," or "tastiest." The use of common phrases and descriptions should demonstrate that many competitors tend to use a similar voice. Every organization should attempt to use distinctive language for its products and services. However, it's still important to use words and phrases that stay true to an organization's unique personality, as opposed to current trends.

Bringing It All Together

Although an understanding of the competition is an incredible advantage to any organization, it should never be taken as a substitute for the insideOUT[4] methodology outlined above. Some organizations merely examine the market, determine what is lacking, and then develop a brand to fill that niche. However, without first achieving a comprehensive, holistic understanding of an organization, it is very difficult to establish a brand that is authentic. The first step should always be getting to know one's own

organization, and only after this should competition be taken into consideration. This ensures that an organization understands what makes it truly distinctive from others, as well as how it may continue to distinguish itself.

What Are the Parts of a Brand?

A brand is the sum of its parts. One part of brand is the content. The other part is the identity or the logos and other visual elements that are consistently associated with that brand. The following are the key elements that make up the content of a brand.

BRAND ESSENCE: Brand essence refers to the underlying values and beliefs that motivate and inspire members of an organization. A brand essence serves as a litmus test for all activities, transformation, and growth within an organization. Pivotal decisions should be made with this essence in mind.

BRAND PROMISE: The brand promise sets expectations, both internally and externally. Internally, a brand promise sets the goals to which team members, management, and stakeholders can aspire. Externally, it sets expectations and allows customers to know where a brand stands, as well as what they have to gain by being associated with it.

BRAND PERSONALITY: This is a representation of the qualities for which an organization is recognized. It is reflected in the organization's communications and interactions. It is also reflected in its culture, values, quality of service, customer perceptions, and its unique identity within the marketplace. Keeping this personality in mind lends clarity and consistency to an organization's practices while also gaining it external recognition, as well as distinguishing it from others in the market.

BRAND POSITIONING STATEMENT: This statement outlines the specific qualities and attributes of the brand. It is the brand's key message.

VISUAL ELEMENTS: The other part of a brand is its visual elements. These refer to all of the visual elements that help to convey the message of a brand, and which make it both recognizable and memorable. The most prominent visual identity of a brand is the logo. Other elements of a brand's visual identity are color palettes, graphic standards, typography, photographic styles, and so on, which also play key roles.

Conclusion

Brands speak volumes about an organization's identity. To establish and develop a brand that is truly unique, it is most effective to look within one's own practices and culture. Matching what an organization is on the inside to how it presents itself on the outside allows others to understand it. This understanding builds both confidence and trust. This essential match also allows an organization to differentiate itself from its competitors. A brand built from within allows an organization to be absolutely unique, and this breeds success.

Notes

1. www.appliedstorytelling.com, accessed November 2008.

2. www.instinctbrandequity.com, accessed November 2008.

3. www.lovemarks.com and www.vertebrae.us, accessed November 2008.

4. insideOUT™ is a trademark name and trademark process belonging to Studio Pinpoint Consulting © 2008

Resources

Studio Pinpoint Consulting, www.studiopinpoint.com

Applied Storytelling, www.appliedstorytelling.com, accessed November 2008.

Instinct Brand Services, www.instinctbrandequity.com, accessed November 2008.

Lovemarks, www.lovemarks.com, accessed November 2008.

Saldanha Branding Business, www.saldanha.com, accessed November 2008.

Siegel + Gale, www.siegelgale.com, accessed November 2008.

Vertebrae, www.vertebrae.us, accessed November 2008.

A Decade of Design: JJ Falk Design LLC

In 1998, after twenty years as a leader in nationally known interior design firms, JJ Falk, IIDA, established her own design practice in New York City. Today, JJFD is a midsize firm providing full design services, from initial project strategy through the final details of construction and implementation, to clients in a variety of businesses on a broad range of projects locally and globally.

In 2008 New York–based designer JJ Falk celebrated the ten-year anniversary of her eponymous firm, JJ Falk Design LLC. The occasion provided not only reason to celebrate, but also an opportunity to step back and examine the practice's past, present, and future and ask a few questions. Was the firm, in its present iteration, still true to the core values Falk had established at its beginning? And was it on a path that would remain consistent with these tenets in the future?

Like many entrepreneurs, Falk's journey into self-employment was an extremely personal effort. Her individual philosophies about design and business serve as a foundation for her own career as well as for her practice—both internally, in its organization and processes, and externally, in the message it presents to the A&D community and potential clients.

Recognizing that a brand goes beyond a logo or piece of letterhead, Falk set about creating an operation that was anchored in her deep involvement in day-to-day operations. Having spent nearly fifteen years designing for two large-scale entities, Gensler and The Phillips

Group, Falk focused on creating a small studio that, while it would aim to have the capabilities to take on large-scale projects, also would keep its headcount well below one hundred, allowing Falk to be deeply invested both financially and creatively. This ideal could be closely monitored internally through hiring policies and project management, and to support it externally Falk deliberately chose her firm name to send a message to the industry and clients. At JJ Falk Design, Falk wasn't just managing principal and founder; she was, and remains, invested in all aspects of the firm. "My name was important, and putting the company in my name is a sign," Falk explains. "I am involved in every single project. If I named my company 'Great Design Inc.,' people would ask who is in it. I used my name to show it is my business." By contrast, she says, clients seeing her name up front "know that the head of the firm will be taking care of them. When they read my name on the front, they know they can call me even if they have a broken chair. That's what makes this company different from larger firms."

In addition to branding the firm in her name, Falk created an official mission statement that would guide the practice:

> Under the direction of JJ Falk, the firm collaborates with clients on a broad range of project types. These include technology, broadcasting, real estate, advertising, publishing, financial services, law and retail spaces. The studio has a personal, hands-on approach to providing the design services that create lasting value for our clients. The firm is committed to the principle that well crafted work environments can foster the excitement and energy necessary to make business grow. As our team listens to our clients, we form an understanding of their human and business goals, which allows us to design spaces that offer simplicity, clarity and beauty. Projects designed by JJ Falk Design reflect not a single, firm defining style; every project is informed by the same set of complex, deeply held principles. Our leadership is rigorously business-like and architecturally visionary. We are as committed to our clients' goals as we are to producing exceptional design. The firm holds to its founding vision of becoming the best at our craft by balancing service, design, technology and process. It is our mission to deliver the greatest possible value to our

clients, while improving the quality and reliability of our practice. The process of discovery provides the core of our design process.

The brand also developed an external face. As it turned out, when Falk was organizing the practice in 1998, she was working on a project alongside a Chicago-based graphic designer who also offered branding services. Bartering her design skills for branding assistance, Falk hired him to help create JJ Falk Design's external image.

The resulting logo and corporate identity system is a direct representation of Falk's portfolio of work from Chicago to New York, which she showed to the graphic designer as background. To signify her personal preference for the stylings, materials, and colors of Modernism, Falk focused on silver and gray as the firm's brand color palette, a subtle nod to Modern design's abundant use of metals like aluminum, stainless steel, and silver. Continuing the Modernist theme, the logo became simply a single vertical line against a solid colorblock that holds the firm's name. "The logo is modern, refined, simple, and functional. There is no décor or decorative font. It is consistent and can be used in different ways, but it always represents function," Falk explains. "It's so simple it is almost a brand logo that is not a logo at all." It says, she adds, "JJ Falk, Modern designer, clean and simple."

In addition to the logo and corporate letterhead, the firm developed straightforward and simple brochures and a website featuring high-quality photos of past work. Everything, Falk says, had to remain true to that refined Modern influence.

For the first few years, the brand's marketing materials remained spare as word of mouth brought in a number of clients. Internally, the strong mission statement served as a constant guide to the practice, and at the end of each year Falk would conduct a full review of the business to ensure that what had been accomplished over the preceding twelve months remained true to her core goals. Indeed, by 2008 the mission statement had adopted new language, but at its heart it remained essentially intact:

> To create natural, humane environments, born out of the use of organic textures, color, natural light, and

JJFD

INTERIORS • ARCHITECTURE

JJ FALK DESIGN LLC 315 FIFTH AVENUE 11ᵀᴴ FL, NEW YORK, NY, 10016 **T:** 212.685.1913 **F:** 212.685.6471 **www.jjfalk.com**

Figure 3-1

The corporate identity and logo of JJFD was crafted to reflect firm owner JJ Falk's Modernist sensibilities. The simple line in the logo and silver coloring pay homage to Modern design's dedication to form and use of materials like steel.

JJFD

JJ FALK DESIGN LLC
INTERIORS • ARCHITECTURE

FIRM PROFILE   BACKGROUND   SERVICES   PRINCIPALS   PRACTICE AREAS   DESIGN MANAGEMENT   WMBE
PORTFOLIO

JJFD NEWS

CONTACT

SERVICES

JJ Falk Design LLC provides full interior design and architecture services to support our clients' needs in every phase of their real estate and facilities cycle, from initial project strategy through the final details of construction and implementation.

Strategic Planning   LEED Services
Site Evaluation   Programming
Code and Zoning Analysis   Space Planning
Pre-lease and Workletter Analysis   Schematic Design
Space Standards Development   Design Development
Furniture and Equipment Inventory   Furniture Specification and Procurement
Building Security Design   Construction Contract Documents
Pre-built Office Design   Bid and Negotiation
Identity Design   Contract Administration

JJFD supports sustainable design and construction and is a member firm of the U.S. Green Building Council. Our project teams include a LEED Accredited Professional.

Figure 3-2

Further building on JJFD's corporate identity, the firm's website carries on the company's color palette and simple stylings.

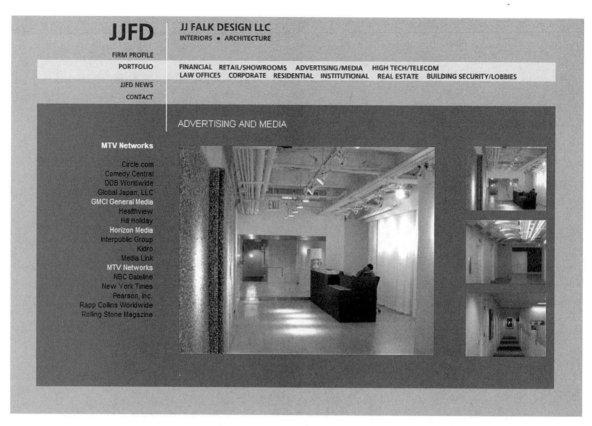

JJFD

JJ FALK DESIGN LLC
INTERIORS • ARCHITECTURE

FIRM PROFILE
PORTFOLIO
JJFD NEWS
CONTACT

FINANCIAL RETAIL/SHOWROOMS ADVERTISING/MEDIA HIGH TECH/TELECOM
LAW OFFICES CORPORATE RESIDENTIAL INSTITUTIONAL REAL ESTATE BUILDING SECURITY/LOBBIES

ADVERTISING AND MEDIA

MTV Networks

Circle.com
Comedy Central
DDB Worldwide
Global Japan, LLC
GMCI General Media
Healthview
Hill Holiday
Horizon Media
Interpublic Group
Kidro
Media Link
MTV Networks
NBC Dateline
New York Times
Pearson, Inc.
Rapp Collins Worldwide
Rolling Stone Magazine

Figure 3-3

In addition to including background information about JJFD as a whole, the firm's website also includes up-to-date photography of its work over ten years in business. Organized within a larger portfolio section, photos are categorized by project type and then further broken down by specific client and project.

human scale. To create "green" spaces through the use of recyclable materials, low emissivity products, and a high standard of air quality. JJFD is dedicated to delivering creative space solutions as an outgrowth of insightful thinking. The firm works with clients in a broad range of businesses, including technology, broadcasting, real estate, financial services, media and advertising, retail and law.

JJFD's design philosophy exhorts working environments that foster positive, productive human activity. To reach that goal we follow a rigorous process of listening to our Clients' needs to develop creative design solutions that offer simplicity, clarity and beauty. These solutions are grounded in an

understanding of the physical infrastructure of the space itself, the specific type of work performed, and aiding the Client to determine a vision of corporate identity.

Monitoring the brand's authenticity on an annual basis has also allowed Falk to check in with herself regarding her goals. For example, after about five years in business, Falk was faced with an important decision that had the potential to deeply impact the firm's brand. Up to that point, the firm had done well and grown to twenty people. "We had to make a decision about the next five years," Falk recalls. Would the firm continue to expand in headcount, possibly diluting

Falk's involvement in each project? Introducing additional principals and leaders would affect the brand both internally and externally. Going back to her mission statement and her goal of being personally involved with each client and thus a true representation of the name JJ Falk Design, Falk chose to keep the headcount low.

Five years later, the official ten-year anniversary provided another opportunity to reexamine the firm's brand, and this time a little tweaking, at least on the public side, was in order. Over the years the practice's name, though officially listed as JJ Falk Design, had often been shortened to JJFD, especially on construction documents where space was limited. Embracing this, Falk commemorated the tenth anniversary with a marketing effort that announced JJFD as the new brand name, and sent out new brochures celebrating current projects as well as listing expanded areas of practice.

Extolling the brand benefits both employees and clients, Falk has learned. "The benefit of having a strong brand is that clients have a predetermined understanding of who I am and what the company is before they come in contact with us. They have an expectation of the brand, which can otherwise require a lot of time to make sure they understand who you are and how you can service them differently than other firms. It's not just a logo or talk, it's also the projects that tell who we are," Falk explains. "They can get the sense that JJ Falk is not as huge as Gensler or SOM, but that we have high-level standards."

Repositioning, Rebranding, Reinventing: Pallädeo

Founded in 1970 in Calabasas, California, as Brown Bunyan Moon and More Inc., today the Glendale, California–based business is known as Pallädeo, a leading design, retail strategy, décor fabrication, and construction partner for America's top retailers. Through three distinct operating divisions—Envision, Create, and Construct—the three-hundred-person firm designs, accessorizes, markets, brands, fabricates, installs, and builds retail experiences, providing a range of services for clients in the retail realm, including Jelly Belly, Bristol Farms, OfficeMax, and Ralphs.

It is one thing to develop a firm's brand strategy and mission statement when the business is in its infancy and the focus is entirely on what is to come. It is quite another challenge, however, to reexamine an existing brand with a successful track record and emerge with a renewed focus and a new identity. If it isn't broken, how do you know what to fix?

Such was the challenge facing the leadership of Pallädeo in 2003. At that time, the business was known as Brown Bunyan Moon and More (BBM&M), a retail design firm founded in 1970 by its namesake partners, Jerry Brown, Al Bunyan, and Russ Moon (with the "More" representing the contributions of the firm's employees). For thirty-four years, the business had prospered and grown, blossoming to several hundred employees working on projects ranging from 2,500-sq.-ft. inline retailers to 120,000-sq.-ft. projects with million-dollar budgets.

By the early 2000s, however, the playing field had changed. Consolidation across the retail industry meant many of BBM&M's clients were now operating in a more corporate atmosphere with less regional control, and BBM&M would likewise have to communicate on a more corporate level. Within the firm itself, the founding partners were no longer involved, and the BBM&M name had the inflection of a bank or accounting firm rather than a creative entity. In addition, the firm was perhaps hurting from its own success: BBM&M had done so well in its retail rollouts that design was no longer at the forefront of its practice. "There's always some sort of pain that drives a transformational process, and what really started it here was that clients were changing, financials were changing, the way customers were doing business was changing—and we had to find a way to be a decision that an executive would make," explains Paul Rottler, executive vice president of Pallädeo Envision, the firm's environmental design and retail strategy division.

The decision to reexamine the brand, however, was not taken lightly. "We were a successful practice and our employees saw that success. We were continuing to get pats on the back for jobs well done, and we were growing," recalls president and CEO Bob Bautista. Recognizing this past success, Bautista recruited Rottler, then an external consultant and owner of Angeles Marketing Group (AMG), to do a deep dive. The goal: to filter out the best of what BBM&M was, and position it for the future.

"There were two key ingredients required for this consultant relationship to work," Rottler notes. "First, the client had to give the consultants permission to say the hard things. Second, they had to commit themselves to act on the conclusions. They could not go back to places that were comfortable just because they were familiar."

AMG launched into assessing the firm's core values, its competitive advantages, past successes, processes, and other attributes or functions that played into its brand, both internally and externally. Key executives were recruited to explore internal dynamics. Externally, secondary research gauged BBM&M in terms of exposure, graphic coverage, and image in comparison to its competitors. AMG also reached out to customers, suppliers, and competitors to find out their true impressions of the firm.

Several weeks later, the consultants presented their findings to BBM&M. "That assessment triggered many, many long-range goals for the company, starting with a business plan," says Bautista. "As we wrote the business plan, we started seeing the meat in it and all the different things we would evolve into, and so we started investing back into the company, trying to take a business that had worked really hard for thirty years and no longer knew its market share, and realign it as a company that could establish very strong parameters, goals, and objectives for the next three to five years and start investing for that."

A comprehensive rebranding had not been on the initial agenda, but as the results were examined, it seemed an opportunity in the making. "Through the assessment phase, we learned a lot about what was not on the radar. As loved as Brown Bunyan Moon and More was, the wider industry didn't know us, so there was a window of opportunity to boost the rebranding effort," Rottler says of the research phase. "We didn't expect to go down this road, but we thought it was an opportune time to use a name change to capture who we were becoming rather than who we had been."

Playing off the idea of greatness, the firm chose to rename itself Pallädeo, inspired by Andrea Palladio, an Italian Renaissance architect. And Palladio's influence went beyond the name on the firm's door. Palladio may be best known for his creation of the three-part Palladian window. He approached projects with a three-part solution: dramatic exteriors, economical materials, and internal harmony and balance. Taking this trio to heart, Pallädeo created three distinct operating divisions: *Envision*, a full-service environmental design and retail strategy consultancy; *Create*, a one-stop manufacturing hub for the custom development of specialty products; and *Construct*, a full-service retail construction management and general construction division.

Changing on paper, however, was only one component. Getting employees on board from the first day would be essential to the new brand's success, as they would be the ones living out the brand's mission statement each day. To conquer this hurdle, AMG and Pallädeo leadership presented the new brand by leading off with what would remain the same and then explaining how things would change for the better. The design studio, lobby, and other office areas were redesigned to reflect the new brand, as were all other company components, from trucks and facilities to equipment and hard hats. An internal video was created to showcase Andrea Palladio's work and philosophies. To celebrate the change, firmwide events were held at the main office in Glendale, the satellite office in Chino, and at multiple job sites in the field. And within twenty-four hours, the firm also reached out to its vendors and clients. A new website and capabilities brochure were created and launched, as was a media relations campaign focusing on Pallädeo's design work and capabilities. "We have

BROWN BUNYAN MOON & MORE, INC.
The Art *and* Business of Store Design

Figure 3-4

Although Brown Bunyan Moon and More was a successful brand for more than thirty years, the company owners sought to reenergize the business in all facets, from its processes to its identity and brand. As a result of these efforts the old Brown Bunyan Moon and More logo was retired.

Figures 3-5 and 3-6

The reinvention of Brown Bunyan Moon and More into Pallädeo necessitated a company-wide overhaul that included new logos and external branding.

people out in the field in arenas all across the nation. We had to let everyone know about the change in a short period of time, or else there would have been a disconnect," says Bautista. "It wasn't just saying the name and saying what we would be. We started living and breathing what we would be."

This focus on living the brand is seen as essential to continued success. "*What* we do is not what's special in the marketplace. It's *how* we do it," explains Rottler. Pallädeo is engineered to provide the infrastructure to support Pallädeo's core values—creativity, relationship, honesty, dependability, and quality—and the

Figures 3-7 and 3-8
Pallädeo's branding efforts also necessitated space changes that communicate the firm's identity both internally (as seen in the firm's lobby) and externally (as evidenced not only on the exterior of the firm's office but also on company trucks).

Figure 3-9
Pallädeo's branding efforts also necessitated space changes that communicate the firm's identity both internally (as seen in the firm's lobby) and externally (as evidenced not only on the exterior of the firm's office but also on company trucks).

focus is on the client's bottom line, providing results the firm can deliver.

The brand is treated as an evolving entity. It is under constant evaluation internally by all employees, perhaps even more so since 2005, when Pallädeo acquired AMG and integrated the consulting business into *Envision*. Former AMG consultants, who are now Pallädeo employees, have built a team within Pallädeo known as the Retail Strategy Group, a full-service marketing agency and retail consultancy providing clients with strategic services in advertising, public relations, branding, and tailored retail strategies.

New employees are brought up to speed through an on-boarding process that still includes the original

Palladio video, and all employees, new and old, are continually trained to be the best they can be.

"Internally, Pallädeo is a sought-after company to work for, and that's because of our brand and because we do what we say we will do," Bautista says. Externally, Pallädeo now enjoys a national reputation that is driven by authenticity. "The next business driver is authenticity: Are you really doing the things you say you'll do?" Rottler says. "Clients and their customers are more sophisticated about whether or not something is delivered, and whether it does what it says it will. I don't know exactly what authenticity will look like in the next ten years, but we're excited about it because that's how we now are wired."

To Market, To Market: Marketing and Public Relations

As discussed, one benefit of having a set brand that truly reflects the core values of your firm is that it provides a distinct message, which can then be sent out to the industry and potential clients to differentiate your practice from competitors. But how exactly does a firm owner go about doing this?

There are countless marketing and public relations–related books, websites, and articles online and in print that can help the individual business owner approach marketing, from something as simple as *Public Relations for Dummies* to more design-oriented sources. Likewise, there are hundreds of ways—some free, some reasonably inexpensive, and some extremely expensive—to promote a brand or business. Finally, there are many independent consultants to assist in the PR process. The ready availability of so many choices may be overwhelming, but luckily a basic marketing strategy need not be that complicated. What it does need, however, is consistency.

Marketing and public relations should be more than a one-time event or effort. It is important to recognize that although marketing is often grouped with sales in general discussions, the two are different functions. While "sales" often relates to techniques and tactics that may be used to turn a potential lead into a solid client, "marketing" often refers to the methods that generate those potential leads in the first place. The more frequently a designer's or firm's name is seen in the industry, the more colleagues, clients and potential clients, and employees will think of that person or firm in a time of need. In an article focusing on marketing for design firms that ran on the design website Core77, author Adam Lerner distilled the concept down to the following formula: "attention + frequency = memory."[1]

Whatever your budget, there are many options available for reaching out to build name recognition. Consider the list given in Table 3-1.

The challenge for many firms is time, and for principals strapped for time, outsourcing marketing efforts to an external consultant or public relations firm may be worth the investment. Look for ways that marketing and PR efforts may already be underway: Are employees already involved in industry organizations or local charity events? Is the firm currently involved with charity events where participation helps spread the business name? Is the business approaching a milestone anniversary or important accomplishment that deserves recognition? It is also helpful to take the time to identify exactly whom you are targeting with your outreach efforts.

One ally for all firms is the press. Believe it or not, many media outlets, from national trade magazines to local newsletters or regional television stations, are constantly on the lookout for new sources and perspectives. Think small to start. If you've got experience with the latest software, can you volunteer to write a product review for a design website or trade magazine? Would you be willing to pen an advice column for the local paper's weekly home and garden section?

Whether you are reaching out to the media or to new clients, it is important to do competitive research on the market: Who are the firm's main competitors, and what sets your business apart from them? How are its services different, and what benefits would the client receive in choosing to work with your firm as opposed to firm X, Y, or Z? Similar to a branding exercise, it is essential to identify and trumpet competitive advantages.

Table 3-1
Ways to Build Name Recognition

$	$$	$$$
• Become an expert in a specific market segment or niche.	• Enter design competitions.	• Hire an external public relations agency to manage and execute ongoing outreach programs.
• Volunteer to speak at industry events.	• Create a media kit for the firm, including up-to-date brochures showcasing the firm's latest work, a current list of its capabilities and services, and a list of recent clients alongside testimonials on jobs well done.	• Hire a permanent employee devoted to marketing and public relations.
• Reach out to local design schools and volunteer to speak to a class, mentor students, or host a class at your firm for the day.	• Professionally photograph your most successful projects (note: this can easily become $$$).	
• Become involved in industry organizations like ASID, IIDA, or AIA, and volunteer for committees.		
• Create a periodic email newsletter to announce firm news.		
• Create a blog with a professional tone and useful content.		
• Reach out to local media outlets as a potential forum for writing articles or advice columns.		

Findings should be used to create a concise, up-to-date press kit that can be emailed or mailed on short notice. Consider it to be a more visual resume that includes the following:

- One paragraph describing the firm as a whole with a bulleted list of services offered

- One paragraph on the top leader's or leaders' experience, background, certifications, and affiliations

- A bulleted list of select clients and projects

- High-quality, professional photographs of the best (and preferably most recent) work

- Contact information (phone, fax, URL, and email)

When it comes to marketing and public relations, it's also important not to underestimate the power of word of mouth. Collect client testimonials after projects are completed. Become an expert on a subject of personal interest, whether it be business planning, designing for assisted living, or building client relationships, and volunteer to speak at industry events, both local and national.

Being a Professional: Networking and Professional Organizations

There are a number of ways to market a company and its services at a very low cost in terms of dollars expended. One such alternative: in lieu of budgeting large amounts of money for advertising or a high-tech website, designers can commit their time to networking and volunteering both within and outside of the profession. Networking as a low-cost, low-tech marketing tactic can be very effective if done correctly. However, even low-budget efforts like these should be approached strategically. Simply joining several groups to be out meeting people and talking to them about your business and services can be a waste of time. Ideally, start by investigating and evaluating two or three select groups to ensure that their members are actual customers or professional contacts you want to meet. This type of focused networking and volunteering can do much for a designer with a tight budget and willingness to spend time instead of money to meet the right people.

Consider the experiences of Ken, a high-end residential designer who was an expert at this type of marketing. Knowing that the patrons of the local symphony orchestra offered a perfect demographic match for his targeted potential customers, Ken became an active supporter. He attended every concert and networked extensively at the theater before each performance and during intermissions. He also became involved with the symphony support group, actively participating in major fundraising events and designing the spaces for the symphony's gala events. Working side by side with the wives of many local captains of industry, getting to know them and letting them know about his design business, he was able to create a long list of potential clients. Other volunteers became familiar with him and his work long before they had projects of their own. At the concerts, they would introduce him to friends and family, further expanding his network of connections. Ken's volunteering and networking placed him top of mind with the exact clientele he wanted.

Another area where volunteerism can pay off is within the profession, volunteering for one of the professional associations like ASID or IIDA, or a related group like the National Council for Interior Design Qualification (NCIDQ) or Council for Interior Design Accreditation (CIDA). All of these groups depend on local and national volunteers to operate, so there are many ways to get involved with these organizations at all levels. Students of interior design nearing graduation may take advantage of student chapter leadership development programs. Networking at professional meetings puts soon-to-be graduates in front of those potential employers they want to meet. Fledgling designers recently out of school can get involved with the local chapter, serving on a committee or task force or as a liaison to one of the local student chapters, helping recruit speakers and professionals to attend meetings. Any of these volunteer positions can help raise a young designer's visibility in a local chapter at no cost aside from their time, dedication, and annual dues.

With more experience and involvement, volunteering for a chapter's board of directors gives a designer a stake in framing the chapter's activities as well as its community influence, and also continues to improve personal visibility among designers, educators, and other industry professionals. Locally, the president often serves as the spokesperson for the chapter, thus offering opportunities for access to the press, doing interviews and writing articles, and so further increasing exposure to the profession and the public.

For some designers, local involvement naturally transitions to a more national role. Often, professional organizations provide access to leadership training in business skills—learning to motivate people and delegate work, resolve conflicts, run meetings, and become an effective interviewee and public speaker, among other's—all of which can be easily transferred back to one's own business efforts. ASID's chapter leaders attend national training sessions and meetings where valuable business skills are taught, and opportunities exist to meet and network with other design professionals from all over the country, enabling the volunteer leaders to develop a professional network that stretches from coast to coast.

There are many ways for a practitioner to become actively involved in one of the professional organizations. If viewed strategically as part of a firm's marketing plan, designers can find volunteer positions that will provide the skills and exposure they want to develop. Volunteerism can provide a win-win situation for both the designer seeking to improve her business skills or publicity opportunities, and the organization needing dedicated volunteers to help it achieve its goals.

Integrating Technology

Another inherent part of every modern firm, small or large, is technology. From online product catalogs, current industry news and trends, and other helpful research tools, to project management software, file-sharing services, and in-house machinery like photocopiers and printers, there are myriad ways to integrate technology into a practice. How each principal chooses to do so depends on her individual needs and work habits.

The Wired Practice

Lena L. West, CEO, xynoMedia Technology

Lena L. West is the CEO and chief strategist of xynoMedia Technology, an award-winning business owner, Entrepreneur.com columnist and blogger, and an experienced speaker. After cutting her "technical teeth" in the realm of computers and networking consulting with Fortune 50 companies like IBM, Pitney Bowes, Philips Magnavox, Hyperion Software, and MasterCard International, West founded xynoMedia in 1997. Her firm helps growing companies figure out their place in the social media landscape and effectively navigate the new world of blogs, podcasting, and online communities to shorten sales cycles, refine product development, and increase word of mouth.

When most interior design practitioners think about technology for their businesses, their thoughts go immediately to computer-aided design (CAD) programs, or to a basic office suite of software programs for word processing, database management, email, and presentations. But according to Lena L. West, CEO of xynoMedia Technology, there is far more technology to consider when starting a design practice.

Some of the basics designers often overlook in terms of technology are telephone systems, Internet connectivity, and business machines like copiers, fax machines, scanners, and printers—all of which are integral elements in today's business environment and should be carefully selected. Once pricey, not all options for these systems are horribly expensive. A firm starting out with multiple employees or one that will add staff over time may manage with a phone system available at local office supply stores, rather than a phone system costing thousands of dollars. These systems take a $150 investment, can be inexpensively expanded to handle up to a dozen handsets as needed, and offer a host of traditional features like customizable voice mailboxes, a virtual attendant, and call-follow features.

All-in-one office machines that combine the functions of copiers, printers, scanners, and fax machines can be a boon for an entrepreneur strapped for cash and space. They cost far less than three or four individual machines that perform the same tasks, and take up much less space. One potential drawback, however, is that if one feature goes down, the entire machine will be down for a visit to the repair shop.

Internet connectivity today really needs to be high speed and, if possible, wireless. Security issues revolving around wireless connectivity in the past are a much smaller threat to privacy and security today. In a business with so much online product research and image downloading, high-speed Internet access is mandatory, as dial-up connection for this type of work is painfully slow. Design firms sending CAD drawings and other construction documents to clients and project team members need to have the ability to send those large files quickly and efficiently.

Hardware

Beyond the office basics, technology breaks down into three categories: hardware, software, and online. Depending on how an office will be set up, the number of computers, and the number of employees, it is best to have a server for networking that allows data to be shared from one central source. The server acts as a reposition for all company data, and through it access to data can be controlled, keeping sensitive files like financial records and human resource files secure while allowing general access to job and project files. If more than two people will have access to computers, it is best to set up a client-server network to support productivity. Buy the most computer capacity that you can afford. You will use it up more quickly than you can imagine as your firm begins to grow. On this note, West strongly suggests equipping a business based on the business you want to have in the future, not on the business you have today. Assume that your firm will grow, and provide technology that will allow you to grow in an efficient and productive manner. In the long run, it will be a more cost-effective investment in your technology.

Software

In addition to the basic office suite software packages mentioned earlier, every firm needs financial management software to deal with the financial aspects of a business, such as job estimates and proposals, purchasing, invoicing, accounts receivable, and accounts payable, as well as budgets and financial reports. QuickBooks by Intuit and Peachtree by SAGE Software are two popular off-the-shelf programs that are relatively easy to learn and operate. "QuickBooks allows for more growth within the firm, and has a smaller learning curve than Peachtree," West notes. "QuickBooks has also done a lot of work in terms of making sure their product really works for small businesses." In addition, there are industry-specific programs available that incorporate financial management within a broader software program specifically for running a design firm.

Project management software is another product that can be of value to interior designers. It helps create timelines, track the status of a project, and keep projects on time and on budget. This software also allows for project contingencies and tracks required resources to complete jobs. Project management software is available off the shelf or in online formats.

Some industry-specific technology interior design firms may find valuable include a larger printer capable of handling project drawings, CAD software, and 3-D modeling software. If these types of software are beyond your level of expertise, West recommends bringing in younger designers or interns. "They can bring you up-to-date on what is happening in the world of technology, and ways you can implement some of the new advances in your firm. They can turn you on to creating projects in virtual worlds like Second Life that will allow clients to put themselves into the spaces you are proposing, looking from different points of view, and walking around. They can also show you how to share project documents online with clients and project teams," she says.

Human resource management programs also may be helpful as a firm grows. HR software keeps track of employee records and key backup information. Should you be involved in a lawsuit with an employee or former employee, all the records of your employer-employee relationship will be on hand for legal use, providing needed protection. These programs manage information you need for government compliance rules and standards, basic information such as Social Security numbers and employee hire dates, as well as other pertinent data about legal situations, performance reviews, disciplinary action taken, and benefits packages and options. Firms that bill clients based on hourly rates, or those that just want to track hours spent on projects, may also make good use of time tracking software. Timeslips by SAGE Software and ClickTime by Clicktime.com Inc. are two such programs. Some financial software, such as QuickBooks Pro, also includes this feature.

More and more software is being provided in software-as-a-service (SAAS) format, where instead of purchasing software in a box off the shelf, it can now be used directly from a manufacturer's or developer's website and be paid for like a rental. In these cases, customers pay a set amount to use the software over a clearly defined time frame, on a per-person or a per-use basis. One such program designers might use is YouSendIt (www.yousendit.com), which helps transmit large files.

Security Issues

Every business, regardless of what field it is in, needs peace of mind that its computers and data are secure and safe. Even within a company, certain data should not be accessible by all. It is imperative to create strong passwords and change them on a regular basis to assure that confidential files like financial data and personnel records are secure.

Another layer of security critical for those with access to the Internet is a firewall. The purpose of a firewall is to keep those on the outside out of your computer and to protect your data from potential theft or damage. There are numerous dangerous or annoying codes that can invade an unprotected computer. It is not uncommon for a website to plant "cookies" in a computer to track a user's movements around its site and the Internet in general. Other things that can be planted in a computer include adware, spyware, malware, and thousands of viruses. These invaders can be everything from useful (cookies) to annoying (adware, pop-ups) to dangerous (malware, viruses, Trojans, worms) to a hard drive and everything on it. In addition to the firewall, good antivirus software is imperative. As the world of hackers and their viruses becomes a billion-dollar business, antivirus software needs to be constantly updated and virus scans run on a regular basis.

Backing up data and taking it off premises for safety is another task that must be done with regularity. Should a fire, flood, or other disaster hit a business, that offsite backup of all the computer data will go a long way toward getting you back in business quickly. In addition to individual desktop and laptop computers, it is also critical to back up the main server. There are several common media types for backing up a hard drive. CDs and magnetic tape are two of the most common, but also the most vulnerable to erasure or corruption. For a secure backup it is best to upload all critical data through an Internet site, to a server located away from your company. These services use the exact same security as major online banking institutions, and are cost-effective and easy to use.

Technology is changing at an astounding pace. Practitioners of all disciplines should stay in touch with new technology coming on the market. Technology news is readily available in magazines, newsletters, and Internet blogs, so it pays to take time yourself, or assign someone on your staff, to keep in touch with changes that can help your business run more smoothly and productively; will translate into better service to clients. Don't overlook younger staff members as sources of information on the latest technological innovations. Whatever your efforts, it will be time and money well spent on the future and success of your firm.

The Communications Business: Domus Design Group

Bruce Goff, ASID, cut his teeth in his family's retail home furnishings and design business. Following his graduation from the University of Nevada – Reno, with a degree in interior design, the retail outlets were closed down to allow complete focus on interior design. Domus Design Group, with a staff of three, was born in 1983. A second office was soon opened in San Francisco, poising the firm to serve the broad West Coast market in corporate, hospitality, and large residential projects. Today Domus Design operates with a staff of fifteen, creating award-winning projects.

"We're not in the design business," offers Bruce Goff, president of Domus Design Group. "Our company is in the communications business. We take in information from clients, add to it, manipulate it, interpret it, translate it, then communicate it all back to contractors in a format that they can create for the client, and to the client in the form of a completed project."

This is certainly not the usual response from an interior designer in describing his firm. But then, Goff is not what one might call a typical interior designer. One thing setting Goff apart from the pack is his use of technology. In fact, his firm has been built on technology since day one, and he works hard to stay on top of technological innovations and identify how they can be incorporated into the firm in ways that will keep them ahead of the competition.

Integrating technology is not new to Goff. He got his first taste of it working in his family's retail home furnishings business, in operation from 1948 until 1983. Goff took over management of the family business in 1975 while still in high school. They began implementing early computers to track store inventory and sales. "Before the computer was introduced, our inventory wasn't even on a spreadsheet, it was on graph paper," Goff recalls. When he started Domus Design Group in 1983, Goff continued to embrace technology, buying his first computer, a Hewlett-Packard Vectra (all that was available at the time) for about $10,000. At that price, he could afford only one stand-alone unit, meaning everyone had to wait his turn to use it. Today, however, Domus Design operates with a much higher level of technological assistance in order to do everything better, cheaper, and faster than competitors.

Technology and Basic Business

The main driver behind Goff's use of technology is the ability to work remotely. For the most basic office functions like communication, copying, and printing, all offices are networked with centralized copying and printing. There are two copiers—large, freestanding Xerox multifunction machines that do color and black-and-white copying as well as scanning, faxing, and emailing—which have replaced multiple smaller single-function machines. In addition, the firm's office manager has one small personal printer used to print

checks that also serves as a backup when the larger machines are down for servicing.

When it comes to new software and hardware, many of Goff's clients who have technology-driven operations provide him with an inside view of what works well and what does not. "I blatantly steal ideas discovered by my clients to incorporate into our business," jokes Goff. "They have IT staff that I don't, so they tend to be on the cutting edge when something new becomes available." He also frequently surfs the Internet for new software applications that can help his business, including programs not specifically intended for use by interior design firms.

Among Goff's software choices is Desktop Tools, which is installed on Domus's servers to standardize everyone's tools. The servers also hold everything that is used on a daily basis, such as templates for stationery and proposals, with no one permitted to save anything in personal files. As things are updated regularly, another software program, Push, sends out updates to all desktop units. Domus also uses Jamcracker software to maintain its systems remotely. A monthly per-user fee covers backup storage off-site, update installation, and a help desk. Accordingly, all records are now backed up safely and securely every night on the Jamcracker servers. In their offices, Domus Design's staff can archive samples and other project materials in a small box, with all digital files and data saved to a CD.

For internal project controls Domus uses Function Fox, an off-the-shelf software program usually marketed to creative firms and consultants in advertising and public relations. A web-based system that tracks project time and costs, it is accessible from virtually anywhere. Financial data and time budgeted for and spent on project phases, along with project dates, phases, and areas of responsibility, is entered into the main system. As time expended on the project is entered, it is charged against the appropriate project and project phase. This program can also track project history, time spent, costs, and other elements that can be useful in future project proposals, and allows for backing up the firm's data off-site.

Technology and the Design Process

When it comes to design-focused technology, Domus Design utilizes programs and processes that drive collaboration and standardization. This way, designers can deal with the aesthetic, emotional, and technical aspects of a project while "the system" provides a structured process. When a new project comes in, it is entered into Domus's computer system using standardized templates. Each employee is trained on the system so that everyone is operating in the same manner throughout each project.

Through technology, client collaboration—as well as distance from the home office to the client's location—has become less of an issue. In the past, Domus had a client who lived in northern California but traveled extensively, and who was building a home at Lake Tahoe. Domus developed a way for such clients to check in on their projects remotely. Goff learned of a software development firm with offices around the globe that used a virtual private network (VPN) that allowed multiple offices to access a project at different times. When one office would close for the night, another office could pick up where it left off and continue working, with yet another office picking up the project later on. Along these lines, a feature called Client Tools was installed on the Domus Design website, providing a secure, password-protected area where everything about a project, including pictures, videos, drawings, and specifications, is uploaded to that client's area. Clients and others working on a project can access information from anywhere in the world, 24/7. As everything is on the Internet, there are no bandwidth issues when sending or receiving large documents or images. In fact, Domus no longer even has to send email messages to clients or project partners. Domus Design has been using this system successfully for twelve years.

Technology and Marketing

First developed in 1992, Domus Design's website is now in its fifth iteration. The first version focused on showcasing computer programming skills, not necessarily quality content. The second version came about when Goff realized clients wanted to see examples of past projects. Unfortunately the firm had only a few images, which hadn't been taken with website use in mind. Now, however, images on the current site are far better. The first thing prospective clients see are project photos and the firm's contact information.

Site information is organized according to the tag line "Live Better—Work Smarter." "Live Better" focuses on the firm's residential work, while "Work Smarter" represents its commercial work. Clicking through, visitors not only get the attractive images they expect, but also details about how each project's goals were achieved. The majority of the firm's marketing efforts are focused on driving traffic to the website. One marketing tactic used was sending clients boxes of customized M&M's that had the firm's Web address printed on them.

Technology and Staying on Top

Goff realized long ago that technology can make even a solo design practitioner seem, feel, and look like a multinational firm. Domus continues to focus on how technology can set the firm apart from its competitors. "Since we still face situations where anyone can call himself an interior designer in many parts of the country, we use our technology tools to show what we can do beyond the 'decorator' level of interior design—what we can do for clients that others cannot," Goff explains. Every other year, Domus Design includes IT and technology in its annual budget, and in 2008, budgets included adding customer relations management (CRM) software and related training. Goff is still researching available programs, comparing features and capabilities. He envisions this addition improving the firm's client outreach, as it will help manage plans for staying in touch with clients by creating touch points—opportunities for Domus to "reach out and touch" their clients as a means of maintaining and building relationships—using surveys, press releases, and small gifts that tell the Domus Design story.

Next on tap: replacing AutoCAD with Revit software in 2010. This state-of-the-art software will be used mostly in consultant mode when the firm is not the lead on a project, bringing the team to a higher level of collaborative ability with the lead consultants (often A & E firms) on a project. For Domus, technology will lead to the future, with Goff firmly believing that "our profession will only stay viable if we embrace technology."

Log On

As seen in Domus Design's experiences, the technology involved in the day-to-day operations at a modern firm extends far beyond a printer or fax machine. In fact, interior designers as a whole seem to be increasingly embracing the online world as a means of both managing internal processes and communicating with clients and managing projects. Consider this: In 2005, an ASID survey of interior designers in small and medium-size firms found that just one in four designers used the Internet for his or her design practice. By 2007, however, a new survey saw that number jump by 300 percent, with 92 percent of designers reporting that they were active online.

So how are successful designers using the Web when it comes to business? Certainly they're looking at products. When ASID asked its survey participants which single source of information they would choose if they could only use one source, the largest group of respondents—30 percent—chose the Internet over other options like showrooms and design centers, catalogs, and sales representatives.

Designers are hardly the only ones logging on. With more than 174 million Americans online, an increasing number of potential clients may also be lurking out there, a fact that has prompted a sizable number of designers to launch a website. In its 2007 survey, ASID found that 38 percent of respondents had their own sites. At that time, 61 percent of respondents did not have a Web presence, but as technology continues to evolve, along with the ways in which designers incorporate technology in their day-to-day practices, these numbers will likely change.

Going Global, Going Mobile: Retail Clarity Consulting

Bruce J. Brigham, FASID, RDI, IES, is the founder of Retail Clarity Consulting, a firm specializing in retail brand development and strategy, store planning and design, visual merchandising, graphics development, and marketing consulting. Brigham launched Retail Clarity in 2001 after relocating to Sayulita, Nayarit, Mexico, following nine years practicing retail design and brand development at Planet Retail Studios in Seattle, Washington. Serving clients around the globe on projects that range from 500 to 20,000 sq. ft. in size, Brigham's client list includes Cartier International in Paris; Cartier Inc., in New York; TSL Jewelry International Ltd., in Hong Kong; Benjamin Moore and Company; Miller Brewing Company; and Nike Inc.

As a designer who began his career in construction as a hands-on master carpenter, Bruce Brigham has grown into a technologically savvy interior designer.

Following his construction experience after finishing college, Brigham joined the interior design division of Westin Hotels, cutting his teeth on commercial and hospitality design projects. He then moved to Callison Architecture in Seattle, where for six years he served hospitality and retail clients. In 1992, Brigham left Callison and joined a Seattle designer practicing in the residential arena. Together they formed a partnership, with Brigham opening a separate office as a retail interior design specialist under the banner of Planet Retail Studios.

It was during his time at Callison that Brigham first en-countered workplace computer technology. Although he created his project drawings by hand, he took to completing project paperwork on a large, cumbersome laptop computer roughly the size of a small suitcase. At the outset of Planet Retail Studios, the technology wasn't much better. The only way Brigham convinced his partner to get a personal computer installed was by promising to paint it to match the décor. But opportunity to advance soon came knocking.

Through his involvement with the American Society of Interior Designers, in 1994 Brigham met Jerry Harke, then director of marketing for ASID. At the time, Harke felt it was important to get ASID's practitioner members turned on to the Web and its marketing opportunities, and he offered to create a free website for Planet Retail Studios in exchange for permission to use it as an example for ASID members. Brigham agreed, provided some Planet Retail marketing collateral pieces for content, and within a couple of weeks the firm had an online presence.

Brigham felt as though a miracle had been visited upon his firm. Physically, it was a small, five-person entity in the northwestern United States, but if the content of its website was topcaliber, that same small firm could appear as powerful and professional as any of the bigger players around the world. Indeed, within a short period of time Planet Retail Studios was discovered by Cartier jewelers in Paris, which had been trolling the Web for a designer with retail experience. Well positioned by search engines, Planet Retail appeared high in Cartier's search results.

Running on the knowledge that they'd been found by the illustrious Cartier organization, Brigham knew the firm's presentation would need to be as high-class as the firm's website suggested. Working on a proposal based on an allegory of the creation of the universe, it was clear to Brigham that for the proposal to appear as high-class as Cartier itself, he would need high-quality color copying and printing capabilities. Among other things, Brigham wanted to print the proposal on fine linen paper stock and incorporate two-sided printing on architectural vellum. Knowing that they could never afford to purchase a copier with these capabilities, Brigham convinced his partner to lease a $120,000 state-of-the-art copier for $800 a month. The investment paid off handsomely: Planet Retail signed a contract with Cartier to assess its stores globally, creating a design brief in excess of 600 pages that set the direction for the future of the Cartier brand, its style, its customer approach, and its worldwide store designs.

By 2000, Brigham decided Planet Retail needed a better online presence. He convinced his partner to invest $40,000 in a new, interactive website incorporating nonstatic technology including Flash, video, and music. Brigham contacted a family member active in Web development for help, and within four to five months the firm's new site, along with CD-ROM marketing pieces that were developed concurrently, was live. "It was huge for us," Brigham says recalling how the firm's Web presence impacted his perspective on return on investment. "It was everything."

In 2001, life changed for Brigham. That year, he left Planet Retail and set out as an independent retail design consultant. Adding to the challenge, Brigham decided to move to Puerto Vallarta, Mexico. Although Brigham and his wife were no strangers to functioning in unique environments—they had previously lived aboard a 50-ft. trawler-style yacht for seven years—life on the water in Seattle did not prepare him for life south of the border.

Setting up his new firm, Retail Clarity Consulting, shortly after the move to Mexico, Brigham found himself attempting to operate his business with nothing but a cellular telephone for communication. With the surrounding area still under development, the phone was Brigham's only connection to the

Internet, and its inability to efficiently send attachments or documents limited Brigham's ability to function. Attacking the phone and Internet access challenges as he would a design project, Brigham found a Hughes dish system capable of providing satellite connectivity. Implementation, however, would take a healthy dose of creativity. Residential models of the Hughes disk were not yet licensed for use in Mexico, the system required a very precise signal to operate, and a telephone landline was critical to accomplish setup. To circumvent these challenges, Brigham found a source in Canada that would sell him a commercial dish and provide service for it. He set up the system in Seattle and then transported key parts of the program to Mexico via computer disk, flying a technician down to Puerto Vallarta three times to get the system up and running.

Phone and Internet problems addressed, Retail Clarity Consulting commenced business. Just prior to Brigham's move to Mexico, a customer in Hong Kong who owns more than 120 jewelry stores in China contacted Brigham about retaining him as a retail consultant. The duo had worked together during Brigham's partnership in Planet Retail Studios, and the client was eager to continue their relationship.

It is technology that supports the relationship between this client with stores in Hong Kong and a home near Paris, France, and his design consultant living and working from Mexico. In addition, drawings for projects are completed in Hong Kong, project production is completed in Shanghai, graphic design is done in San Francisco, and visual merchandising design is done outside of Paris. Through technology, however, the projects turn out just as if all elements were handled locally.

This relationship has shown Brigham just how valuable knowledge has become in the global economy. Many of the routine functions and tasks of an interior design firm can be obtained for pennies on the dollar overseas, but it is the knowledge designers bring that has the most value to global customers. "It's no longer about selling products or doing drawings as a part of the design process," he says. "It's about my selling knowledge and solutions that make my global clients successful, that holds the most value in today's global marketplace."

Brigham's marketing efforts are entirely Web-based. He no longer creates printed marketing collateral but instead directs potential clients to his website, whose offerings are focused on solid content about retail, branding, and connections. While much of his global work is done from his beachfront home office in Mexico, Brigham is still somewhat of a road warrior, with client locations around the world—and technology aids him here, too. He travels with his Hewlett-Packard laptop with a backup battery and power cord, Blackberry, and a Bose speaker to play music off of his iPod, as well as a small portable printer. While he doesn't consider himself a technogeek, he uses technology in practical ways that allow him to live the life he wants to lead, while still remaining a global player in the design community.

Using the Web to Market Your Firm: Resolve Digital

Barry Harrison is managing partner at Resolve Digital, a website design and marketing firm located in San Francisco, with an office in New Zealand. Founded in 2001, the firm includes a staff of six that serves three primary market areas: design and building, travel and tourism, and the corporate and nonprofit sectors. In addition to website design, other services provided by Resolve Digital include search engine optimization, Web marketing and public relations, Web copywriting and graphic design, and website evaluations.

How important is it for an interior design firm to have online representation in the form of a website or another online identity in this Web2 world? Barry Harrison, a former architect, interior designer, and product designer, says it is absolutely essential. "Without a Web presence," he notes, "a firm is immediately suspect. Potential clients will wonder, why aren't they online? If a firm doesn't have its own website, at the very least it should be represented on a design community site like DesignFinder (www.designfinder.com) that will enable potential clients to find it online."

As the managing partner of Resolve Digital, a website design and Internet marketing firm in San Francisco, Harrison sets and maintains standards to guide clients through the process of designing and marketing a successful website that will attract, retain, and engage a target audience. In addition, the company also provides services that help customers optimize their online presence through blogs, HTML newsletters, and other online marketing tools.

In the past, it was enough for a design firm to launch a website that was little more than an online brochure. And while this may still be a useful way to communicate a designer's or a firm's capabilities, simply posting a digital version of a printed brochure is no longer enough. Most people today have high-speed Internet connections and larger monitors, and they are increasingly tech-savvy and demanding. When they log on they often expect, at the least, larger, professional images of current work.

Increasingly, clients use the Internet to search for a design professional, and having a Web presence allows these potential clients to find you, see your capabilities, and peruse your portfolio without committing to an in-person meeting. This saves designers time as well, as it cuts out meetings with prospects who may not be a good match for the designer's style or capabilities. "It's more about quality than quantity," Harrison notes. "If you only have three well-photographed projects, just post those three. Poor-quality images undermine your message and do more harm than good."

For a website to be an effective marketing tool, a firm's message must be communicated clearly to the target audience. As succinctly as possible, it should state who you are and include an appropriate, professional headshot, Harrison recommends. Try to answer the potential client's primary question: Why should I hire you? Build credibility by offering information about your education, design experiences, professional skills, testimonials and references, professional affiliations, awards, published articles and books, and, of course, your contact information.

How to get started? When looking for someone to design a site, Harrison recommends seeking someone with domain expertise, meaning firms that have created sites for other interior design firms, as they will have a better understanding of the industry and your visitors' goals. An ability to work with online portfolios is a must. It is also important to consider how your site will be updated: Will the site designer provide a content management tool so you can update the site yourself, or do they offer ongoing maintenance? Above all, it's important to look for a Web design firm that is interested in showcasing your design work, not just its own.

It should go without saying that you need a Web designer who is easy to reach and communicate with. In this virtual world, it is no longer necessary to work locally, but no matter where the designer is located, he or she should be accessible, should listen to you, and should understand you and your business. Ask for and check references, and look at their online portfolio. "If the Web designer doesn't have experience in your field doing work that you want, don't be their guinea pig while they learn," Harrison cautions.

Another top concern is cost: How much a site costs depends on the scope of the project. Digital Resolve, for example, designs sites that start at around $6,000, but has also completed projects in the $25,000–$35,000 range. The complexity of your requirements and the scope of the work affect pricing. Many lower-cost Web design firms don't include adequate time to refine details to get the site right or provide important additional services like content editing or search engine optimization (SEO), which helps drive site traffic. Getting a site up is one step; showing up in search engines like Google and Yahoo! is another. A Web designer and/or copywriter should know what keywords and phrases potential clients may use to search for you and how to maximize your ranking in search results. After all, a basic search for "interior designer" can return millions of results. Will your site appear in the first few pages? Even if most of your clients come from word-of-mouth referrals, SEO remains critical to a site's success. Utilize opportunities to link to professional organizations like ASID or IIDA, and sign up on DesignFinder or other similar sites listing and linking to design professionals.

Participate in blogs and other online discussion groups, as your comments, when accompanied by your name and company name, may increase your likelihood of being noticed.

Those without the patience to implement a long-term SEO strategy can sign up for pay-per-click marketing, where you bid for placement in search engines. In buying a small ad on a search results page, you pay each time someone clicks through your ad. On one hand, this method can be extremely expensive, but on the other hand, it may be the only way to get your site listed immediately on the first page of results.

Once your website is launched and attracting visitors, how do you make those visitors take action? For most designers, this means asking prospects to submit a form or call for more information. With this in mind, it is good practice to include a contact form with an automated "thank you" reply, rather than just have an email window open in a visitor's browser. Not only does this tactic allow you to gather additional information—how the customer would like you to respond, what time of day is best to reach them, what specific information they desire—but the names and contact information from the form also can be added to a database for future communications like newsletters or special offers.

Launching an online presence, however, is just the first step: Don't just launch your site and forget about it. It needs to be reviewed regularly. Add new services, update your portfolio, change staff information. And although for many today the Web is a primary communications tool, it should not be a firm's only marketing channel. Public relations, articles, networking, and community and professional involvement are all still important facets, as websites do not replace the human interactions that close deals.

Marketing through the Web: Merlino Design Partnership Inc.

Bruce Hurowitz, IIDA, has practiced interior design at Merlino Design Partnership Inc. for nearly twenty years. The firm, named among the top twenty-five U.S. design firms in 2005 by StarNet and *Floor Covering Weekly* magazine, is headquartered in Gulph Mills, Pennsylvania, near Philadelphia, with a second office in Orlando, Florida. Its areas of expertise include senior living, retirement communities, assisted living, skilled nursing, and healthcare, with projects ranging from smaller renovations budgeted around $100,000 to major projects of between $100 and $200 million.

Merlino Design Partnership Inc. is no stranger to the power of marketing. Devoting 4–5 percent of its budget each year to marketing, the firm actively reaches out to clients and potential clients both in person and in print. Merlino has participated in trade shows, created editorial-style advertisements, and presented lectures and seminars to targeted audiences. The firm's projects are often entered in design competitions, and funds are sometimes set aside for project coverage in pay-for-play publications such as *Design for Senior Environments* and *Trends in Senior Living*. The marketing budget also supports the sponsorship of client-requested events like golf outings and annual dinners. Merlino's efforts, however, are not limited to print pieces, conferences, and competitions. The firm also actively markets itself online.

The firm first launched its online initiatives in 2004. That year, Merlino went through the process of relocating to its current space in Gulph Mills, Pennsylvania, and took the move as an opportunity to retool its printed marketing materials. Given these changes and revisions and the ever-growing interest in the Internet, developing a Web presence seemed like a natural addition to the process.

This task of establishing an online identity fell to Hurowitz who, as managing partner, not only worked on interiors projects but also oversaw the firm's marketing efforts. Although he holds a B.S. in business administration and a B.A. in interior design, Hurowitz is not a trained Web designer, so he began by surfing the Internet and assembling a variety of images and websites that appealed to him. Although the firm used an IT consultant to handle its computer server and other in-house needs, Hurowitz sought out a consultant specializing in Web design to help craft this new presence. Through his research, he came upon Digital Resolve, a website design and Internet marketing firm in San Francisco. Digital Resolve's experience in working with architects and designers was a key selling point. "I felt that they would know the difference between what we were trying to portray versus another type of business," Hurowitz explains. "The graphic quality and overall feel of the site gives users insight to our design sense."

Over a three-month period, Hurowitz and Barry Harrison, managing partner at Digital Resolve, developed Merlino Design's site to address three basic questions:

- Who are we?

- What do we do?

- How well do we do it?

To showcase the Merlino Design Partnership brand identity, the firm posted a variety of high-quality project images alongside the partners' credentials and corporate philosophy. Images of the firm's own offices were included to support the "Who are we?" question, while the project portfolio, which was divided into three sections with mini slideshows of completed work in retirement, senior care, and commercial facilities, quickly and visually answered the "What do we do?" query. Augmenting this was a list of the firm's services and its procurement capabilities. To further bolster this online portfolio and address the issue of quality raised by the third question, the designers also made sure the site featured the firm's design honors and awards, as well as its media coverage.

While the process may not have been cheap—Hurowitz estimates the firm invested about $20,000 along with hundreds of hours of time—it is seen as a well-made investment that continues to grow in value. The original agreement with Digital Resolve included software that allows Merlino, and Hurowitz specifically, to update the site as needed. Since

launching the first iteration, Merlino has modified the site to include added functionality, Flash, and the capability to publish an HTML newsletter.

Like many new websites, Merlino's online home took time to garner a serious number of hits from potential clients. To build traffic, the firm worked on getting its site listed in search engines and directories and instituted search engine optimization techniques to increase the site's likelihood of appearing in search results. When participating in buyer guides, the firm ensured that its URL was added to its listing, and key links were added online to build connections with other Web-based sources. The bimonthly e-newsletter also helped drive traffic, as did word of mouth as employees began referring people to the site for information. However, while the site now garners successful results from online searches, driving traffic remains an ongoing effort, and Hurowitz feels the firm could still improve its search engine optimization.

The firm is also careful to market across a variety of media and not just online. "The bigger investments only take one good lead or project. The less expensive items, such as the website and newsletter, yield more traffic with fewer sizable projects," Hurowitz notes. "The ROI percentage may be better with the Web-based solutions, but the real marketing for real projects comes through relationships." That isn't to say, however, that the Web may never bring in big work. In fact, Merlino's big payoff from its online investment came from a Tokyo-based client that used the Web to locate qualified firms. In this case, Merlino's site gave its designers the opportunity to sell themselves for a project they may otherwise never have known about.

Conscious of this potential across various media, Hurowitz recognizes the opportunities that may result from reaching out in print, in person, *and* online, rather than choosing one channel over another. "The more visible we become, the more we lecture, the more publications we are in, the more people are drawn to our website, the more we are selling a service to a fairly distinct group of clients."

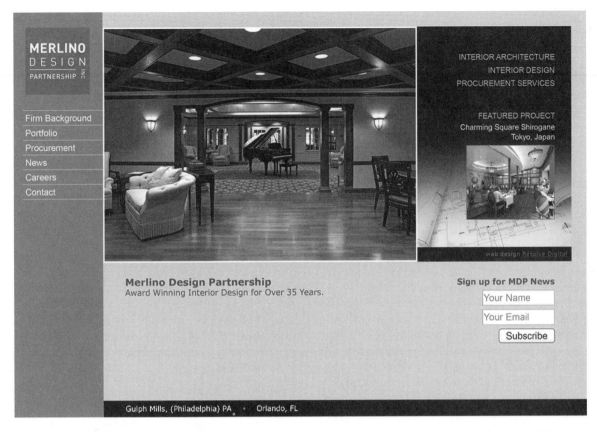

Figure 3-10

Merlino Design Partnership website home page. Merlino Design Partnership first launched its Web presence in 2004. Working with Digital Resolve, Merlino managing partner Bruce Hurowitz, IIDA, created the first iteration to address three questions: Who are we? What do we do? and How well do we do it? To build traffic, the firm incorporates its Web address into all marketing materials and is continually working to improve its search engine optimization.

Plugged In: Slifer Designs

Beth Slifer hung out her shingle as a sole practitioner of interior design in 1984, and over the past twenty-four years molded and built her company to a level of success that now includes sixty-two employees. Slifer Designs, located in Vail, Colorado, offers interior design and interior architecture services while operating a high-end showroom featuring unique products that are changed as often as every week. In addition to a strong focus on sustainable design, the firm provides award-winning

design solutions through two divisions: residential interior design (ID); and interior architecture and hospitality (IAH), dealing with hotel and luxury resort design projects. In 2002 the firm formed an in-house Green Team to address sustainable design through education for not only its staff, but also its surrounding community, with the goal of incorporating green elements into all of aspects of its business.

It is small wonder that Beth Slifer, armed with a master's degree in business administration and an entrepreneurial spirit, managed to turn a one-woman operation into a highly successful sixty-two-person, award-winning interior design firm celebrating its twenty-fifth anniversary in 2009. Slifer built her firm around the principles of luxury and lifestyle, operating under the philosophy that the final product of design is, ultimately, lifestyle.

Slifer Designs has consistently been ranked in the top three of residential interior design firms by *Interior Design* magazine, and over the years has earned awards and accolades from the industry for its high-quality residential and hospitality work. But it is not luck that keeps this successful firm in the limelight year after year. Slifer Designs understands the value of aggressive and active marketing efforts.

The firm allocates a marketing budget of between 1.5 and 3 percent of gross revenues annually to keep its name front and center. For a number of years, Slifer used typical printed materials like company brochures and direct marketing to reach prospective clients, but in 1999 the firm also embraced electronic and digital marketing media, launching its first website that year. Developed in less than six weeks, the site was small, grew slowly, and was handled in-house, with the firm letting its Web designers have creative control. The strategy was to limit information so that customers would have to call and arrange a face-to-face meeting to complete the sale.

In 2005, however, a major updating effort was launched. The second version, which was developed over about nine months, was a much larger, more complex site, with more projects and messages to represent Slifer Designs. The strategy changed from "make someone pick up the phone and call us" to "tell people as much as we possibly can online."

To take more control of the site's look, the firm added a graphics person to its team. Realizing the need for high-quality photography online, the firm undertook a significant photography effort, which turned out to have more than just online payoff, as the images could also be repurposed for print advertising and basic brochures. What's more, when the sustainability movement began, the Web grew in importance as the firm began backing away from the use of printed materials and direct mail in favor of marketing through its website.

Pictures and biographies of the entire staff were added, as well as increased information about the company and its design process, a much larger portfolio section, and a page on sustainability. The portfolio section was divided into sections that would highlight residential, hospitality, and remodel projects. Multiple layers were created for the site, allowing for archiving of images and case studies of older projects. The rationale was that the more information on the site, the more time prospective clients would spend there.

Slifer Designs contracted a reasonably priced, local Web designer to upgrade its site about once a month. New articles about the firm, memos, press releases, and new project images are added to keep the site current and keep customers coming back. In addition, articles, memos, and press releases in PDF format are retyped so that search engines will pick them up. The site as a whole successfully uses search engine optimization tags to raise its search rankings, eliminating the need for pay-per-click marketing.

Indeed, the relaunched site began to get hits immediately, and to supplement search engine traffic, Slifer also promotes the Web address in all of its marketing materials: business cards, showroom shopping bags, infomercials, mailings. In 2007 the firm also added an e-newsletter feature to the site. Because some of the firm's customers don't have email access, it was determined that there would be five annual issues: three on the website and two sent to a database of ten thousand clients and potential clients by direct mail. The print versions go out in the spring and before winter holidays, while the online versions are posted at three of Vail and Aspen's peak times: over President's weekend, the Fourth of July, and Christmas.

Carol Johnson, director of marketing, is responsible for the newsletter. She keeps the email version to one page, while the printed version is six pages long. It includes a personal message from the president, one article each from the residential and hospitality divisions, a new project feature, published articles about the firm, and announcements about firm awards. There are also shopping tips featuring pieces from the Slifer showroom, alongside some type of special offer

Welcome to Slifer Designs

Creating Luxury Living Experiences

ABOUT | BLOG | PORTFOLIO | SERVICES | SHOPPING | SUSTAINABLE DESIGN | CONTACT

 Slifer Designs Printable Brochure
You must have Adobe Reader to print or view PDF documents.

HOME

Slifer Designs is the nation's top authority on luxury resort mountain interior design. Offering full-service interior design and interior architecture and hospitality services for over 20 years, Slifer Designs has consistently been ranked in the top three of residential interior design firms by *Interior Design* magazine. Luxury resort design is Slifer Designs' specialty, which continually results in happy clients, and beautiful, comfortable and enjoyable living spaces. Design teams approach each project by keeping their client's vision, needs and budget as top priorities. Based in Edwards, Colorado, Slifer Designs has completed projects throughout the Vail Valley, Aspen, Telluride, Jackson Hole, Lake Tahoe, Park City, as well as Hawaii, Cabo San Lucas, Nantucket and Sonoma County, California. Please explore the website to see their impressive portfolio as well as information about the designer showroom located in Edwards, next to Starbucks.

Resources : XML Sitemap

Slifer Designs : Famous Interior Design Firm in Colorado offers Resort, Restaurant & Residential Interior Designs.

Slifer Designs : Top Interior Design Firm in Colorado offers Resort & Residential Interior Designs.

Figure 3-11

Slifer Designs' website home page. Each year, Slifer Designs allocates 1.5 to 3 percent of gross revenues to marketing, which includes maintenance and continual development of its online presence. Over the years, the site has expanded to include more photography, firm information, an email newsletter, and a company blog.

to drive traffic into the showroom. It seems to pay off: Johnson believes that the high-quality photography and the clean layout brought in a couple of jobs from the print newsletter in 2007.

Late in 2007, the Slifer team decided to add a blog, with Beth Slifer in charge of creating content. Blog entries are archived and available on the Slifer Designs website, and in the future individual designers may also contribute articles to the blog. In addition, as Slifer prepared to step down as CEO and creative director (while remaining involved as chairman of the board), Yvonne Jacobs, vice president of interior design and Slifer's leadership replacement, took over blog duties with input from Johnson.

Always looking for ways to improve online marketing effort, Slifer hopes to do a major site upgrade in 2009.

YVONNE JACOBS BLOG

YVONNE JACOBS, VICE PRESIDENT FOR SLIFER DESIGNS, IS SHARING HER THOUGHTS AND VIEWS
ON VARIOUS INTERIOR DESIGN TOPICS. AS VICE PRESIDENT OF ONE OF THE TOP RESORT
RESIDENTIAL AND HOSPITALITY DESIGN FIRMS IN THE NATION, SHE IS A EXPERT IN HER FIELD
AND HAS INTERESTING INSIGHTS ABOUT THE INTERIOR DESIGN INDUSTRY, PARTICULARLY THE
RESORT INTERIOR DESIGN SECTOR.

MONDAY, OCTOBER 9, 2008

Back to Solid Ground Equates to Simplicity in Design

I just returned from the City of Lights, where I attended the annual Maison & Objet: Paris Fall/Winter Home Trends trade show. The show offers a lush picture for 2009. With only four days to soak it all in, I navigated the seven massive halls, each holding acres of exhibits. I ventured into a feast for the eyes and inspiration for the mind. It's my pleasure to share my observations with you.

There was a wonderful display by Elizabeth Leriche called "Farm Life," which is a movement for updating countryside living. Aptly titled "Back to Solid Ground," the display communicates the quiet migration of city dwellers toward the rural spaces that surround them into objects in real life. In my view, this translates to new ideas of living as opposed to the same old standard. Leriche believes that "the simple pleasure of rural life is about reviving a belief in local produce and setting down roots."

Throughout all of the exhibits, I observed an emphasis on natural materials and organic objects. Messages being conveyed at the majority of the displays evoked a quest to rediscover the relationship between designer and function. I saw many locally hand crafted objects, and artisan works related to age-old rituals, such as farming. Collections of curiosities (coral, terrariums, fossils) were everywhere.

The new colors are lavender and lime green. Both of these tones were paired in separate displays with neutrals, mostly white. Lavender can be soft and soothing, a perfect shade for the new movement of simplicity in design. Lime green, perhaps not as tranquil, is a great color to accent with white or blue. It's vibrancy calls attention to the "Back to Solid Ground" theme previously mentioned. Subtle ways to add these colors were also presented for those seeking a little less commitment. Lavender dishes, or a lime green pillow, as opposed to painting an entire room in one of these shades, is a good solution.

BLOG ARCHIVE

▼ 2008 (1)

   ▼ October (1)

      Back to Solid Ground Equates
      to Simplicity in Desi...

Figure 3-12

Slifer Designs' blog. Launched in 2007, the Slifer Designs blog provides a forum to discuss industry issues and firm experiences. Originally written by Beth Slifer, it is now overseen by Yvonne Jacobs, who succeeded Slifer in 2009.

Under consideration are black page backgrounds that require less electricity, a change that supports the firm's sustainability focus. Another plan is to add an online retail (or e-tail) component so customers can purchase from Slifer's showroom online.

Slifer also continues to explore offline options, and one marketing channel aggressively used by the firm is television. It is a market the firm embraced even before tackling the Web, and as a big proponent of electronic marketing, Slifer considers television a perfect tool for sharing the firm's messages. Creating a half-hour editorial piece, otherwise known as an infomercial, allows the use of outside experts and opinions from architects or clients to support Slifer's messages.

By 2008, Slifer had done three editorial infomercials with much success. The second version of its infomercial, entitled *Evolution of Design*, was an historical piece covering the past, present, and future of design. That production ran locally in Vail, Aspen, and Telluride, Colorado, for three years. A third version was divided into nine segments, each about eight minutes in length, covering topics like green design, luxury residential design, before-and-after remodels, Slifer's showroom, and hotels, spas, and restaurants. Recognizing the shorter attention spans of today's customer, these pieces cover very specific topics in a much shorter time frame, and in addition to running on local television can also be easily interwoven on Slifer's website.

The feedback on the television pieces was phenomenal, according to Johnson, who knows of at least two jobs that resulted from them. In an effort to contain costs and expand the shelf life of the expensive TV pieces, Slifer Designs includes still photos of current projects and adds voice-overs. As these are expensive pieces to create, the plan is to keep them valid for three years. The investment, after all, is worth the rewards.

Being a Professional: Ethics

One last issue that every professional interior designer must consider throughout their career is that of professional ethics. It is a topic that touches all aspects of a business, from its finances and accounting policies to its employee relationships and human resources management, its sales and marketing, its delivery of services, its client relationships, and the individual designer's intellectual property. Consider the scope of ASID's Code of Ethics, which is reprinted in full in Appendix A. It addresses a designer's responsibility not only to the public and his clients, but also to other interior designers and colleagues, the profession as a whole, and to his employer. For many, documents like these provide starting points for individual designers to craft their own internal values and moral principles.

Ethics in Business: The Designers Furniture Gallery

Marilyn Schooley Hansen, FASID, is owner and CEO of The Designers, a $1.5-million furniture gallery and interior design business located in Omaha, Nebraska. The Designers has been operating continually for twenty-eight years at two locations in Omaha, and today has a staff of eight. Hansen and a team of three interior design professionals work on award-winning residential and commercial projects in Nebraska, Iowa, Florida, Oregon, and California. Hansen's belief in strong ethical standards led her to participate in developing and delivering an award-winning continuing education program on ethics and contracts with attorney Alan Siegel and fellow designer Michael Thomas, FASID, which has been presented across the country.

Like many of her colleagues, Marilyn Hansen had parents and teachers who helped instill a strong moral and ethical compass that influences not only her business activities today but her entire life. The Merriam-Webster online dictionary (www.merriam-webster.com) defines ethics as "the discipline dealing with what is good and bad and with moral duty and obligation," and also as "a set of moral principles." For Hansen, an active participant in the interior design field for more than forty years, presenting herself and her business, The Designers furniture gallery, at the highest professional standards is key, and being trustworthy and dependable top her list of characteristics necessary for success.

Along her journey to becoming a true professional, in 1973 Hansen joined AID, one of the predecessor organizations that became ASID, and found that the ASID Code of Ethics (whose observation is required by all members) provided a framework from which Hansen could grow as a professional and as a designer. Hansen finds that using the ASID Code of Ethics as the basis for her firm's policies regarding ethical behavior allows for a broad, universal understanding between Hansen, her staff, and other design professionals.

In addressing ethical behavior related to customers, The Designers' mantra maintains that the customer is always right, but it also throws in a healthy dose of protection for the firm. Contracts clearly spell out the scope and goals of each project, and lines of communication are constantly open during all project phases. The tenets of the ASID Code of Ethics add further support to this client-firm balance. Does this approach to clients pay off? "Absolutely," Hansen states firmly. "I would not choose to run my business in an unethical manner for pure financial gain. First of all, it's wrong, and second, I've worked too hard on the trustworthiness of my reputation to throw it away." As Hansen sees it, the greatest benefit of treating customers in an ethical manner is the building of trust and respect in the designer-client relationship, a vantage point that enhances project success.

Recently, Hansen's ethical treatment of a customer helped save a relationship in peril. For this specific project—a hotel—a large light fixture was ordered, but when the fixture arrived on site, it was 30 percent larger

than previously discussed. Although the fault was not Hansen's or her firm's, the business relationships with both the client and the supplier were at risk.

Although financial gain for The Designers was not at issue, Hansen felt strongly that her reputation and the future of the relationship were at stake. In response, Hansen hopped on a plane at her company's expense and flew to the site to focus on addressing the situation. "Sometimes it's not much fun doing the ethical thing, but you must uphold your business ethics over everything else," states Hansen.

The Designers' employee handbook clearly states that all employees, regardless of their roles at the store, are expected to abide by the ASID Code of Ethics, and they routinely share staff experiences as a means to reinforce those rules. New employees are given the handbook, which covers ethical customer treatment, and the ASID Code of Ethics is explained in depth during new-employee orientation. "It's our goal to mentor and grow our employees ethically as they mature in their design careers," notes Hansen.

Not content to extend ethical behavior and treatment solely to customers, Hansen also includes her employees and their contractors, vendors, and suppliers under her ethical umbrella. Her belief is that treating employees ethically builds trust and long relationships. "Doing what you promise develops a sense of security on both sides, which is necessary if a business is going to thrive," asserts Hansen. Unfortunately, not everyone maintains the same level of ethical standards. As important as ethical behavior is in client dealings, it is just as important to have policies and procedures in place to protect the firm from unethical employees. Several years ago, Hansen's seemingly successful business began having unexplained financial problems. Hansen knew money was coming in steadily, but bills were not being paid, resulting in significant unpaid balances on company accounts. When Hansen began investigating a number of odd incidents, she found her bookkeeper had been embezzling money totaling over $300,000 for more than eighteen months. She had concealed her activities by delaying financial reports, falsifying financial records, and even bringing another employee into the deception. The case was turned over to the police and taken to court. The former employee is on a repayment program and the firm is back on its feet, but it was a long, grueling process Hansen won't soon forget.

Hansen was devastated by this betrayal of trust, and questioned her own managerial abilities. She hired a business coach to help review her management approach as well as her internal policies and procedures to keep this kind of situation from reoccurring. Realizing she can't be in the store and out in the field working on design projects at the same time, Hansen also interviewed and hired a new manager who is in the store at all times, overseeing operations.

In addition to treating customers and employees in an ethical manner, a number of positive benefits can also result from dealing ethically with suppliers and contractors. In general, better treatment from vendors can result from a history of trust and dependability. Faster customer service, quicker shipping, better financial terms on orders, and more appreciation of your business by the suppliers and contractors can result from dealing ethically with them. In difficult times, Hansen's firm has enjoyed hands-on service from presidents of a number of furniture companies based on the trust that has been built over her firm's history.

Hansen believes that ethical behavior is not optional, and advises that temptation to behave otherwise should be avoided at all costs. While the world may never learn of your transgression, you will know—and that knowledge can follow you throughout your career. She advises: "If you wouldn't want the story exposed to the world, don't do it. Stick to your ethics no matter how difficult it may seem at the time—then you'll have no regrets."

Being a Professional: Licensing and Certification

Any practicing interior designer today must also be aware of professional licensing and certification requirements in the states in which he or she practices. These professional registration and licensing laws do not determine whether a designer's work is "good" or "bad." Rather, these legislative efforts determine a minimum level of competency that one must meet in order to safely practice one's profession.

The education, experience, and testing required to be a professional interior designer differs by state or jurisdiction. At the time this book was written, twenty-six states and eight Canadian provinces had laws recognizing interior design as a profession, either through a title act or a practice act. In early 2009, nineteen U.S. jurisdictions had title acts, six had practice acts, and one state had a permitting statue.

A title act protects the use of a term like "interior designer," "certified interior designer," or "registered interior designer," and restricts use of the specific titles in the act based on requirements outlined in a local statue. A practice act is a form of licensing that limits who can practice interior design based on requirements included in the local statue.

Each state has jurisdiction over how, exactly, the government regulates its certification, but in general, to be recognized as a certified or licensed interior designer in these states, an interior designer must pass the National Council for Interior Design Qualification (NCIDQ) exam. The exam tests six areas: project organization, programming, schematics, design development, contract documents, and contract administration.

Before sitting for the NCIDQ exam, candidates must accrue a certain amount of education and experience, most often totaling a minimum of six years. Some states also require a state-specific code exam, and many require certified and licensed interior designers to obtain continuing education unit (CEUs) in order to renew their certification.

Interior Design Registration Laws

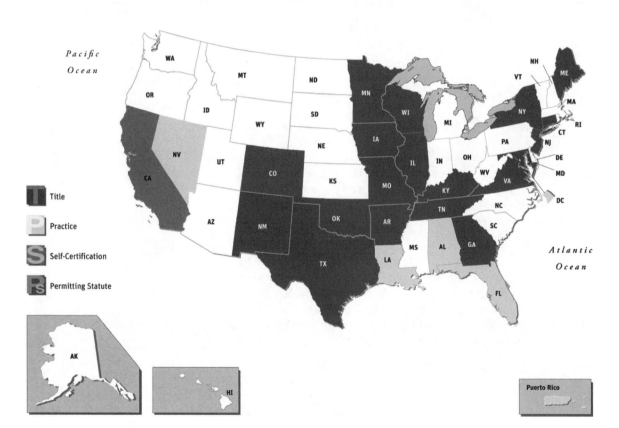

Figure 3-13
Interior Design registration laws, by state. © *American Society of Interior Designers. Used with Permission. All rights reserved.*

Table 3-2
Interior Design Registration Laws and Requirements, by State

State	Type of Law/Title Registered	Minimum Post-HS Education	Total Education Plus Experience Required	Continuing Education for Renewal	Year Passed
Alabama[1,6]	Title/Practice "Interior Designer"/ "Registered Interior Designer"	60 quarter hours or 48 semester credit hours, 4 years for the registered level	6 years	Yes	Title Law: 1982 Practice Law: 2001
Arkansas[1]	Title "Registered Interior Designer"	4 years	6 years	5 hours per year	1993, amended 1997
California[1-4]	Self-Certification "Certified Interior Designer"	None	6-8 years depending on education	10 hours every two years	1990, amended 1991
Colorado[5]	Interior Design Permitting Statute	2 years	6 years	None	2001
Connecticut	Title "Interior Designer"	Follows NCIDQ	Follows NCIDQ	None	1983, amended 1987
Florida[1]	Title/Practice "Interior Designer"	2 years	6 years	Not less than 20 hours every two years	Title Law: 1988, amended 1989, Practice Law: 1994
Georgia	Title "Registered Interior Designer"	4 years or first professional degree	4 years (no experienced specified)	12 hours every two years	1992, amended 1994
Illinois	Title "Interior Designer"/ "Registered Interior Designer"	2 years	6 years	None	1990, amended 1994
Iowa	Title "Registered Interior Designer"	2 years	6 years	Yes	2005
Kentucky[1,7]	Title "Certified Interior Designer"	Follows NCIDQ	Follows NCIDQ	12 hours per year	2002
Louisiana[1]	Title/Practice "Registered Interior Designer"	2 years	6 years	5 hours per year	Title Law: 1984, amended 1990, 1995, 1997 Practice Law: 1999
Maine[1]	Title "Certified Interior Designer"	4 years	6 years	None	1993
Maryland[1]	Title "Certified Interior Designer"	4 years	6 years	10 hours every two years	1991, amended 1997, 2002

Table 3-2
(*cont.*)

State	Type of Law/Title Registered	Minimum Post-HS Education	Total Education Plus Experience Required	Continuing Education for Renewal	Year Passed
Minnesota[1]	Title "Certified Interior Designer"	Board determines	6 years	24 hours every two years	1992, amended 1995
Missouri	Title "Registered Interior Designer"	2 years	6 years	10 hours every two years	1998, amended 2004
Nevada[1]	Title/Practice "Registered Interior Designer"	4 years	6 years	None	1995
New Jersey	Title "Certified Interior Designer"	2 years	6 years	Yes	2002
New Mexico	Title "Licensed Interior Designer"	2 years	6 years	8 hours per year	1989
New York[1]	Title "Certified Interior Designer"	2 years	7 years	None	1990
Oklahoma	Title "Interior Designer"	2 years	6 years	None	2006
Puerto Rico	Title/Practice "Interior Designer"/ "Interior Decorator"	2 years or 480 hours	2 years (no experience specified)	4 1/2 hours per year	1973, amended 1976
Tennessee	Title "Registered Interior Designer"	2 year	6 years	24 hours every two years	1991, amended 1995, 1997
Texas[1]	Title "Interior Designer"	2 years	6 years	8 hours per year	1991
Virginia[1]	Title "Certified Interior Designer"	4 years	6 years	None	1990, amended 1994
Washington, DC[1]	Title/Practice "Interior Designer"	2 years (as required by NCIDQ to take exam)	6 years	5 hours every two years	1986
Wisconsin	Title "Wisconsin Registered Interior Designer"	2 years	6 years	9 hours every two years	1996

Footnotes: No jurisdictions require residency. All states' current interior design legislation requires passage of the NCIDQ to be registered [license or certified] as an interior designer.

---

[1] Seal or signature required on interior design documents.
[2] California has an independent self-certifying board (i.e. not a state run board).
[3] California's independent board allows either the NCIDQ, CQRID, or both NKBA exams.
[4] Additional code exam required in California (CCRE).
[5] Colorado interior designers who have met the education, examination and experience standards are permitted to prepare interior design documents for filing and obtaining building permits.
[6] "Sealed Level" exam required in addition to NCIDQ exam for Alabama registered interior designers and for permitting privileges.
[7] To become certified in Kentucky prior to July 15, 2006 interior designers need ten years of interior design experience or eight years of experience and two years of interior design education, and successful completion of the Building and Barrier-Free Code Life Safety section of the NCIDQ exam. To become certified in Kentucky prior to January 1, 2009 interior designers must have a total of seven years of interior design education and experience. After this time, interior designers will need a minimum of a four-year degree from a FIDER accredited school and two years of interior design experience.

Note: Michigan Board of Architects keeps a list of qualified interior designers. Contact board for additional information.
© Copyright American Society of Interior Designers, May 2006

Do you know your state's certification requirements? It's important to not only be up-to-date on your home state's requirements, but also to make sure your certification and licensing is acceptable for all states in which you practice. For example, an interior designer living in Connecticut, and practicing in New York, New Jersey, Connecticut, and Pennsylvania must be fluent in all four of these regions' requirements.

Luckily, ASID maintains a comprehensive and up-to-date listing of each state's licensing status, alongside a breakdown of required education/experience, accepted examinations, details on continuing education requirements, and contact information for each state's board or agency overseeing interior design registration and licensing.

Part II:
Sustaining and Growing Your Business

Chapter 4:
Taking Your Business to the Next Level

N ow that the initial planning and research is out of the way and your firm is up and running, it's time to sit back and reap the rewards, right? While that may sound like a good idea at first, it may not be a recipe for long-term success. Continual success requires constant investment and examination. Thus, it is essential to treat a business as an ever-evolving entity, one that may need to grow or constrict to respond to market fluctuations, project load, new economic or market opportunities, or old-fashioned ambition.

Deciding When to Grow

For most business owners, one of the biggest decisions is whether to grow at all. After all, once you've reached a certain level of comfort, why rock the boat? Some obvious answers include increased revenues, higher industry status, and the ability to take on more work thanks to additional employees and technology. There are also, however, an array of challenges related to business growth.

First things first: In mulling over the decision to grow a business, it is essential to determine whether the timing is right. Moving a firm to the next level isn't something that should be done on a whim. Before embarking on a growth plan, consider these logistical questions:

- Do you have the funds to grow? Is your business, as is, financially secure?

- Are you comfortable with your existing situation, not just financially but also in your ability to handle project requirements?

- Do you have a desirable work/life balance? Will expanding your business compromise this? Will you be able to deal with any changes caused by growth and the necessary commitment that comes with it?

Are you comfortable with your responses? If so, put those professional concerns aside, and next consider whether you are personally ready to grow. Ask yourself:

- Do you have sufficient, if not superior, business management skills?

- Are you a visionary? Can you envision the future of your growing business?

- Are you a business strategist?

- Do you understand formal recruitment and hiring practices?

- Can you develop employees' knowledge and skills?

- Can you deal with difficult situations and make hard decisions?

- Can you delegate responsibility to others?

Deciding How to Grow

Just as complicated as deciding when to grow is deciding exactly how to expand. The average firm offering interior design services has between two and six employees. Larger firms, however, especially those with multiple offices, may employ sixty, eighty, or one hundred designers or more. The definition of small, medium, and large firms varies widely. According to the 2002 economic census and ASID's 2007 report *The Interior Design Profession: Facts and Figures*, the fifty largest interior design firms employed about sixty people on average, but the four biggest firms employed about 153 each on average. How big do you want your firm to be?

There are myriad ways to grow a business, and some are more complicated—physically, emotionally, organizationally, and legally—than others. While Chapter 5 will take a more in-depth look at some of the processes and paperwork involved in growing from a small entity to a midsize or large firm, this chapter takes a more conceptual view and first looks at some of the common ways designers might choose to grow their businesses.

Essentially, there are two types of growth: organic growth and acquisitive growth, as shown in Table 4-1. Organic growth applies to methods that grow a business from within, including adding staff to an existing team or adding another location. It may also include diversifying business offerings by adding services like client moving management; branching into another design specialty, such as product design; or targeting new market segments. Acquisitive growth, on the other hand, is just as it sounds: growing a business by acquisition outside of the original business model. These options may include buying into a franchise operation; acquiring or merging with another practice; or setting up a strategic alliance with a manufacturer as a dealership, or with a related business such as an architectural firm or a developer.

Table 4-1
Growth Strategies

Organic Strategies	Acquisitive Strategies
• Adding staff	• Franchising your business
• Adding another location	• Acquiring another practice
• Diversifying your business offerings	• Merging with another firm
• Targeting new market segments	• Forming an alliance with a related business or dealer

Both organic and acquisitive growth can happen over the course of years or within a few short months, but all growth processes have long-term ramifications and thus should be undertaken only after serious analysis and contemplation based on each business owner's individual situation.

On Her Own, but Not Alone: Mosaic Design Studio

Based in Columbus, Ohio, Mosaic Design Studio is a boutique firm specializing in interior design related to senior living, independent care communities, healthcare, corporate office space, and hospitality. In addition to being a full-service interior design firm, Mosaic also provides turnkey services that encompass pro forma development, facilities planning, project management, move management, construction management, strategic planning, and capital assessments. Mosaic also offers a complete line of senior-friendly furniture called "Designed For Life." Lisa M. Cini, ASID, IIDA, IFMA, is the founder and president of Mosaic Design Studio and Designed for Life. She is a native of Ohio and began her interior design and management career after graduating from the Art Institute of Dallas.

After a number of years as director of the Interior Design division of Karrington Health, a Columbus, Ohio–based developer specializing in assisted living and dementia facilities, Lisa Cini found herself at a crossroads: Karrington was being acquired by another firm. At first, Cini planned to go along with the merger, but after thinking it over she decided instead to venture out on her own, operating out of her home

or a small office, perhaps hiring a support person to help carry the load. This plan, however, was short-lived.

Karrington's chairman of the board, Rick Slager, had another idea. Over the years, he'd been impressed with Cini's design skills and had also noticed her tendency to approach design projects from a business point of view. Her knowledge level and logical approach to design, he felt, would serve her well in building a business of her own. Hearing of Cini's decision to start her own firm, Slager suggested she take four other Karrington designers, which Cini agreed to with some trepidation. Her vision of a small, one-person firm growing over time had instantly become a company of five.

Starting out with a concentration on the assisted living and dementia facilities market got the firm up and running for its first two years. In fact, in the first year alone, Cini and her group brought in $1 million in revenue from projects across the country. Unfortunately, shortly thereafter the market became overbuilt and business dropped off. The healthcare field in general, on the other hand, continued on an upswing, and in response Mosaic Design Studios refocused its target market. In addition to these interior design projects, the firm added nondesign services, including relocation assistance for clients, move management, and wayfinding system design for healthcare facilities.

In hindsight, Cini admits that taking on the first four employees at the company's formation was nerve-wracking. Contrary to this fast-paced start, she sees herself as a very risk-adverse business owner whose philosophy is to hire slow and fire fast. Now, whenever possible, she prefers to let attrition handle staff cuts, and until the entire staff is working a significant amount of overtime and weekends, or there is a demonstrated need for a specific skill set or personality type within the mix, she doesn't think about adding staff.

With herself and four other designers to support from the get-go, Cini found herself not only acting as the chief designer but also serving as the marketing manager. As such, she was responsible for bringing in projects, a role that during her tenure at Karrington had been filled by someone else. To address this, Mosaic Design Studios became active in trade shows targeting its potential client base, and as the company's brand recognition grew, speaking engagements and writing articles in trade publications were added to the marketing plan with some success. As it became apparent that the best project leads were coming from Cini's speaking opportunities and articles, Mosaic cut back on the costly trade show circuit.

Through these means, much had been accomplished in getting the company name out to its target markets. In 2001 Cini's husband, Greg, came on board as the firm's official marketing arm, strengthening the emphasis on brand building. In his role, Greg focused on the basics, collecting client testimonials and letters of reference. Adding these pieces to the firm's marketing toolbox brought in additional business, and allowed Cini to dive back into the creative side of the business. Three years into business, Cini began to see a need for additional staff to handle project load. Utilizing a system involving design student interns, Mosaic identified the stronger students and offered them full-time employment upon graduation.

Since its founding, the firm's size has fluctuated between eight and fifteen employees, settling into an arrangement some may consider a bit heavy on the administrative side. Whereas some design firms tend to hire more designers than support staff, Cini oversees only three other designers, as well as one or two interns. In addition, one senior designer provides managerial assistance by supervising day-to-day design operations. The rest of the firm includes one administrator, a marketing person, and a purchasing and accounting employee.

Initially, design staff was paid a salary; profit sharing was added as the workload and net profits increased. However, profit sharing became more difficult as administrative help was added to keep the firm running smoothly. On the one hand, the firm's systems were vastly improved by the addition of administrative staff, but costs also rose significantly. However, Cini maintains profit sharing when she can, and uses bonuses to offset low profit shares and keep key staff members satisfied. Administrative staff now includes an assistant to the president, as well as purchasing and marketing staff, who support the design staff. Over the years, Cini has noticed a generational shift. Younger designers, she finds, are less willing to work overtime and are more interested in quality of life than the extra money earned by working extra hours. Another change spurred by this generational shift affects project management. In the past, each designer was responsible for managing her own projects. As designers who despise project management duties have come on board, project managers with no design background have also been hired.

Cini maintains her practice of hiring only full-time employees rather than hiring on a contract or per-project basis, feeling it is better to have a full-time employee who is trained in the firm's documents processes. However, she is also exploring subcontracting as a means to address future staffing issues.

Before bringing on additional staff, Cini considers the workload, as well as any new technology, office space, furnishings, and equipment that would be required. The firm also conducts personality profiles, team interviews, and background checks to assure a good fit with existing staff. Word of mouth often brings in a number of candidates, but Cini also uses recruiting firms when seeking candidates for administrative positions.

Now that the firm's growth has slowed to a manageable pace, Cini wishes that she'd known to specialize and market to her strengths early on. It took nine years for her to realize she could hire consultants to help her determine the firm's core competencies and how to package them to attract the customers she wants. Business finance is another area she wishes she had been well versed in from the beginning, and she admits that being a manager also took some getting used to. As the firm owner, Cini envisioned she would be the "good" boss, creating an environment that was warm and friendly to its employees, where she, in fairy-godmother-like fashion, would bestow rewards such as raises and bonuses. She soon found, however, that in reality, there also are times when the boss has to say "no"—and during those times, employees didn't react as if a magic wand had touched them. It was difficult not to take these situations personally. To remedy this, Cini hired an office manager to act as an administrative buffer between her and her staff, taking on the more difficult and distasteful tasks that arise.

Other changes that have come with growth have been in the way Mosaic bills for services. Starting out, hourly fees were routine for projects, but as overhead has grown with staff additions, flat fees and "not to exceed" fees became the norm. Net profit has been reduced, but gross revenues have grown along with the size of the firm. A huge increase in healthcare benefit costs is a major factor leading Cini to consider outsourcing over hiring more full-time employees.

One thing that has not changed since Mosaic's doors opened is Cini's control over project and work allocation to her employees. All team members report to the president, while interns report to the full-time associates within their respective areas.

Having learned from her experiences, Cini continues to plan for growth. In 2007, she was planning for staff numbers to double over two years in response to a number of significant contracts, and also anticipates growth as necessary over five to ten years, to keep challenging herself and her team to operate at their best.

Jumping Right In: Catlin Design Inc.

Juliana Catlin, FASID, is principal of Catlin Design Inc. in Jacksonville, Florida. The full-service interior design firm offers services in both commercial and residential interiors with specializations in corporate interiors, hospitality, and healthcare design. An ASID member since 1976, Catlin served as ASID national president from 1999 to 2000.

Like many working women, Juliana Catlin faced the challenge of juggling work, marriage, and family. Working in Jacksonville, Florida, for a developer specializing in high-end corporate projects, her schedule included frequent 7:30 a.m. meetings—an arrangement that eventually became unfavorable. Although her employer made accommodations like allowing Catlin to bring her children to work, the overall stress was taking its toll.

Reaching her breaking point in her struggle for a work/life balance, in 1984 Catlin decided that leaving the development company and starting her own firm would provide the control she lacked. Being her own boss, she felt, would help her to better manipulate her schedule and juggle client and contractor meetings and job site visits with family duties. She envisioned completing drawings after her children went to bed in the evening, and setting meetings at times when she had someone to stay with them during the day. She felt confident that should the situation arise, she would be in a position to take half a day off to attend a school program or chaperone a field trip.

Delivering the news to her boss, Catlin was shocked when he suggested she take the rest of the company's design staff—a total of five other designers—with her. This was certainly not a suggestion she had anticipated. However, to help the fledgling new firm gain traction, Catlin's soon-to-be-former employer agreed to provide projects for a set period of time, and to continue their business relationship.

With a string of employees on board, Catlin opened up Catlin Design Inc. with ambitious visions of building a large practice with one hundred employees. In preparation, she structured the firm as an S Corporation, meaning that all profits—or losses—would funnel directly through her personal income tax forms.

With her ambitious plans in mind, Catlin immediately set out to brand her business. Drawing on knowledge gained from her father, a graphic designer, Catlin took steps to ensure that every aspect of her business supported the detail-oriented nature of the Catlin Interiors brand. With a laugh, she demonstrates this precise nature by recalling a client visit where, after the presentation, Catlin asked for feedback. Instead of critiquing the presentation, however, the client lamented that he couldn't find his cup of coffee on the tabletop. Catlin, it seems, had matched the cups' color to the exact finish of the table, so the cups seemed to disappear.

An important element of the Catlin Interiors brand revolves around exceptional customer service, and Catlin has trained her staff to go above and beyond for their customers. If that means helping a client find a plumber for an emergency long after the project is complete, it is done. In a perhaps extreme example, a client once tasked Catlin with designing their home while the family took a six-week vacation. The project also included having the family moved in upon their return, which happened to be Thanksgiving Day. Not only did the firm complete the project and the move, but it also arranged to have Thanksgiving dinner ready for the family when the clients arrived home.

As for that vision of a hundred-employee firm? Twenty years after starting out, Catlin has learned that in order to do what she wants to do in the design world, and manage it at the level where she is most comfortable and satisfied, she needs to maintain her staff level at around a dozen employees. Going beyond that number by even one employee, she says, puts her in a place where she feels disconnected from the projects and the people. On the other hand, managing

twelve employees maintains Catlin's sense of control. An added bonus of keeping the firm at this size is that the team remains close-knit. Everyone takes care of each other, Catlin says, whether it is providing some additional help to a staff member who is behind on a project phase, or offering support for personal problems and challenges.

Catlin needed support personnel for her original staff of five designers, so assistants were added to provide support and take on job tracking and management tasks, and a bookkeeper was added to keep the business running smoothly. All of these additions were brought in on a full-time basis and paid an hourly wage. By 2007 Catlin Interiors included Catlin as principal, one senior designer, three project designers, two design assistants, a project coordinator to track projects, two administrative assistants, and one person to handle deliveries. This staffing mix has worked well for the firm for the past ten years.

Staff roles have generally remained unchanged, except that senior design staffers now take on projects with less oversight from Catlin. Catlin continues to hire staff outright, avoiding contracting employees on a per-project basis, and staff additions are made based on workload and the firm's ability to support additional hires. As Catlin has found personnel issues may take up valuable time, she hires carefully and double-checks candidates' references. For nondesign staff positions, recruiting services have been helpful, but when it comes to design staff, word-of-mouth recommendations and the local interior design programs have been excellent sources of talent.

Financially, Catlin's greatest challenge over the years has been controlling overhead. The customer service the firm provides can take a sizable chunk out of profits, but the hope is that this level of service will result in repeat business and high-quality referrals. Another challenge for Catlin is an offshoot of the firm's close-knit culture, as being in such close touch with employees can create levels of stress and turmoil within the firm at any given time.

Looking back over her years in business, Catlin, like many business owners, wishes that she had delegated earlier. Empowering people to capitalize on their own strengths often removes layers of stress from management and provides opportunities to grow successfully. Once Catlin learned to manage in this manner, she found that she could have a more creative role in the firm's projects, with strong staff backing her up on administrative tasks. She now hires employees that are her creative opposite: people who enjoy the number-crunching tasks of a business. As for the pace of growth, Catlin aims to keep it at a "humane" level, hiring conservatively because, she admits, she doesn't have the heart to fire people if times get tough.

Looking ahead, Catlin is moving into a new business phase, focusing on removing herself from such an active role in the firm. Still thinking design but not necessarily in the interiors realm, she is considering opening a retail outlet to provide specialized pieces of furniture, lamps, and accessories that are hard to find in the Jacksonville area. While her interior practice would continue to function as a separate entity, Catlin would then be free to travel and search for the specialized pieces she has in mind, finding joy and creativity in the hunt along the way.

A Deeper Look at More Complicated Means of Growth

As noted earlier in the chapter, some means of growth are inherently more complicated than others. Into this category fall franchising, dealerships, and mergers and acquisitions. All of these business models involve outside entities and personalities that may be difficult to deal with or control. Some also come with a lot of predetermined structure and rules of operation.

Deciding to Franchise

Technically, a franchise is a legal and commercial business relationship between the owner of a trademark, service mark, trade name, or advertising symbol and an individual or group wishing to use that identification in a business. What this means for an interior design firm may be interpreted in two ways. On one hand, a business owner can choose to become a franchisor, licensing out a business to a franchisee—which, it must be noted, is not the same as opening a secondary office. It involves allowing an unrelated group or individual to operate under the same company name and brand for a set franchise fee or other financial arrangement. Developing a business as a franchise is a big investment that requires drafting a franchise agreement and a very specific business model, preparing marketing and operating materials as well as operations and policy manuals, and an array of management and legal preparation.

The other franchise option is to become a franchisee and buy into an existing franchise. One benefit of franchising in this regard is the opportunity to build upon an existing brand name and its past success. According to the U.S. Department of Commerce, the success rate for franchise-owned businesses is high: In studies conducted from 1971 to 1987, the Department found that less than 5 percent of franchised businesses failed or were discontinued each year.

Picking a Franchise

There are a growing number of interior design–oriented franchise options available, and finding the right one requires some research and legwork. First of all, talk to those in the trenches. Asking potential franchisors for a list of their other franchisees offers a starting point to hear firsthand reports about how the franchisor operates with its partners. Go beyond a quick call: visit them, spend some time observing their operations, and don't be afraid to ask about their expenses and relationship with the "mother ship," so to speak. More specifically, the U.S. Small Business Administration recommends asking the following questions:

- How long has the franchisor been in the industry? How long has the firm granted franchises?

- How many franchises are there? How many in your area?

- Examine the attitude of the franchisor toward you. Is the firm concerned about your qualifications? Are you being rushed to sign the agreement? Does the firm seem interested in a long-term relationship, or does that interest end with the initial franchise fee?

- What is the current financial condition of the franchisor? Check the franchisor's financial statements in the disclosure document. If the franchisees are paying their upfront fees but not their royalties, this may indicate that franchise units are being sold to investors but that they fail to open or perform too poorly to pay royalties.

- Who are the principal officers, owners, and management staff? What is each person's background? How much experience in franchising do they have?

- Compare sales promises with existing documentation. Be certain that the sales presentation is realistic and that major promises are clearly written into the contract. Be alert for exaggerated claims and pressure tactics.

- For newly established franchises, make sure the franchisor has registered the company's trademark. If not, the company's name and logo may have to be altered, forcing you to change your market identity after you have established yourself.

- Verify earnings claims and compare them with other business opportunities. Investigate all earnings claims carefully. Earnings claims must (1) be in writing; (2) describe the basis and assumptions for the claim; (3) state the number and percentage of other units whose actual experience equals or exceeds the claim; (4) be accompanied by an offer to show substantiating material for the claim; and (5) include certain cautionary language. Treat this opportunity like any other investment. Does the franchise offer the return you require? If not, you may want to look at a different business.

- What is the legal history of the franchisor? Have any of the executives been involved in criminal or civil actions? Is any litigation pending, particularly involving any restrictions on trade that may affect the franchise?

- Is the franchise a member of the International Franchise Association (IFA)? If not, why not? The IFA has a strict code of ethics that must be met before a company can become a member.

Evaluating a Franchise Package: Questions to Ask

Upon choosing a franchise option, it is important to closely examine the package you're buying. Be sure to review all the variables with your attorney, accountant, and/or business advisor prior to legally committing to a franchise. Chief among these considerations is the financial commitment. Franchise operations may involve not only a franchise fee, but also a territory fee, promotional fees, building construction or renovation fees, and training and educational fees, among other costs—these costs can amount to thousands of dollars. Does your agreement require you to invest in a starting inventory or an initial set of equipment? It is important to determine all fees up front, as well as whether these costs are one-time payments or repeat expenses. Ongoing costs may include royalties paid to the franchisor, insurance, and interest payments.

Think long term, too: What is required for a franchise renewal? What is needed to resell the franchise? Some franchise operations require that you get approval from the franchise corporation of any person before selling your franchise to them.

Further, just as it is important to meet with other franchisees ahead of time, it's also essential to examine your role in the bigger picture. How will your franchise be expected to operate within the franchise framework? Will you be restricted from competing with other franchises in any way?

A Franchise in Practice: Designs of the Interior

After completing bachelor's degrees in interior design and communications, Stephanie Bruss began her design career working at a studio in Barrington, Illinois. Shortly thereafter, the firm's owners decided to turn the operation into a franchise program, offering their knowledge and experience to other designers across the country. Bruss became a designer for two of the early franchise operations before deciding to jump on board as a franchisee herself. As owner of Designs of the Interior

(DOTI), in Green Bay, Wisconsin, Bruss employs eight people. The firm's projects run the gamut from small to large in both the residential and commercial fields of remodeling and new construction.

Stephanie Bruss always knew she would one day own her own firm. What she didn't know was exactly what form that business would take.

In 1993 Bruss was working as a designer/manager at Designs of the Interior (DOTI, pronounced "dottie"), then a Barrington, Illinois–based interiors firm. That year, the owners broached the idea of growing the

---

business by transitioning it into a franchise structure. Although Bruss had qualms about the potential success of such a model, she remained on board as the company developed its franchising plan, assisted in getting the first few franchises up and running, and served as an independent interior designer for some of the new franchises.

In exchange for an initial investment, in addition to use of the corporate name and identity franchisees are guaranteed a protected franchise territory, signage and fixtures, showroom inventory, office furnishings, some leaseholder improvements for their studios, and some working capital. From assistance in selecting a site for the DOTI location and negotiating a lease, to owner, manager, and design staff training, the DOTI corporate offices provide everything necessary to get a franchise up and running, as well as additional training and support to help grow the business.

In 1999 Bruss moved to Green Bay, Wisconsin, and became an independent designer in conjunction with the training and development of new DOTI stores. That same year, she left her corporate position with DOTI to open her own franchise, Design of the Interior Green Bay.

At the beginning, Bruss incorporated the franchise under the original DOTI design studio franchise model and began operating out of her home. Soon enough, she moved the business into a studio and added another designer to help handle the workload. Although she recognized the growth opportunities through a franchise, she was hesitant to stick with the old model. Instead, Bruss set about modifying the franchise concept into a storefront setup that offered retail opportunities.

Moving the business into a storefront operation gave Bruss the space necessary to grow her team, but also required extra staff to support the higher overhead costs. As a result, the business blossomed to twelve employees before shrinking back down to eight. Balancing business with design, the team split in half, with 50 percent of the staff focusing on the creative tasks while the remainder held support positions. A

business manager oversees managerial tasks, with one full-time and several part-time employees operating the store while designers are out on client calls. The business also added an IT technician, who manages the firm's website.

By 2007 most DOTI franchises were operating under Bruss's storefront model. Although the concept is rolled out in numerous locations, each franchise owner receives individual support from the DOTI corporate office. For their initial investment of $325,000 to $450,000, franchisees also receive protected franchise territory, showroom inventory, signage and fixtures, office equipment and furnishings, leasehold improvements, and working capital. Each week, corporate conference calls are held to address specific educational business topics concerning business operations. In addition, an annual owners' meeting provides a forum at which to discuss ownership issues, as well as explore additional educational opportunities. New franchisers have the option of receiving training from the national level, and personalized visits may be arranged to focus on a franchise's strategic and marketing plans. The company also assists franchises in managing vendor relations. "It's like having a mentor to guide us through the hurdles," Bruss notes.

Additional benefits of the franchise model include having access to greater buying power, a variety of product lines, merchandise discounts, and the ability to purchase pieces without manufacturer-imposed minimums. Bruss also relishes the power of name recognition. "Being part of the larger corporation gets us a lot of attention from vendors at shows like High Point," she explains. "It's nice to be part of that bigger corporation and be able to get hands-on help from the home office, but still own and control your own company." The brand's strength, however, can also prove challenging to strong-willed franchisers. "Your brand is going to be the corporate brand. You can't come up with your own logo or advertisements," she notes, adding that "this aspect takes a bit of your ownership away. As a franchise owner, you have to hope that the same level of quality and service will be maintained as the home office continues to grow and expand."

Let's Make a Dealership

Most commonly involving manufacturers, dealership arrangements may be more informal than franchise arrangements. Typically, design firms sign on to be dealers of a specific manufacturer's goods; then, with an agreement in place, the firm buys product from the manufacturer at wholesale prices with the intent to resell it.

A dealership arrangement comes with special considerations. It often necessitates the firm setting up some sort of showroom to display goods, which may mean increased financial burdens. In addition, the manufacturer may make the relationship contingent on the dealership meeting sales quotas.

The benefits of a dealership arrangement are mutual: The manufacturer reaps the geographic representation of the dealer, while the dealer may benefit from the manufacturer's reputation and brand power, as well as its support network.

Finding the Right Mix: Elements IV Interiors

Since founding Elements IV Interiors in Dayton, Ohio, in 1990, Kim Duncan has grown the business from five employees to a team of sixty-five. The firm specializes in commercial, K–12, and government design and sales, and has operated as a Haworth dealer since 1989. It has been recognized twice by *Inc.* magazine's Fastest Growing Companies in America list and also by the Dayton Top 100 Companies list.

When asked why she decided to start her own business instead of continuing to work for someone else, Kim Duncan replied that it was just part of her personality. A self-described self-starter who likes adventure, "I just had faith that I could start a business and be successful," she recalls. As far as working for someone else, she had reached her limit of putting in long hours at firms with little room for advancement.

In 1990 Duncan took the first steps toward owning her own office furniture dealership, joining three partners to launch Elements IV Interiors in Dayton, Ohio. They coined the firm's name in honor of its four owners. The quartet also hired two full-time designers and one furniture installer.

In the beginning, Elements IV Interiors set up shop as an installation firm, collaborating with a local moving and storage company and servicing other Dayton area furniture dealerships. The team worked primarily with clients seeking to reconfigure their existing systems furniture. Given the small full-time staff, the company hired help as needed, contracting local off-duty firefighters to assist with installations. With two of the business partners actively marketing their installation services, in very short order additional full-time installers were added to meet demand.

The business's evolution into a dealership operation happened by chance. While completing an installation that required some additional Haworth components for the new layout, Duncan and her partners contacted the manufacturer to see what would be required for them to purchase the necessary pieces. They found out that only authorized Haworth dealers could do so. Over the course of learning about the process, Elements IV became a limited Haworth dealership. Given the firm's Dayton locale and its prior experience working with Wright Patterson Air Force base nearby, the dealership arrangement allowed the firm to service a government contract for the base.

To Duncan, it seemed a natural arrangement. "Office furniture dealerships were all that I had ever known," she recalls. "I did a college internship at an office furniture dealership, and I got my first job after graduation at a Knoll/Kimball dealership. Following the philosophy of doing what you are best at seemed the best course of action."

Shortly after the limited dealership agreement was arranged, a major project came along that involved the design and furnishing of a full floor at a local hospital. But before Elements IV could accept the project it was necessary to obtain Haworth's approval, as the lucrative project was outside of Elements IV's very limited territory. Seeing the value of the hospital project and the concurrent furniture sales, Haworth approved the firm's participation on a one-time-only basis. This arrangement was fleeting, as Elements IV's reputation grew and additional projects came in. Eventually, Haworth advanced the business to the level of a full-preferred dealer covering a larger territory. As a full dealership, it was assigned a generous geographic region in which to freely operate as a Haworth office furniture dealership, opening the door to growth and expansion for Elements IV.

By 2007 the firm was operating as an independent business representing Haworth. Over the years, Duncan has been extremely happy with the relationship between her dealership and Haworth. Her success led to an opportunity for Duncan to represent her region as one of twelve dealership owners on Haworth's Dealer Council for North America, which meets regularly to discuss issues affecting dealerships. As part of this role, Duncan served as an intermediary between the manufacturer and other dealers in her region.

The firm also has continued to evolve. Growing from its initial job with Wright Patterson AFB, the business holds two furniture maintenance contracts with the base and is responsible for maintaining the base's furniture inventory, which meets the needs of 22,000 employees. With three designers generating sales and projects, the firm hired additional support staff, first bringing on an administrator who evolved into a receptionist/bookkeeper/HR manager/administrative assistant and general jack-of-all-trades. Until this key staff member came on board, the designers and sales staff had done all quotes, paperwork, and purchasing. As revenue increased, another full-time salesperson was added, and the firm now adds part-time installation staff as needed.

In 1998 Elements IV purchased Office Furniture USA, a franchise providing an even wider range of products, access to deeper discounts, and a dependable shipping and freight system. In 2003 a customer support specialist came on board to assist the sales and support staff with quotes, order entry and follow-up, and other clerical duties, and in 2006 full-time project managers were brought into the mix to focus on larger construction projects and their installation.

Since 1990 three of the original partners have left the business, so that Duncan remains as the only founder. Originally an equal partner with the three cofounders, when one partner left Duncan acquired shares to achieve a majority interest of 65 percent in the business. This change in ownership allowed the firm to quality for Women's Business Enterprise (WBE) status—national certification from the Women's Business Enterprise National Council—which opened up new markets and business opportunities.

Joining Duncan in a leadership capacity are President Jack King and Vice President of Sales and Marketing Mark Williams. The firm as a whole has grown from six employees to a staff of sixty-five that includes the three owners (Duncan, King, and Williams), an eight-person sales staff, and seven interior designers (four senior and three junior designers). In addition, there are two project managers, six administrative support staff members, and thirty to forty team members who support the sales and design teams in an operations/installation/delivery capacity.

While a part-time designer assists with project spikes, the sales and design staff are mostly full-time employees to ensure their commitment to Elements IV and its sales plan. When additional help is needed, the firm subcontracts to independent designers on a per-project basis. As would be expected in any startup, staff additions have taken a toll on the firm's bottom line as payroll expenses and benefits costs have escalated. However, with cross-training and product training programs in place, employees generally grow into their positions and generate sufficient revenue to not only cover their salaries but also add to the organization's bottom line.

With costs related to hiring full-time employees rising, many issues are considered before adding staff. Duncan

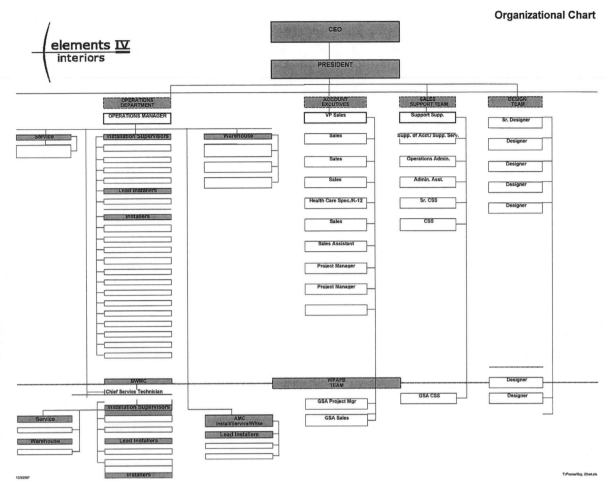

Figure 4-1
Elements IV organizational chart and mission. Elements IV
organizational chart clearly delineates a chain of command within the firm.

carefully watches the designers' workload. If it appears to be backing up with excessive overtime and the trend appears to be lingering, hiring decisions are made. When it comes to hiring, the use of services like Monster.com helps bring in a plethora of applicants, but very few meet the company's criteria and seldom does Duncan find more than one or two people worth interviewing from this pool of candidates. To

supplement such sources the firm maintains relationships with colleges and student interns, and now offers a bonus to current employees who refer someone that eventually becomes a full-time employee. However, even those who pass the rigorous screening process are hired on a part-time or probationary basis to assure they will be a good fit for the company.

Ownership Transition: Contract Office Group

Contract Office Group (COG) is a full-service contract furniture dealership and the largest Haworth preferred dealer in Northern California. The dealership offers a complete suite of products from the Haworth Architectural Interiors line, including lighting, access flooring, movable walls, and furnishings. Leonard and Sue Alvarado bought COG in 2001, just when the dot-com bubble burst in Silicon Valley. Alvarado, who has a background in interior design and experience as a director of sales for Haworth, was targeted by Haworth as a part of its corporate strategy to establish a dealership in the San Francisco Bay Area. With his wife, Sue, who also holds a degree in interior design, Alvarado took ownership of the dealership and created a business model that highlighted a new direction for the firm and Haworth dealerships.

The history of Contract Office Group (COG) dates back to 1976, when Wayne Gianotti and John McCabe started the San Francisco–based company. For two decades the business prospered in the Bay Area, growing through a merger with another entity, eventually building a strong portfolio during the dot-com boom of the 1990s, and blossoming to 197 employees.

Unfortunately, the company's fortunes ran into a roadblock in the late 1990s. Like many Silicon Valley and Bay Area businesses heavily invested in the technology sector, COG was deeply impacted by the dot-com bubble burst. Drastic reductions in the demand for office furnishings necessitated major cuts at the dealership, and the two-hundred-person firm shrank to sixty. Shortly thereafter the business took on new owners and, with them, a new life.

The evolution of COG came as part of a bigger strategy of a larger entity, namely Holland, Michigan–based furniture manufacturer Haworth. In 2001 Haworth executives sought to establish a dealership in the Bay Area to highlight new directions for the company.

Based in Los Angeles at the time, Leonard Alvarado was the successful western director of sales for Haworth who, before joining Haworth, had spent ten years working at a Herman Miller dealership. Seeking his experience—and enticing him with the San Francisco–area climate—Haworth approached Alvarado about running the new Bay Area venture.

In December 2001 Leonard and his wife, Sue, who is also trained in interior design, purchased Contract Office Group, effectively buying out Gianotti and McCabe in a deal financed through Haworth. Buying an existing dealership had both pros and cons. Thanks to its long history, the company had name recognition in the region, but new owners meant new relationships needed to be established with the local A&D community. In the 1980s COG's owners had operated the business as a direct competitor to architects and designers in the region, something the Alvarados sought to change. Instead of competing with the A&D community, the new owners sought to be a resource. The transition from competitor to colleague, however, took work. "I think that we were most surprised by how important it is to have the kind of relationships and networking skills required to be 'rainmakers' for the company," Sue recalled. "To thrive in our market it is critical to have both principals engaged in local events, as people do business with those they know and trust."

Once the purchase was finalized, business restructuring began. Leonard took the helm as CEO while Sue undertook the task of rebuilding relationships within the A&D community. Internally, COG was restructured into three divisions: sales and marketing, design and construction, and services. The goal was to reinvent the company as a dynamic dealership that could offer clients a staff that was highly educated and experienced in design and construction. Since customers require a broad knowledge of both construction and design, half of COG's sales staff consists of educated designers; the director of the San Francisco office is an architect.

Although by 2007 the firm was not yet back up to its 1990s staffing levels, COG employed ninety-three staff members, many of whom joined during a 30 percent increase in staff over a two-year period. This staffing increase was split among operations, sales, design, project management, project coordination and order entry, accounting, IT specialists, receptionists, warehouse staff and managers, and installers and installation managers. During the downturn in the economy, customers were in less of a position to purchase new furnishings, so COG added designers, move specialists, project managers, and installers to take advantage of client moves and changes to their existing furnishings and space. Most employees join the dealership on a full-time basis, but the business also employs contract labor during uncertain economic times so that its labor force can continue to expand or contract to meet market needs. Whether hiring full-time or on contract, the Alvarados carefully consider customer needs, market conditions, and improving operating efficiencies before making additions. Nonetheless, COG is once again in growth mode with a focus on hiring the essential people needed to aggressively move forward.

Since the ownership transition in 2001, COG has opened a second office and now operates both in San Francisco and in Milpitas, California, near Palo Alto.

Rather than providing a standard showroom featuring a few select Haworth pieces, COG's facilities are designed to showcase the Haworth story, including many of its extensive product lines. It is a strategy that has paid off: The business is one of the ten largest Haworth dealerships nationwide, and its business model has been copied as the formula for the "new" Haworth dealership.

For the Alvarados, their goal is to be known as part of a team providing sustainable solutions, and owning a dealership is their vehicle to do so. The firm's motto is to provide S.M.A.R.T. facilities: that is, Sustainable, Manageable, Adaptable, Reusable, and Techno-logically savvy work environments. Looking to the future, the duo hopes to maintain COG's position as the leading furniture dealer in its area, although "leading" doesn't necessarily mean "biggest." Still focused on the importance of local relationships, the management's driving force isn't to rack up the most sales but rather to have the local A&D community embrace them as partners.

Residential Roots: Barbara Goodman Designs

Barbara Goodman Designs operated for thirty-one years in Greenville, Delaware, under management by Barbara Goodman Cresswell, providing complete interior design and architectural design services for residential clients and hospitality clients, including a number of country clubs and private executive offices. Twenty-nine years into her business career, Cresswell partnered with Drexel Heritage to open a dealership in Wilmington, Delaware. Over the years she had sold a number of the Drexel Heritage lines. Since beginning as a sole practitioner in 1976, through three businesses, Cresswell has grown her staff to thirty-three.

Despite having thirty-one years running a successful high-end residential design firm under her belt, Barbara Goodman Cresswell still looks for opportunities. In the mid-1970s Cresswell was a newlywed and a recent transplant to Greenville,

Delaware, where she didn't know a soul. While settling into town, she met a local craftswoman who operated a window treatment workroom in her home and, over time, Cresswell began taking part in the work. At first she worked for no compensation, but eventually she decided there was no reason she couldn't do the work herself and make a profit.

Capitalizing on her passion for design, Cresswell launched Barbara Goodman Designs in 1976, and although she initially sought to focus on window treatments, word of mouth soon encouraged her to expand to full design services. Despite her success, a financial mishap quickly made it clear that she needed to expand in a more businesslike manner. Busy with her designs, Cresswell received a call from her banker, who was wondering why she was bouncing checks. Puzzled at her lack of funds in light of all her success, Cresswell quickly found the source of the problem: a stack of undeposited client checks in her desk drawer. Three years into her business, it was time to hire a secretary to manage paperwork and bookkeeping.

Cresswell's first employee led to others, although the firm continued to operate out of Cresswell's home. After hiring her secretary, Cresswell added staff to help with drafting and otherwise free up her own time. While clerical support personnel came on board in full- and part-time capacities, during the first five years the drawing and drafting assistants were hired on a freelance contract basis. However, after running into difficulties scheduling part-time employees, Cresswell began hiring on a full-time basis only. Under this policy, she added junior designers to help manage projects for a growing client list.

In the early 1990s a new business opportunity arose, and Cresswell entered into a partnership with a firm in Wilmington, Delaware, but after three years the partnership dissolved as a result of philosophical differences between the partners regarding customer relationships. Cresswell returned home with her own business, clients, and staff.

Barbara Goodman Designs continued to grow and, to Cresswell's surprise, drew from her home again. In 2001 her son Christopher (called Chip) announced he wanted to join the firm. There was, however, a condition to Chip's participation: the firm would have to move to a real business location. Thinking she could buy a year or two's time in looking for a new location, Cresswell agreed, but less than two months later the business broke ground on a 3,500-sq.-ft. studio that would also house a showroom and design center. By 2005 the firm had expanded into nearly 7,000 sq. ft. of space.

Over the years, Cresswell began stocking a number of product lines in the showroom, including Drexel Heritage, a home furnishing and fine furniture manufacturer. In late 2004 Drexel Heritage representatives broached the idea of Cresswell opening a Drexel Heritage store to become a full-fledged preferred dealership. Already busy with her design firm, Cresswell was unsure about taking on another major business commitment, but in researching and discussing the opportunity with her son, she eventually chose to take part in the venture and operate the two companies—Barbara Goodman Designs and Drexel Heritage—separately. The next year, in December 2006, Cresswell's 16,800-sq.-ft. Drexel Heritage store opened.

The difference in operating the dealership, Cresswell says, is simplicity. At the store, she notes, a Drexel table may come in only three sizes and three finish choices, while at Barbara Goodman Designs custom solutions abound, which in turn require drawings, specifications, and meetings with tradesmen.

Opening the dealership wasn't the end of Barbara Goodman Designs' growth or its homespun roots. Shortly after the Drexel Heritage store opened, Cresswell's daughter, Kim, joined the business as head of sales and marketing.

In response to problematic delivery and installation service, in 2006 the company bought a warehouse and started its own receiving and delivery service. Now, in addition to handling all of the receiving, delivery, and installation for its own businesses the company also, under the name Furniture Services Unlimited, provides "white glove" services for other design firms in the area.

On the personnel side, the firm blossomed to thirty, with a balance that leans more to the design side than the clerical. Cresswell's reasoning is simple: Designers generate revenue; support staff generally does not. As a result, the firm's staff includes nine interior designers (four at a senior level, five at a junior level), alongside six managers, four clerical employees, five laborers and installers, and one in-house accountant. In addition, the firm employs three external consultants on a weekly basis: a bookkeeping service to balance the accounting work done in-house, a CPA, and a business advisor. Cresswell maintains control over the mix, assigning all projects with occasional input from her daughter Kim.

Although she has not put a cap on the firms' growth, Cresswell sometimes thinks she should have frozen the size when she had fewer employees and a higher profit level. She's found that it takes a full year to get new designers trained on the job and for them to begin generating revenue that sufficiently covers the cost of their compensation. Hiring new employees also requires space planning, as management personnel require private office spaces, while designers are able to share workstations and computers. There must also be sufficient clerical staff on hand to support the new employees.

Recruiting talented designers has also been a challenge, as Cresswell has come to find that Internet sites are not much help, and many of the accredited interior design programs skew to the commercial end of the industry, limiting candidates for this residential design business. An in-house person has helped Cresswell locate prime job candidates, but in the end she has found that her best employees come with their own marketing package.

Given the challenges, Cresswell has no specific plan for growth or for the size of her firm as she looks to the future. By 2007 Barbara Goodman Designs operated in two shops: the one in Greenville and another seven miles away in Wilmington. Instead of planning by numbers only, Cresswell now prefers to run the business less around planning and strategies and more around a flexible framework that allows the business to be open to opportunities.

A + B = C: Mergers and Acquisitions

One of the more complicated means of growth is a merger or acquisition. Some situations involve two separate, friendly entities merging their businesses to form a larger one. Oftentimes, however, this may involve one larger, more successful or well-known company legally taking over the controlling interest of another company. A merger can be less complex and not necessarily involve the transfer of money, remaining a legal joining of two companies and their staffs, assets, and liabilities to form a new, larger company. An acquisition, on the other hand, generally involves one company purchasing another and taking over management of the other firm due to holding controlling interest.

The benefits of a merger or acquisition may include increased revenues, market expansion, the potential to build on an established brand, increased staff size and number of customers, and product and service diversification. The process, however, brings with it its own challenges. Are you looking to purchase controlling interest in another firm and absorb it under your name, or would you rather sell your business into a bigger practice? How will your employees react? Will your customers follow you? There are many variables to consider.

Buying In: Larry Wilson Design Associates

In 1987, after more than a decade of designing for firms in Houston, Washington, D.C., and New York, Larry Wilson, ASID, IIDA, founded Larry Wilson Design Associates in Jacksonville, Florida. Thirteen years later Wilson merged his practice with Rink Reynolds Diamond Fisher Architects to form the interior design arm of Rink Design Partnership Inc. Wilson is principal-in-charge of interior design for the sixty-five-person firm, which focuses on commercial, restaurant, hospitality, retail, and resort design. He has won numerous awards for his design, including the Gold Key Award of Excellence in Hospitality Design, 26th Annual IIDA National Interior Design Award, DuPont Antron Award, and Solutia Doc Award, as well as the ASID Medalist award. He is a past chairman of ethics and appellations for ASID, past president of the ASID's Florida North chapter, and past director of the ASID Jacksonville chapter.

Like many creatives in the design field, Jacksonville, Florida–based interior designer Larry Wilson did not get into interior design because of a love of bookkeeping and managerial tasks. However, in the late 1980s that is exactly where his focus unintentionally fell as he found himself overwhelmed by business duties for his firm, Larry Wilson Design Associates.

Larry Wilson Design Associates opened shop in 1987 with three employees—Wilson himself, his wife, Laurie (also an interior designer), and a junior designer. The Subchapter S corporation worked out of a 400-sq.-ft. office rented from an architectural colleague. Although the office was filled with passion, what it didn't have was a plan. "I'll be very candid: I was absolutely clueless," Wilson says. "In retrospect, I really didn't know what I was getting into. We didn't have a formal game plan and we didn't have a formal business plan or any kind of marketing plan." However, several clients had followed Wilson from his previous firm, providing a small bit of financial assurance.

The firm took any work that came its way, which was mostly residential at the start. After the firm's first restaurant project won a Gold Key award, hospitality projects soon joined the flow. Although Wilson sought to keep the firm at a "mom and pop" level, the firm added two additional—and essential—staff members: a CADD technician and a receptionist/clerk. Laurie, who had previously owned an art gallery and was thus more familiar with managerial procedures, handled the business side, while Larry focused on design. The firm operated under this arrangement for thirteen years.

Over the years the firm's reputation continued to grow, as did its project load, until things reached a breaking point. "It got to the point where I was constantly stressed and thought if I didn't do something differently I was going to die. At that point,

though, I was so stressed that I didn't have the wherewithal to realize I could step back and grow the business differently," Wilson says. "I wasn't looking for anything in particular, but the time I made that comment about dying happened to coincide with the opportunity of a merger."

For various projects over the years, Wilson had partnered as the interior designer for a number of architecture firms, one of which was Rink Reynolds Diamond Fisher, a thirty-five-employee entity. In 1999, around the time that Larry Wilson Design Associates was struggling with its workload, the firm partnered with Rink Reynolds Diamond Fisher on a large-scale project for Ponte Vedra Inn and Club. "Word had gotten out around then that I was talented and could design, but I was having trouble getting work out of the office. One of Rink's principals approached me to come on board as the interior designer for the project, which would be contracted through their firm," Wilson says. "Technically, I was still independent, but we would do the project's work together."

After one of the project's weekly meetings, Jack Diamond pulled Wilson aside and broached the idea of continuing the firm's collaboration permanently. Although he played it cool at first and remained nonchalant, Wilson later went home and made a classic pro/con list. Potential "cons" of the deal included a possible lack of control when it came to design, as well as less personal interaction with clients. Being an owner of a larger entity could mean higher debt responsibility and carried a bigger sense of accountability among the partners. On the "pro" side, the merger would offer the ability to handle larger jobs and would provide more design muscle as well as a larger talent pool. It also offered the potential of a higher income, a higher profile, and a more flexible schedule.

For Wilson, the pros far outweighed the cons, and he agreed to the merger. However, joining the practice wasn't as simple as just saying yes. Structurally, Wilson demanded 100 percent equal partnership. As an interior designer entering a business comprised of architects, he was concerned that coming in as anything less than a full partner would lead to challenges. Specifically, he was concerned that the other partners would challenge the way he wanted to approach his work, and without similar standing he would be in a weaker position to argue his beliefs. To make the even partnership happen, Wilson bought into Rink Reynolds Diamond Fisher by purchasing stock shares over a year and a half, instead of having the firm buy out Larry Wilson Design Associates. "What can happen when you are bought out is that you may lose control, and all of a sudden you are a possession. You are no longer a strong voice. By buying into the larger firm, even thought it hurts initially, you can remain a strong voice," he says.

After involving attorneys and external consultants, including one who specialized in company buyouts and mergers, the deal was finalized on paper. Because all involved were concerned about losing Wilson's name recognition as well as work with other architecture firms, the new entity began by operating under both firm names. Letterhead was crafted featuring both names and logos, and the firm maintained two different phone numbers—but kept one set of joint books. After about a year, however, the firm became Rink Reynolds Diamond Fisher Wilson.

Inside the firm, though, a lack of preparation led to culture shock. Both sides of the equation underestimated the amount of team building necessary before the actual, physical merger. "When we came on board the architectural staff wasn't ready for it, and we came across some hostility and confusion," he recalls, noting that his team moved into Rink's offices immediately after the merger and were seen as outsiders.

One specific barrier was the architectural employees' unfamiliarity with the depth of interior design processes and of the need for collaboration with the interior design team. Taking charge of the assimilation process, Wilson had to be quite vocal, explaining what an interior designer does and demanding that an interior designer be involved on a project from the initial meeting through job completion. He made sure not only that the project teams were budgeting for interior design services, but also that these fees were broken out from the architectural services so that they could be tracked. Wilson's persistence worked: the interior design studio, he notes, has in many cases become the benchmark for the rest of the office.

Another challenge for Wilson was—and still is—balancing the administrative tasks with the opportunities for design. Rink Reynolds Diamond Fisher Wilson (which became Rink Design Partnership in 2005) continues to grow. Since the merger, the interior design department has grown to eleven, while the overall firm has expanded to sixty-four employees.

This growth sometimes forces Wilson to step back from the design process and into a more managerial role. In response, he strikes a compromise between the two realms: in a perk afforded to senior level managers and partners, Wilson has become selective with his project participation, digging into certain hospitality and restaurant projects—his two favorite realms—while divvying up the remainder of the projects around the department. In return, this owner-level arrangement allows the designer-at-heart to remain involved in the creative process.

Preparing for an Acquisition

Charles B. Schelberg

Charles B. Schelberg is a principal at Miles & Stockbridge P.C. in Baltimore, Maryland, where he concentrates on the representation of regional and international clients in complex business transactions such as mergers and acquisitions, financings, and joint ventures. In addition, as outside general counsel he advises clients on a wide array of issues, including contract matters, commercial disputes, corporate governance, business entity formation, and regulatory and real estate issues. In 2007 Miles & Stockbridge represented the Baltimore-based, privately owned architectural firm RTKL Associates in its acquisition by the international engineering and consulting company ARCADIS. Schelberg led the legal team handling the transaction.

Your interior design business is successful and has grown steadily over the years. Your firm has talented employees, satisfied clients, and a strong reputation. But you have concluded that organic growth alone will not enable the company to reach quickly enough the size, financial performance, markets, or other milestones that are necessary for long-term success. So you have decided to grow by acquiring one or more other design firms.

An acquisition can take anywhere from a few weeks to many months to complete, depending on the pace of negotiations and the complexity of any business, legal, or other issues that may arise. The parties may seek to maintain the secrecy of negotiations until closing. Spread of word of the negotiations could lead to raids by competing firms on key employees, disquiet among important clients, or bids for the target firm from rivals in or outside the industry. Considerations like these often lead the parties to proceed with the transaction as quickly as possible. However, the likelihood that an acquisition ultimately will meet your strategic goals will be boosted with careful preparation. Before starting a sprint through negotiations to closing, taking the following steps can help you achieve a successful acquisition:

- Assemble a team of professional advisors with strong experience in mergers and acquisitions. An experienced lawyer can help you create and negotiate the optimal structure for a deal to minimize legal risks and maximize tax advantages. You will need skilled accounting input to evaluate the financial condition and performance of a target firm, and to understand the financial impact that an acquisition may have on your business.

- Gather information on the prevailing methods for valuation of interior design firms. In order to decide on a price range you are willing to pay for a target firm, and then negotiate that price, you should understand how companies in the industry are valued. This can vary with economic and market conditions. A knowledgeable accountant can provide invaluable advice here. You can also meet with firms that provide business consulting or advisory services to interior design companies to obtain useful information on valuation methodologies and pricing of comparable transactions.

- Identify your long-term business strategy and how a proposed acquisition will help you achieve your goals. Be specific. What milestones must be met or goals achieved after the acquisition is completed in order for it to be a success? For example, if you are making an acquisition in order to reach a new category of clients not served by your firm, then employment and noncompetition agreements with the target's key employees serving those clients may need to be an essential term of the deal.

- If possible, become familiar with the target's business before negotiating the specific terms of the deal. By offering a confidentiality agreement to the target, you may gain access not just to its financial statements but also to key employees. Discussions with the owners and senior employees will provide insights into the target's strengths and weaknesses, its corporate culture, and how well it might fit into your business organization. A more complete "due diligence" review of the target should be made before closing the acquisition.

- Determine how the acquisition will be paid for. If the price will be paid in cash at closing, unless your company is in the unusual position of having sufficient cash to pay from its own resources, then financing will be necessary. A new credit facility with your current bank or a new lender may need to be obtained. If the seller is willing to defer payment of part or all of the sale price until a point after closing, this may provide much or all of the needed financing. The issuance of stock of the acquiring company to sellers is relatively uncommon except in acquisitions by publicly held companies. If stock or other ownership interests in your company will be part or all of the consideration to the seller, compliance with the securities laws can impose complex and expensive disclosure burdens.

- Consult with your lawyer and tax advisor before agreeing in principle to a legal structure for the transaction such as a purchase of the stock of the target company rather than a purchase of its assets. Different structures can result in very different tax, financial, and liability consequences for the buyer. In some cases it is possible to design a structure that enables both buyer and seller to achieve substantial tax savings.

- Be prepared to sign a letter of intent outlining the purchase price and basic terms of the acquisition before proceeding with a final due diligence review of the target and preparation of the acquisition contract. A letter of intent is usually drafted as a (mostly) nonbinding statement of the parties' understanding of the deal, to ensure that there is a meeting of the minds before incurring the expense and effort of the full acquisition process. Be sure to involve your legal counsel in the preparation of the letter of intent in order to include all legally advisable terms, including a right to abandon the deal before closing if the

negotiations or due diligence do not advance satisfactorily.

- Above all, do not make the common mistake of allowing the deal to take on a life of its own. Always keep in mind the business and financial objectives to be served by the acquisition, and use them to guide your decisions as you work toward closing.

A Successful Future: Sustaining Growth

As evidenced in the case studies collected in this chapter, many firm owners find that growth is hardly a one-time consideration, but rather is best regarded as an ever-present variable. Indeed, a continual focus on a firm's composition with regard to business climates and personal ambitions or desires can provide the flexibility needed to survive the market's cyclical ups and downs.

Suite Success: Cole Martinez Curtis and Associates

Jill I. Cole is the cofounder, president, and managing principal of Los Angeles–based design firm Cole Martinez Curtis and Associates. During her time leading the firm, Cole has received numerous industry honors, including multiple Gold Key, Designers Circle, and ARDY awards, as well as the 1993 Platinum Circle award, which recognizes exceptional achievement in the hospitality design industry.

In 2007 Los Angeles–based design firm Cole Martinez Curtis and Associates (CMCA) celebrated its fortieth year in business, a milestone for any business and four

decades of adventure for the firm's cofounder and president, Jill I. Cole. Since taking on its first hotel project redesigning the Adolphus hotel in Dallas, the firm has emerged as a prominent hospitality practice, consistently designing premiere hotels, resorts, clubs, and spas around the globe. And just as a hospitality property redesigns itself over the years to meet the needs of an ever-changing clientele, so too does CMCA constantly examine its size, structure, and practice to fine-tune its own formula for success.

Forty years ago, when Cole first set out to start the practice that would evolve into CMCA, she and her business partner, Milton I. Swimmer, did so with the familiar desire to be their own bosses in a friendly business environment and dreams of creating a thriving firm with a range of exciting clients and projects. Their first and foremost goal for the firm, however, was more nuts-and-bolts oriented: they simply wanted to make payroll.

When the two partners decided to venture out on their own, they were colleagues at another Los Angeles firm, where Swimmer was the design director and Cole a designer. One day, while chatting about her frustrations with their work environment, Cole broached the topic of leaving to start a new firm. Swimmer, it turned out, had been thinking the same thing and suggested that if Cole could find a project to support her for one year, she could go with him.

Armed with a project and some of Swimmer's clients, the two rented a small office from a client and set up Milton I Swimmer Planning and Design Inc. Alleviating their initial concerns about being paid, the firm started with a bang, growing from the two-person base to four employees within the first year. "It was pretty explosive," Cole recalls. With both Swimmer and Cole running around with clients, they quickly hired a receptionist to answer the phone. "In those days nobody had cell phones, and you had to be at a phone to answer, so it was important that we had a living, breathing person to field phone calls." Next on board was a draftsperson, and the firm continued to blossom from there.

Employees continued to come on board thanks to an ever-increasing workload, and at its most dynamic point topped out at 135 employees specializing in four different markets: office and commercial interiors, retail design, hospitality design, and office purchasing. Although CMCA had not begun with specific markets in mind, the group specialties were created to achieve long-term business stability. "We started all these different groups because as time went on we felt that it was good balance, as the real estate industry on which we depend is so cyclical," Cole says. "We thought that if we were in different specialties, we'd have a better chance at overcoming slowdowns in particular sectors. If offices weren't busy, retail could be—and if retail wasn't busy, hospitality could be." To reflect the diversity of the practice, the firm name was changed to Swimmer Cole Martinez Curtis and Associates.

This multimarket approach served the firm for more than twenty years, during which time Swimmer left the firm and two principals, Leo Martinez and Joel Curtis, became full partners. The business name was then changed to Cole Martinez Curtis and Associates.

In business, the partners divided specialties by personal passion: Martinez oversaw retail planning and design, Curtis directed commercial projects, and Cole took charge of hospitality. In addition, CMCA formed a strategic alliance with an interiors firm in London to start branching into European work. The firms shared a fifty-fifty partnership, with CMCA sending employees to work in the London office for up to three months at a time.

However, maintaining a firm of that size and scope requires a number of variables to remain in line, and when a severe real estate recession hit in the early 1990s CMCA suffered alongside the rest of the architecture and design industry. "Every sector died at once, and the vacuum created a huge upheaval in the design and architecture community. So many people left the industry it was sad," Cole recalls. "The entire industry was hurt badly and, in my lifetime, I think it was the worst we'd ever gone through."

At CMCA, the team hunkered down, taking any project it could to keep the firm going, but shrinking in the process. Management shifts also affected the firm's operating structure. Over several years, both Curtis and Martinez decided to leave the firm, and in response Cole decided to refocus. "When the firm had 135 people, there were four partners who were all bringing in business, but it's very hard for one person alone to support that many people." And so, as Curtis departed, the firm shuttered its commercial division, and likewise the retail practice when Martinez retired.

Given the trauma of the economic downturn, CMCA morphed into a specialty firm, shrinking from 135 people to 15, most of whom are devoted to design. Three of these fifteen are purely administrative staff, and for some matters like IT issues and accounting CMCA employs external consultants.

Maintaining her hospitality focus, Cole retained the core employees in her group and retrained some of the firm's other original staff for hospitality work, which would become the firm's sole focus. Little did Cole know that downsizing and refocusing would lead to such long-term success.

Dedicating the firm to the hospitality market, Cole has spent the past decades focusing on growth of quality, not quantity, working to build the brand's reputation for meticulous attention to quality and customer service. The results have brought in projects like The Lodge at Sea Island, Zagat's #1 Small Hotel of 2006 and Best Golf Club Resort in America for 2006 by *Golf Digest* magazine; Rum Cay Resort Marina, a luxury residential and resort marina community on Rum Cay in the Bahamas; the Renaissance Hollywood; and the historic Jackson Lake Lodge in Moran, Wyoming.

Despite CMCA's success, Cole isn't content to churn out the same projects year after year. Although she has little intention to branch back into the variety of markets CMCA once embraced, the firm is dipping its toe into the senior living market, capitalizing on its hospitality expertise to answer client requests for more resortlike environments. They also reopened their London branch, which closed down during the early '90s recession. Ballooning the firm up in terms of headcount, however, isn't on the agenda. There are no plans to open an additional office unless a principal-level person were on board who would be willing to take the responsibility of running it, something Cole herself would rather not do. Instead, she focuses on maintaining the familial culture of the firm, hiring as needed, but not on a per-project basis. Growth remains cultural rather than structural. "It's important that we permit new people with younger ideas and new points of view to come in without drowning them in the rhetoric of "well, this is the way we've been doing it all these years," Cole says.

Although she has no plans to retire, Cole recognizes that at some point, the firm has to go on without her. With this in mind, she says, "My personal goal is to create a platform where the younger people here see an opportunity to eventually take over. I want people to feel that they can run the business and keep it going. After all, it's their home as well as my mine."

Riding the Tide: Mancini Duffy

Founded in 1986 by the merger of Ralph Mancini Associates Inc. and Duffy Inc., Mancini Duffy first started life in 1920 as the architecture firm Halsey, McCormack & Helmer Inc. Today, the firm focuses on interior design and interior architecture, specializing in corporate interiors. It operates out of four offices in New York, New Jersey, Connecticut, and Washington, D.C.

Considering what can happen to a firm in one year, the contemplation of what can transpire over more than eight decades is potentially mind-boggling. For Mancini Duffy, a New York–based firm with three other regional offices, it would be easy to rest on more than eighty years of success and growth. Instead of dwelling in the past, however, two of the firm's leaders, chairman and CEO Anthony Schirripa, AIA, and president Dina Frank, AIA, IIDA, say the firm's leadership draws from its experiences to focus on the business's continual evolution.

Whether it is expanding its client list, branching into new markets, or recruiting future firm leaders, a modern-day business cannot sit still—and thriving interior design practices are no exception to this rule. And so, over the last decade or so, Schirripa, Frank, and their colleagues have prepared for long-term growth and success by continually monitoring and adjusting the present.

This focus on the future has allowed the firm to weather ups and downs. Successes along the way have included establishing a working partnership with tp bennett of London, International Partners in Design (TPID), and the launching of a building design practice (a revisiting of the firm's origins) in the Washington, D.C., office. Significant obstacles have also popped up along the way. The beginning of the century was particularly challenging, as the firm's San

Francisco office was hit hard when the dot-com bubble burst, and subsequently closed, and then the New York office, located at Two World Trade Center, shrank by about 50 percent following the attacks on September 11, 2001. These occurrences, though challenging, proved to be surmountable thanks in part to a dedication to continual growth, and the firm gradually regrew to its size before the dot-com crash. By the mid-2000s fourteen top-level principals and directors were overseeing roughly two hundred employees across the firm's offices, and despite some constriction following the economic crisis that developed in 2008, the firm's growth plan remains intact.

Boiled down, the firm's growth philosophy revolves around the straightforward desire to never say no. As Schirripa explains, he never wants to be in the position of having to tell a client he can't do their work—and whatever size the firm needs to be to achieve this is how big it will grow. And so, already more than two hundred employees in size, the firm continues to actively expand. As part of its larger strategic plan, the firm has a growth plan in place that is monitored annually. It is defined with broad and challenging objectives, but not specific calendar deadlines or target numbers. One major objective revolves around diversifying the practice's client roster within the corporate market. Twelve to fifteen years ago, more than two-thirds of Mancini Duffy's client base consisted of New York banks, Wall Street institutions, and other financial sector ventures in the area, while the remaining third comprised accounting firms and a small handful of other interiors projects. The firm began actively targeting new clientele with this balance in mind, and today it more closely mirrors New York's corporate leasing activity—so that if law firms are accounting for fifteen percent of the leasing activity in New York, for instance, the firm's client roster is reflecting a similar percentage. In addition, the firm is now looking to transfer its corporate experience into the higher education/institutional and healthcare markets.

While the past eighty-odd years have given the firm a stronghold in the New York area, another major objective is expanding its geographic reach into what the principals call 24/7 financial centers. These areas, including cities like Los Angeles, San Francisco, Atlanta, and Chicago, are primarily metropolises with a stock market and a thriving, around-the-clock downtown community. Establishing beachheads in these areas requires flexibility, Schirripa and Frank say, in order to find the best approach for each situation, whether it's partnering or merging with or acquiring a local firm (such as the firm's arrangement with TPID in London) or recruiting local talent to take charge of the new branch. However the growth is undertaken, Mancini Duffy also takes care to maintain its corporate culture across the offices. The challenge here, the principals say, is instilling the firm's values in the new office without overriding the regional influences that give the office its own personality. To help address this among its current New York, New Jersey, Connecticut, and Washington, D.C. offices, the firm holds meetings throughout the year where the entire practice comes together to discuss planning, goals, and problems.

Of course, to staff all these new offices, the firm is also mindful of how it grows its overall headcount, and has found that when it comes to recruiting up-and-coming designers you need more than a solid history or brand name. Over the next five to ten years, the principals anticipate a talent shortage across the industry, as graduates with interior design or architecture degrees are no longer necessarily going straight into the A&D field. To counteract this, Mancini Duffy is focusing its recruiting strategy, becoming more actively involved in design education and making a concerted effort to support schools. The firm has instituted a disciplined intern program for recent graduates, as well as support programs for recent graduates preparing to take certification exams such as the NCIDQ. After all, Frank and Schirripa note, it's these graduates that are the ultimate tool for growth, as they will become future of the firm.

Open to the Possibilities: Wilson Associates

With offices in Dallas, New York, Los Angeles, Singapore, Johannesburg, and Shanghai, as well as an associate office in Cochin, India, Wilson Associates is an internationally acclaimed design firm that creates interiors for hotels, restaurants, clubs, casinos, and high-end residential projects. Founded in 1971 and incorporated in 1978, the firm has designed and installed more than one million guestrooms in thousands of hotels and offers a full range of interior architectural design services, from initial space planning and design through construction documents and administration. Clients include Kerzner International, Las Vegas Sands Corporation, Four Seasons Hotels, Ritz-Carlton Hotel Company, St. Regis Hotels, Disney, and Armani Hotels. Wilson Associates is a twenty-time winner of the American Hotel and Motel Associates' Gold Key award for excellence in hotel design, and president Trisha Wilson is a recipient of the Manfred Steinfeld Humanitarian Award from *Hospitality Design* magazine, a Distinguished Alumni of the University of Texas at Austin, a member of the Interior Design Hall of Fame, and was named Woman of the Year in 1990 by the Network of Executive Women in Hospitality (NEWH).

As much as there is to be said about the necessity of planning, there is also a case to be built for trusting your gut. Just ask Trisha Wilson, ASID, president and CEO of Wilson Associates.

If someone had told Wilson when she was graduating from the University of Texas that one day she would be running an award-winning and successful interior design and architecture practice with more than 350 employees around the globe and more than $50 million in annual revenue, she, like most recent graduates, would have scoffed at the possibility.

Building a global empire certainly wasn't on Wilson's mind when she first graduated. What *was* a top priority was getting a job—any job. In fact, her first job was not at an interior design firm but rather at Titche-Goettinger, a Dallas department store.

Although the position was categorized in the design department of the store's furniture department, it was, in fact, a sales position.

While it was not the typical stepping stone to an interior design career, that first job inadvertently set Wilson on her path. "I learned so much from having to just get out there and sell," she recalls. These selling skills came in handy: It was through a cold call that Wilson got her first interior design project, a new Dallas restaurant named the Railhead. Hearing about the project, which would have a train theme, Wilson contacted a family friend who owned a model train business to learn all she could about trains before putting together a pitch. Her initiative paid off, and in the wake of that first project additional work began coming in, including the original Chili's and Kitty Hawk restaurants. Branching out into hospitality, Wilson heard about a new hotel, the Loews Anatole, being built in Dallas by Trammell Crow, a well-known national real estate developer. Intrigued, she sent him a letter, insisting she had ideas he couldn't live without. To her surprise, Crow called, giving her a chance to pitch him and win him over.

As her portfolio grew, Wilson hired an employee to help out, Snow Blackerby, who is still with the firm thirty-four years later. Over the years, however, Wilson didn't structure her practice with a goal in mind for headcount, number of offices, or level of revenues. "People would ask me what my goals were and I would say I don't do goals," she recalls. "Or, I would say my goals were to be happy, healthy, and financially secure."

A combination of tenacity, openness to new opportunities, and a trust in her gut instincts helped Wilson expand from that first project to a global venture. Of Wilson Associates' six offices outside of the Dallas headquarters, only one of those, the New York office, was opened with an ulterior motive. "All of the offices were opened in response to workload and new markets, but New York was opened to give us legitimacy," she explains. While she acknowledges that the concept may seem amusing now, in the late

'70s Wilson ran into a range of stereotypes. As she recalls, "Texas was the Wild West to the world. People would truly ask me if I rode a horse, carried a gun, and wore cowboy boots." If you had a New York or Los Angeles office, she explains, you were legitimate. But even that business move came about by a degree of chance, as a friend from high school who had also trained in design was getting married and moving to New York. Wilson approached her about starting the office, which they did as a one-man office out her New York apartment. As work came in, the office expanded, hiring an additional employee and then another and another.

The rest of the firm's offices—which now include Los Angeles, Singapore, Johannesburg, and Shanghai, as well as an associate office in Cochin, India—opened in response to more of a gut feeling than a calculated plan. "Many of them opened because I read something and it felt right, Wilson says. "We opened our first Asia office in 1990, long before the area became the way it is now, but at the time I felt the excitement in the area growing." This gut instinct approach, however, doesn't mean Wilson goes into a new area on blind faith. She starts slowly, which is important both logistically and financially. "Everyone thinks you have to borrow money to grow, but I have never borrowed a cent," she notes. Like the New York office, most of the regional offices opened with one-person bases, and then grew as needed. The Shanghai office, for instance, expanded four times in six years, reaching thirty people. The firm is using a similar approach in the Middle East, where although there is no official Wilson Associates office in the region, the firm has people on the ground managing projects.

In hiring employees, Wilson is adamant about not poaching from firms she respects, and she finds that the practice's reputation, in terms of both design and internal culture, brings a bevy of potential employees its way.

While payroll is issued from the Dallas office, each regional office has an in-house employee to handle human resources issues and who then communicates with a head of HR in Dallas. Wilson maintains a hands-off managerial style across the globe, giving control to the managing directors of her offices to create an environment that's best for their regional culture. "How we do business in the Middle East is very different from how we do business in Japan or China. I don't want to put a round peg in a square hole," she explains. "It's the personality of the leader of each office that sets the example. Our Singapore office is very different from Dallas—one, because of the culture, and two, because the person leading it has a different style than I do." Although there is no centralized command post for all offices, Wilson insists on continual communication. "There is hardly a day I don't communicate with people, preferably by phone or voicemail rather than email, because they can hear inflections in your voice," she says. And although she gives designers creative leeway, she also speaks up if a decision seems wrong for the firm. "I don't visit the offices on a set pattern, but when I'm there I try to go around to see what they're doing, to talk, and to lend an ear. I may chime in on my experience in an area or about things I've gone through and might know or think."

"The biggest challenge," Wilson says, "is to understand the different cultures and different challenges each country faces. In some cases, English may be an office's second language, and even in England we speak differently." An English designer referring to skirting, for example, may be talking about what an American designer calls baseboards, not about bedskirts. It's also important to remember the context of each office. "You may email someone in South Africa and not think to call to follow up," Wilson says, "but they may not have electricity to get their email at that moment. Or, if you send something in the mail, you usually send it to a post office box where someone can pick it up so it is not stolen."

With seven offices under her belt, Wilson remains open to the possibility of more, as well as to opportunities outside the design field. In 1997 she founded The Wilson Foundation (www.thewilsonfoundation.org), a 501c(3) nonprofit organization that addresses the needs of disadvantaged and underserved children, primarily in the area of Limpopo Province, South Africa. Remaining vague about the future of the firm is intentional. "I have no idea where the firm will be in the future. We'll be wherever life and opportunity lead us," Wilson says. "I don't make goals because our imagination is our only limitation. What I believe we may be doing three, five, or ten years from now may not even be conceivable in my wildest imagination right now. If I limit it to what I know or can verbalize today, I'll be limiting my opportunities."

Parting Shot: A Sixty-Second Guide to Managing Growth over the Long Haul

SCORE is a nonprofit organization based in Herndon, Virginia, and Washington, D.C., that is dedicated to the formation and growth of small businesses, and offers small business advice to entrepreneurs. Here, a growth-specific installation of the organization's Sixty-Second Guides shows you how to develop a strategy for managing long-term growth.

0:60 Revisit Your Business Plan

Your business plan doesn't go up on the shelf just because your startup phase is over. Refer to it often to make estimates accurately reflect today's realities. Even subtle changes in the marketplace may require you to alter existing contingencies and develop new ones.

0:44 Watch Those Numbers

Your financial statements provide insights into the health of your business. Project cash flow several months ahead based on reasonable expectations for sales and income, demand for your product and services, regular payments (e.g., loan payments and rent), and other factors. By comparing actual cash flow to projections, you can spot changes that will help improve performance.

0:34 Develop Relationships

Though your business may be gaining a reputation for solid work, it may be premature to bring on additional resources. Stretch your capabilities by building partnerships with other businesses in your field and with specialty consultants. They will also call on you when they need help—perhaps at a time when you could use the work.

0:25 Delegate Time-Consuming Tasks

A growing business is sure to demand more of your time. That's why it's important to identify employees who can take on those routine and managerial responsibilities. They'll relish the opportunity to grow personally and professionally—and you'll be free to focus on the road ahead.

0:13 Watch the Big Picture

What issues or trends affect your business? They may be as far-reaching as a change in the nation's foreign policy, or as seemingly minor as a new stoplight near your store. Stay current with your community, study your sales records, and communicate with customers, suppliers, and colleagues. This awareness will make you less susceptible to surprises and better prepared to capitalize on and even anticipate changes.

0:03 Keep Learning

You're sure to gain knowledge and instincts as your business experience grows. But even veteran entrepreneurs can benefit from the perspectives of others. That's what makes services like SCORE so valuable. Experienced volunteer counselors will serve as sounding boards for new ideas, and provide advice on issues both routine and unexpected. It's all free and available in person at a SCORE office, or online at www.score.org.

Chapter 5:

Transitioning from Small to Midsize and Large Firms

Growth is never easy, and deciding how to go about expanding an enterprise, as discussed in Chapter 4, is just one facet. Taking on employees, whether running an independent firm, a franchise, or a dealership, is complicated. Luckily, there is an array of resources available to help small business owners manage the transition to a larger playing field.

Sprint to the Start: Diane Boyer Interiors

Based in Verona, New Jersey, Diane Boyer Interiors is led by Diane Boyer, ASID, a nationally recognized interior designer who specializes in high-end residential design. Her work encompasses historic preservation, custom furniture and cabinetry, and kitchen and bathroom design. Her award-winning interiors have won multiple Design of Excellence awards from the New Jersey chapter of ASID, including three Gold awards. An active professional member of ASID, Boyer is a past president of the New Jersey chapter, served on the national board of directors, and was a member of the National ASID Homeless Advisory Task Force. She received NJ/ASID's Medalist awards for distinguished service to the chapter and the design profession in 1993.

Having worked for two different firms during her thirty-four-year interior design career—both of which ultimately closed, leaving her seeking employment with a new organization—Diane Boyer determined that in her next venture she would be the business owner. In addition to the financial benefits of such an arrangement, owning a business would provide her with more control over her own—and her clients'—destinies.

Prior to venturing out on her own, Boyer freelanced for another design firm until a number of vendors began suggesting she set up her own business. With two young children and two hundred dollars in the bank, she took the risk, creating a partnership with another designer. That collaboration, however, lasted only three years. Rather than setting up another business of her own, Boyer approached a local dealership about creating a residential division employing Boyer and her staff. The dealership agreed, and Diane Boyer Interiors, a division of Bill Behrle Associates, began.

Boyer worked for the midsize corporation for thirteen years. At the time, the company had eight locations and divisions in the New Jersey/New York region and operated primarily as a contract office furniture dealership, with divisions specializing in hospitality, healthcare, and residential design. Boyer led the residential division, but her group also dabbled in contract work, as well as hospitality and healthcare design.

In 2005, the firm's owners announced that after seventy-eight years in business, the family-run entity would file for bankruptcy the following day. Boyer had twenty-four hours to decide whether to once again face unemployment and another job hunt or take control of the company's residential division and launch it as her own practice.

The decision was not without complications. Although Boyer's division at the corporation had a large client base, it also had $1 million worth of undelivered product on the books. Resolving this issue would be critical to get cash flow moving and keep clients satisfied.

Undeterred, Boyer moved forward with a plan to purchase the residential division, which was subsequently launched as Diane Boyer Interiors, LLC. The firm's ten employees would operate out of their existing 4,500-sq.-ft. office. Logistically, Boyer acquired client assets and company liabilities as well as existing furnishings and the firm's library of resource materials and catalogs. In taking on responsibility for vendor and client debt, Boyer also faced a significant financial outlay that required a substantial amount of capital.

The transition was anything but easy, and for Boyer it was a lesson in crisis management at every level. With the parent organization facing bankruptcy, the buyout required masterful negotiations, including litigation with furniture corporations owning shares of the parent company as well as client lawsuits and personal issues involving owners and employees. When all was said and done, there were twenty-six different signatures on the paperwork sealing the deal.

Boyer had none of the time most entrepreneurs spend on due diligence and planning when starting a business. With only one day to make a decision, she experienced this fast-track event as a time of sheer chaos. Luckily, Boyer was not alone in the process: A stroke of luck came with an angel investor. A long-time client who owned a number of international

companies offered to help Boyer negotiate the complex deal, as well as financially back her new enterprise if necessary. The client had experienced a similar situation when he and his wife started out in business, and just as another "angel" had done for him, he wanted to show his own faith in Boyer's talent and ability to succeed. Once the terms of the acquisition were finalized, financing was arranged with a loan personally guaranteed by Boyer and backed by the client.

Finalizing the deal solved only one part of the equation. On a positive note, each of the parent company's clients agreed to stay on with the new venture, as did all the vendors, including one who had lost a significant sum of money in the bankruptcy. In Diane Boyer Interiors' first few years, both groups passed along new clients to help get the firm on its feet.

During negotiations Boyer's team remained in its old office space, working with clients until the landlord locked the doors for nonpayment of rent. It was a day that escalated the sense of chaos pervading the transition, and initially all ten employees were forced to work from Boyer's home. For several months the business ran from Boyer's dining room and basement with only one phone line, cell phones, and one fax machine. The new firm had its current project files but no access to earlier records. The challenges involved with trying to get clients' previous orders separated from the bankruptcy proceedings, shipped, and delivered seemed insurmountable at times.

Organizationally, Boyer started with what she knew. Pressed for time to sign legal documents in the beginning, she took the organizational chart from the old firm. As the new firm grew, specialized areas of expertise like antiques and CAD operations were added.

The firm operated at a loss for the better part of two years but shortly thereafter began running in the black. With clients' issues resolved and their projects complete or back on track, a strong, positive relationship exists between the designers and their customer base. What's more, Boyer has maintained relationships with the owners of the former parent firm's other divisions, with each new entity supporting one another's achievements and successes.

Getting the fledgling firm up and running required a review of its financial situation and projection of yearly income to ensure the enterprise would be viable. The needs of existing clients were reviewed to assure the firm could complete its projects successfully, and forecasting was done for new areas of growth. A marketing and public relations plan was developed, and plans were created for development of a strategic plan as well as a review of the organizational structure.

In contrast to the significant debt at the firm's beginnings, Boyer's firm has grown to a significant level of billing with high profitability. The days of working in Boyer's home are gone as well, and the firm once again rents its original office space. An external CPA firm handles the monthly review of bookkeeping, payroll, and taxes. The lessons, however, continue. Because the firm was set up as a limited liability corporation (LLC), the profits and losses of Diane Boyer Interiors are run through the owner's personal income tax forms. Boyer was surprised at how quickly the business recovered from its chaotic beginnings to move into profitability. Had she known the practice would so quickly overcome its operating deficit, she would have begun prepaying a larger amount of taxes at an earlier date.

Two years into the new venture, Boyer's most pressing challenges are more common ones. Like most business owners, she struggles with the rising costs of healthcare and insurance. She wants to institute a 401(k) program and find a strong person to oversee the firm's technology needs. As the owner, she has embraced the decision-making process, from handling day-to-day decisions—Should the firm rent or purchase new computers, printers, and color copiers? What do you do when the roof starts leaking?—to dealing with personality clashes among staff members.

With its rocky beginning behind the firm, Boyer is optimistic about the future. Although she has not determined a specific size for the firm, she is open to the possibilities, whether it's designing a new line of cabinetry or perhaps opening a new office in Florida to handle an influx of work from the region.

Getting It Down on Paper

No matter how fast the work is flowing in, it is important to take time to pay attention to the details. Logistical components of growth can be divided into two realms: the paper (comprising legal, financial, and tax issues) and the personal (personnel management issues).

As payroll and overhead costs grow, it is essential to get the firm's books in order. Whether you are still keeping your own books at this point or you have an in-house financial manager, it is time to open up a more frequent line of dialogue with an accountant. It is essential to discuss growth plans with both your financial and legal advisors, to ensure not only that you have the finances to grow but also that you are adequately prepared for any bumps that may appear in the road.

In opening up this communication, Richard Gilman, CPA, CITP, a partner with Baker Tilly Virchow Krause (formerly Virchow Krause & Company LLP) in Chicago, who has worked with interior designers for thirty years, lists the following as essential:

- Straightforward communication. When it comes to numbers, everything is foreign to most designers, Gilman notes. Avoid jargon or slang that's industry specific, and speak up about unfamiliar terms or matters. It is essential that all parties in a conversation are talking in terms the others can understand.

- Honesty. The more your accountant knows about you, the more they can help you. If you're not comfortable discussing the fine details of your business with your accountant or attorney, it's essential to find out why. After all, you're paying an hourly rate, just as clients may be paying you, and you should make the most of your investment. If you cannot resolve this, it's time to find another consultant.

- Thinking ahead. Finances concern more than the monthly bills. They also require big-picture planning. If you are the sole proprietor of your firm, will you be willing to offer a financial portion of the business to future partners?

In expanding the firm, labor will be the biggest expenditure, followed by direct costs and operating expenses. Adding a junior designer earning $35,000 a year isn't as straightforward as simply adding that sum to the annual budget. Each new employee also comes with additional expenses such as payroll taxes, equipment, office space, and insurance, and that $35,000 salary could easily end up costing the firm $45,000 a year once these additional expenditures are tacked on.

In 2007 *Contract* magazine's annual salary survey reported that respondents considered salary one of the top two criteria (alongside benefits) in determining job satisfaction. So how do you even know what to offer a new employee? According to data from the U.S. Bureau of Labor Statistics, the mean wage for an interior designer employed in an interior design firm in 2005 was $46,290, while designers working in architectural and engineering firms earned slightly more, $49,870. Also in 2007, ASID released data for both the mean hourly wage and salary for interior designers by state (Table 5-1), and the median base salary for interior designers in the top twenty metro regions, as determined by number of interior designers employed (Table 5-2). As can be seen from the results, salaries and hourly rates vary widely by geographic location.

The financial picture isn't all about expending, as each new employee also brings in additional profits. Gilman offers this example: A firm hires a new junior designer at an annual salary of $35,000. If the firm owner bills out that designer at $75 an hour for one year, that employee has the potential to bring in more than $104,000 (after calculating in the cost of sick days, coffee breaks, etc.).

The potential profits are enticing when seen so simply, but it is important to keep plans grounded in reality: HR consultants agree that whether a firm has two employees or twenty, from a staffing standpoint things almost always run better with one too few people than with three or five too many. It's a balancing act: Overstaffing leaves people with too much spare time, whereas underhiring can stretch resources and staff thin and quality may be sacrificed. Both situations have a significant impact on firm finances; in this case, staying on the lean side also helps keep cash flow issues in check.

Table 5-1
Compensation for Interior Designers, by State

State	Mean Hourly Wage ($)	Mean Annual Salary ($)
Alabama	23.66	49,210
Alaska	29.14	60,610
Arizona	20.74	43,130
Arkansas	17.27	35,920
California	27.84	57,910
Colorado	20.73	43,110
Connecticut	27.41	57,000
Delaware	20.32	42,270
District of Columbia	28.96	60,250
Florida	22.16	46,080
Georgia	22.13	46,030
Hawaii	29.72	61,820
Idaho	21.76	45,260
Illinois	24.08	50,090
Indiana	20.50	42,640
Iowa	16.13	33,550
Kansas	18.10	37,640
Kentucky	20.12	41,850
Louisiana	20.51	42,660
Maine	20.57	42,770
Maryland	26.97	56,100
Massachusetts	29.45	61,260
Michigan	30.42	63,270
Minnesota	23.91	49,730
Mississippi	14.21	29,550
Missouri	21.68	45,100
Montana	19.64	40,850
Nebraska	27.85	57,930
Nevada	30.16	62,730
New Hampshire	24.95	51,900
New Jersey	28.17	58,600
New Mexico	19.35	58,600
New York	30.36	63,140
North Carolina	20.72	43,100
North Dakota	15.87	33,000
Ohio	19.24	40,010
Oklahoma	19.42	40,400
Oregon	24.85	51,680
Pennsylvania	24.69	51,350
Rhode Island	21.16	44,020
South Carolina	22.34	46,470
South Dakota	18.79	39,080
Tennessee	21.39	44,500
Texas	20.55	42,720

Team in Training

Hiring an employee is only one challenge of growth. Once team members are on board, managers have to work hard to keep them there. What kind of workplace will you keep? Do you want a more businesslike atmosphere, or a familial culture? Will you want to start offering financial ownership in the firm to more senior designers? If you have quality people on staff, are you willing to take money out of your pocket to retain them? Finding the right salary for a new employee is just the tip of the iceberg.

Hire and Seek: Creative Business Interiors

Established in 1991, Creative Business Interiors was founded by co-owners Stephanie Anderson and Gary Zimmerman Jr. to help clients design, build, and furnish their facilities. The midsize firm, which also operates a Knoll dealership, has offices in Milwaukee and Madison, Wisconsin.

Having run their own business for eighteen years, Stephanie Anderson and Gary Zimmerman Jr. are well versed in the impact of long-term relationships on a practice of any size. As the cofounders of Creative Business Interiors, they oversee a complex practice that has grown from an initial team of four in one office to an entity with eighty-five employees in two locations.

Throughout the years, the firm has operated with a constant focus on growth. When first drafting business plans in 1991, Anderson and Zimmerman described in detail—but without fixed deadlines—how the company would evolve into new markets as finances and the industry allowed, operating under the philosophy that if you're not growing, you're going backward.

Specializing in the design, construction, and business furnishings of existing buildings, Creative Business Interiors handles projects in a number of markets, including the corporate, healthcare, financial,

Table 5-2
Median Base Salary for Interior Designers in
Top 20 Metro Regions*

Metro Region	Interior Designer I ($)	Interior Designer V ($)
Los Angeles/Long Beach, CA	41,704	77,287
New York, NY	44,234	81,976
Miami, FL	36,677	67,971
Chicago, IL	40,351	74,780
Washington, D.C.	40,567	75,181
Atlanta, GA	37,407	69,324
Dallas, TX	37,675	69,822
Boston, MA	42,133	78,082
Houston, TX	38,246	70,878
San Francisco, CA	45,420	84,173
Denver, CO	39,159	72,570
St. Louis, MO	37,601	69,684
Minneapolis–St. Paul, MN	39,930	74,000
Orange County, CA	41,806	77,467
Phoenix/Mesa/Scottsdale, AZ	38,823	71,949
Philadelphia, PA	39,710	73,593
Detroit, MI	40,493	75,043
Cincinnati, OH	45,508	68,606
Portland, OR	48,238	75,722
Seattle/Bellevue, WA	41,320	76,576
San Diego, CA	39,643	73,468
TOTAL USA	**37,266**	**69,062**

*As measured by number of interior designers employed

Sources: ASID Interior Design Profession Facts and Figures; U.S. Bureau of Labor Statistics, Occupational Employment and Wages, May 2007; Salary.com, February 2009. © American Society of Interior Designers. Used with permission. All rights reserved.

educational, government, and retail sectors. The firm is also the exclusive Knoll dealership for southern Wisconsin. The practice is structured as a single-source enterprise that employs registered interior designers, a sales force, and administrative staff members, as well as master craftsmen, journeymen painters, and factory-trained furniture installers. In all, about half the firm's employees are in-the-field craftsmen, painters, and installers, while the other half are split between the Milwaukee and Madison offices.

Given the complexity of Creative's business model, Anderson, Zimmerman, and John Norfolk—the firm's third owner, who came on board in 2002—are acutely aware that the old maxim "good help is hard to find" is a challenge that extends beyond the start-up years. Accordingly, the business has made employee relationships a focus from day one.

Launching in the recession of the early 1990s underscored the challenge of hiring and retaining good people as many talented designers left the industry, and to this day Anderson regards hiring as one of the top components of success. Accordingly, the firm is constantly on the lookout for new design talent. In addition to posting job ads when positions become available, the firm's leaders interview candidates whenever they are available, regardless of whether there is a specific spot open at the time. The firm is also continually involved with design schools across the state and has had significant success with second-career students who have left another industry to go back to school and pursue design.

Hiring designers straight out of school, however, also comes with unique challenges. Over the years, Anderson noticed that young people coming into the firm without experience working elsewhere had no baseline for comparison when it came to firm operations or culture. To keep new employees from wondering if the grass is greener elsewhere, the firm's leadership trio places priority on making the office environment one that employees really enjoy. As a result, Anderson, Zimmerman, and Norfolk practice a very hands-on management style, with a focus on making the senior leadership visible to and accessible by all employees. Doing so allows them to foster employees' professional and personal growth by quickly recognizing and rewarding potential.

Hand in hand with the challenge of recruiting talent is the subsequent task of training them in firm practices, something that has been especially critical on the sales side of Creative's business. Given the firm's array of services, the owners recognized from the beginning that hiring and training salespeople would not be a one-time thing that could be addressed in a simple orientation session or packet. Anderson estimates that familiarizing a new salesperson with the firm's services and products across five major service categories to the point that they can assimilate and sell it can take up to two full years. Having spent time in sales positions herself, Anderson focuses on offering a different learning experience from the one she received when, on her first day, a bunch of leads were dropped on her desk along with the blanket assignment "find someone to sell to." In her practice today, she seeks to actively share the knowledge she's gained from her own research, training, and experiences with her team. To augment this, the firm brings in independent trainers or speakers.

Personnel Management Issues: Looking Outside for Internal Help

The experiences of Diane Boyer Interiors and Creative Business Interiors provide a number of interesting lessons. As a firm grows, managers must be prepared to invest increased time on personnel on a daily basis: Bringing great employees into the fold is a big challenge, and keeping them on board is equally as important. At a certain point, employees will want additional perks, including benefits, and principals taking on a more managerial role will also need to institute some new policies for the benefit of all involved.

Fortunately, small business owners can outsource a variety of functions—including human resources issues like payroll, benefits, training, recruitment, and retention—to professional employer organizations, or PEOs. One of the most common mistakes small business owners make, according to the Society for Human Resource Management (SHRM), is not delegating work when possible. It's not often a designer gets into the profession because of a desire to manage others, yet as their firm grows owners often find themselves managing more and designing less.

At first, an HR consultant may be needed no more than three to four hours a week. With the addition of more employees that time will naturally increase, and once fifteen to twenty people are on board an HR person may be needed one day a week or more.

Just as with hiring an accountant or attorney, not every consultant will work for every business. In hiring external consultants or advisors, consider the following:

- Responsiveness
- Business acumen
- Reputation
- Philosophy and approach
- Representative client base
- Billing rates and policies
- Efficiency
- Creativity

Creating Policies and Guidelines

As the firm grows, it is important to institute some standards on how the company will address a variety of issues that come about in daily operations. While the law does not require owners to create and institute an employee handbook, it is recommended by a number of business advisors.

An employee handbook is a written document that describes the benefits and responsibilities of the employment relationship: it lets employees know what the upper management expects from them, and vice versa. A procedures manual, on the other hand, is usually a comprehensive guide that specifically details the supervisory and managerial roles; often lower-level employees are not allowed access to procedures manuals.

Compiling an employee handbook does not have to be complicated (see Table 5-3 for suggestions on information to include). Consider taking the following steps:

1. Research. Rather than just doing things in a certain way because that's the way they've always been done, take time to reflect on whether any changes are in order. Talk to employees. Distribute a questionnaire or do some informal polling. Review past employee complaints.

2. Write. In putting things down on paper, keep it simple: Use direct vocabulary and short sentences, and avoid legal jargon. Be clear and concise, and use language that reflects the formality or informality of the firm's culture.

Table 5-3
What a Personnel Manual Might Contain

When creating an employee or personnel manual, consider including:

1. Who you are. Provide an introduction that describes not only the company's history but also its core business philosophies. Include background on the firm's founder(s), descriptions of its services, and an organizational chart, if available.

2. Work hours. What are normal business hours, and when will overtime pay be authorized? Vacation and leave policies also should be addressed. How, for example, does the firm address holidays, sick leave, and maternity leave? Does the firm provide compensation for jury duty or other types of leave of absence?

3. Benefits. Does the firm offer health, dental, or disability coverage? On a similar note, how does the business address pension, profit-sharing, or retirement plans?

4. Pay and salary details. How are salaries paid, and what is the review process? How does the firm address performance reviews, raises, and promotions? Are bonuses offered? If so, how are these calculated and distributed? What are the firm's expense reimbursement policies?

5. Office behavior. This ranges from the in-office dress code and personal hygiene to personal telephone or computer use and personal visits. Does the office allow smoking? Be aware, however, that rules concerning employees' appearance may be illegal if they discriminate against a particular group.

6. Drug and alcohol abuse, sexual harassment, and discrimination policies.

7. Disciplinary procedures.

8. Employee safety and emergency procedures.

9. The complaint process. How does the firm handle employee grievances, disputes, or conflicts?

10. Intellectual property. Working within the creative realm, all design firms should address intellectual property or copyright laws. Who owns the design concept—the individual designer or the firm? What are employees' responsibilities in protecting intellectual property both inside and outside of the firm?

11. Termination policies. How does the firm handle the termination process? What are grounds for dismissal? Is there a probationary period? How does the firm handle severance pay? Is there a set process for employees when they choose to resign? Does the firm conduct exit interviews?

12. Continuing education and opportunities for advancement. Does the firm require certain certifications? If so, does it compensate employees for educational courses related to the certification, CEU credits, or testing fees? What are the internal opportunities for advancement?

13. A signed form, completed by each employee upon review of the manual, to acknowledge their receipt of the manual as well as their review of it.

3. Review.

4. Approve. Get final approval from an attorney.

5. Distribute. Collect signed forms from employees acknowledging their receipt of the manual.

6. Review on an annual basis and update as needed.

Bringing in Benefits

At a certain point, employees will start asking about insurance, healthcare benefits, or a 401(k) program, and it is important to recognize that as an employer, a firm owner is required by law to provide certain benefits. Employers must:

- Give employees time off to vote, serve on a jury, and perform military service (such time off need not necessarily be compensated by the employer).

- Comply with all workers' compensation requirements.

- Withhold FICA taxes from employees' paychecks and pay your own portion of FICA taxes, providing employees with retirement and disability benefits.

- Pay state and federal unemployment taxes, thus providing benefits for unemployed workers.

- Contribute to state short-term disability programs in states where such programs exist.

- Comply with the Federal Family and Medical Leave (FMLA).

Employers are not legally required, however, to provide:

- Retirement plans

- Health plans (except in Hawaii)

- Dental or vision plans

- Life insurance plans

- Paid vacations, holidays, or sick leave

Although the second list may not be required, many firms offer some or all of these perks. It is common in many industries, for instance, to offer paid holidays for New Year's Day, Memorial Day, Independence Day, Labor Day, Thanksgiving Day, and Christmas Day. Vacation days and sick day policies are individual to each business, but in recent years a number of companies in many industries have switched from the more traditional allocation of sick days and paid vacation days to offering a general paid time-off policy, where employees are given a set number of days to allocate to vacation, personal, or sick days, as needed.

As discussed in Chapter 3, there is an array of insurance coverage that business owners should consider upon startup regardless of staff size, including key person insurance, general liability insurance, workers' compensation insurance, and unemployment insurance; many of these policies are relatively inexpensive and easy to maintain. As the firm grows, instituting a more comprehensive benefits plan or a 401(k) program may become more feasible. Society for Human Resource Management (SHRM) consultants note that many health insurance providers will price out policies for firms of fewer than ten people. Finding out what kinds of programs are available to a specific organization is the first step. Contacting a local SHRM representative or another human resources organization may help; reaching out to providers themselves can also get the ball rolling.

Monitoring Growth and Progress

As many business owners have noted, growth for growth's sake is tempting but most often does not lead to long-term success. Even when it is initially supported by firm finances and a growing project load, not all growth will be successful in the long run, and in many cases a business will both grow and shrink a number of times over its life cycle. Several firms covered in the case studies here, for instance, have had radical fluctuations in size or have taken the gamble of opening additional offices, only to scale back down over time. None of these firms' owners, however, were deterred by the growth decisions they made. There may, in fact, be an upside to downsizing, as it often affords a business owner a chance to reflect, reprioritize, and refocus.

Success in Seattle: EHS Design

EHS Design, formerly Emick Howard & Seibert Inc., is a midsize, full-service design and architecture firm headquartered in Seattle with projects and clients throughout North America. The company provides architecture, interior design, strategic planning, programming, and space planning services for retail, corporate, public works, and financial clients.

After more than thirty years in practice, Jack Emick is reaping the rewards. As the CEO of EHS Design in Seattle, he oversees a firm that employs more than fifty people and offers full-service strategic planning, interior design, and architectural services to clients including AIG Insurance, Accordia Northwest, AT&T Communications, the Cystic Fibrosis

Foundation, Deutsche Financial Services, Hewlett-Packard, London Fog, Range Rover, Safeco Insurance Company, and Toshiba, among others.

The path to success, however, wasn't all smooth sailing. Over more than three decades, the firm's evolving management team has run into and overcome a number of challenges common to growing firms.

In 1977, Emick was a young designer settling into Seattle. Having been there several years, he felt at home in the city, but was becoming disenchanted with his career opportunities in the local market. Emick wasn't alone in his frustration. Another local designer, Mindy Howard, whom he had met through industry connections, felt similarly, and together they decided to leave their positions at bigger firms and create their own opportunities.

Emick Howard & Associates—comprising Emick and Howard, as well as a third interior designer who also handled bookkeeping, reception, and some marketing duties—started off working out of Emick's home. The trio worked incessantly, going on sales calls and marketing presentations during the day and completing other firms' overflow work through the night. Focusing solely on interiors, Emick Howard & Associates targeted two sources of income: architectural firms that didn't have in-house interior design capabilities, and real estate brokers.

Although clients were receptive to the new firm, the tight-knit local design community was not as welcoming. Both Seattle transplants, neither Emick nor Howard had extensive local connections and had little local family support. The firm also drew some pushback because it chose to represent tenants at a time when few firms were doing so. Emick and Howard, however, pushed through by focusing on their firm more than their competition.

The local community may not have been extremely welcoming, but the market was. The firm took off quickly and added two additional employees—a space planner and another interior designer—within the first month, which forced the burgeoning practice out of Emick's house and into a small office in downtown Seattle. Within the next three months, an architect joined the team, bringing the employee tally to six.

The firm interviewed constantly, and although the small business could not initially offer incoming employees the perks of a larger entity, such as benefits packages and 401(k) programs, it could offer different kinds of rewards. In researching the local hiring market, Emick and Howard saw that while many bigger firms could offer benefits and the like, they also suppressed base salaries. To counteract this, the duo focused on creating a familial culture that included on-the-spot performance rewards like bonuses, additional time off, trips, and parties.

As the work flowed in, the firm's growth continued, and within a year and a half of operation the staff was up to ten people. At this point, Emick and Howard faced an important decision: Keep expanding or cap growth? The duo's original business plan had centered on a practice no bigger than fifteen people, so as to keep things manageable without adding additional leadership or partners. To stick with this plan, the firm as a whole became more selective about projects, turning down work that didn't fit its market niche and projects that didn't feel quite right.

With ten employees, the familial business also had to institute more corporate policies. The team contracted with an independent human resources firm to handle personnel issues, a relationship that became increasingly important as Emick Howard & Associates instituted a benefits program. One plus to working with an outside firm, Emick notes, was that it kept the internal staff isolated from the daily HR issues. Another benefit was the external expertise: The external firm and its employees had much more up-to-date HR-specific knowledge than Emick himself could hope to gain or hire, he explains. "Being designers from the beginning who were then forced into being businesspeople, we realized what our weaknesses were, as well as what we liked and didn't like to do," he says. Working with consultants helped isolate the design side from the business side.

By the end of the second year, the firm had also drafted its first employee handbook with advice from its lawyer, accountant, and HR consultant. The document is still in use today and is reviewed every other year or so by the management team along with their legal, financial, and HR consultants.

For fifteen years or so, the firm remained consistent in size and continued to prosper, but not all ventures were successful. In the early 1980s Emick Howard opened a secondary office in San Francisco. It seemed like a good idea at the time. Two employees were relocating to the Bay Area, and the firm was reluctant to lose them. Moreover, two major clients at the time were headquartered in San Francisco, which provided an instant workload for the second office. However, the venture was short-lived. As it turned out, the San Francisco–based clients were executing projects in Seattle and spending more time in Washington than in the Bay Area. This fact, combined with the low cost of doing business in Seattle, made a financial argument against the second office. Looking at the numbers, the firm shuttered the branch after three years.

In 1992 a new opportunity arose that seemed promising. Paul Seibert, a former client who had left town only to come back and launch his own financial facilities planning and design consulting firm, approached Emick about a possible merger. Initially hesitant, Emick declined. However, the benefits of the deal began to outweigh the concerns. Although Emick was comfortable with his firm remaining around twelve to fifteen employees in size, the opportunities presented by merging changed his mind.

The merger of the two entities into Emick Howard & Seibert Inc. took careful planning. In forming the new venture, no money changed hands, but all assets and employees from each business were consolidated so the marketing base could be expanded. The new entity doubled the total personnel count and opened up new market sectors, as both firms had been dipping their toes in the architectural realm. In addition to designing interiors, the partners sought to add more core and shell work.

Although the owners did not seek out a specialized M&A consultant to help with the transition, they did work closely with their individual legal and account-ing firms to work out the details on paper. An outside accounting firm valued each practice's assets and then made a financial adjustment between the three shareholders so that Emick, Howard, and Seibert became equal shareholders in the new business. As the deal progressed, the team also kept a close eye on the cultural transition. While the Seattle design community remained tight, with many local designers knowing each other in passing, the firm went to extra lengths to merge the two cultures, hosting a number of social gatherings before the official merger so that the two staffs could become more familiar with one another. The tactic helped minimize attrition: In the twelve to eighteen months following the merger, the new entity lost only a few employees.

Since then the firm has continued to evolve and grow. In the mid-1990s Brett Conway and Jim Haack came on board to expand the firm's architectural capabilities. At first the duo came on as employees to help handle a substantial increase in architectural work, but within several years both Conway and Haack purchased minority shareholder positions in the firm's ownership. More recently, Howard retired from the practice, which changed its official name to EHS Design. Still, the firm continues to eye growth in terms of market areas, and is once again toying with the idea of a branch office or two. With an increasing amount of work coming in from the Southwest and an ex-employee already relocated to the area, the owners are considering opening up another branch, but after the San Francisco experience are proceeding with caution.

Added Responsibility: Sechrist Design Associates Inc.

Seattle-based designer Melinda K. Sechrist, FASID, and her husband, T. Michael Sechrist, incorporated Sechrist Design Associates Inc. in 1980. Over the last twenty-eight years they have grown the business from a home-based sole proprietorship to a thriving firm with twenty-two employees. Concentrating on senior living, multifamily, and high-end residential projects, the firm generated $3.3 million in revenues in 2007.

Melinda K. Sechrist worked on space planning for Safeco Insurance Company for two years before she decided to start her own practice. In 1980 Sechrist and her husband, T. Michael Sechrist, decided to start a family. At the time, Safeco did not offer part-time work, so Melinda decided to capitalize on her desire to work directly on client projects.

Shortly thereafter, Sechrist and her husband, a landscape architect, incorporated as Sechrist Design Associates Inc. Melinda served as president of the fledgling enterprise, while Mike acted as vice-president, secretary, and treasurer.

Beginning business as a sole proprietorship, Sechrist began adding part-time designers as the workload grew, and in less than three years the firm had expanded to six employees—all of whom worked from the basement of the Sechrists' home. After two and a half years in business, it was time to move. The firm relocated to a 3,800-sq.-ft. office and added a part-time administrative assistant to handle bookkeeping and paperwork.

At the time, Sechrist had no set plan for how large the firm might become. As its reputation grew and more work came its way, the firm added staff to handle the increasing work.

By 2005 the staff had grown to twelve, and Sechrist realized the current structure was no longer working. It was increasingly difficult to schedule projects and ensure that they were then handled properly and at a high level of quality. In addition, Sechrist was struggling to personally oversee the majority of the work. She was working, in essence, two jobs: designing and dealing with clients during the day, then taking care of paperwork and proposals at night. Throughout the firm, designers were burning out at an alarming rate and leaving to work in larger firms that could provide more support.

In a key moment, Sechrist realized she was the bottleneck in the operation. She subsequently began relinquish some of her responsibility, which turned into a major breakthrough for the firm.

By 2007 the venture had twenty-two employees and had grown out of its old space. The firm moved to an 11,000-sq.-ft. office in a contemporary building that matches its corporate identity and also provides room for the firm to grow.

Sechrist and her husband remain as upper management, overseeing three administrative staff members and seventeen designers. A director of design manages senior, midlevel, and junior designers and is responsible for assuring that all projects are completed to company standards. As a whole, the firm is dedicated to providing excellent and innovative design solutions to meet the strategic, functional, aesthetic, and budgetary needs of their clients in a positive, service-oriented manner.

Sechrist continues to explore management operations, and plans are underway to add an operations manager, who will oversee all employees. The goal is to force Sechrist to let go of the day-to-day issues and give more responsibility to middle managers, thus freeing her up to handle the ownership and executive tasks that go with growing and marketing a successful practice. It is also intended to help create an environment where the designers can grow and work on more interesting and challenging projects. In planning for this transition, all project and administrative tasks will become standardized to maintain the high-quality standard for design. Most important, this step will allow for the creation of a company that has a value of its own apart from the designer/owner's reputation.

Sechrist credits volunteer experiences with the American Society of Interior Designers for providing excellent leadership training and an introduction to strategic planning and management that propelled her business awakening. Recognizing her lack of business knowledge, she began attending seminars and joined Excell Executive Leadership Exchange, a CEO support group that provides assistance and resources in a peer group setting.

Realizing the need for expertise from someone knowledgeable about implementing change in an existing business culture, in 2004 Sechrist Design hired an outside consultant that helped put the firm on track. The consultant reviewed the business to identify issues that were holding it back and helped Sechrist prioritize these issues and develop solutions. For several years they have worked together to create a hierarchy for the business, improving existing standards and procedures, creating new ones, developing a strategic plan, and integrating new ideas and methods.

With a better grip on firm management, Sechrist is now able to make future plans, which include creating project-type divisions of the staff. The corporate hierarchy is also poised to shift into a more horizontal model than its current structure. Sechrist is cautious about the project divisions, taking care that designers are not pigeonholed into certain project types and that they are permitted to grow through experience with multiple types of projects.

Job Title: Junior Designer

Overview: A Junior Designer (designer with 1–3 years experience) will work with other team members to develop conceptual designs, plan interior spaces and furnishings, produce sketches and construction drawings, and provide details as needed to implement overall design concepts. This position will select color and materials pallettes to complement the overall design concept. A Junior Designer will also develop specifications and color boards. A three- or four-year interior design degree is required.

This position is critical to project completion, process, profitability, and client satisfaction. Responsibilities include planning, scheduling, and directing daily activities of production personnel.

Reports to: Director of Sales and Project Management, Midlevel Designers, and Senior Designers

Employment/Pay Status & Pay Range: Salaried regular full-time employee. Base salary range is $_____ per year.

Key Responsibilities:
Design
- Programming: attend occasional client meetings with Senior Designer; take notes and gather information to use in developing concept; write up and distribute meeting notes
- Develop concepts with a Senior Designer, dependent on size of project
- Develop preliminary design using sketches and drawings as needed to communicate concept
- Develop color and material options for review by Senior Designer
- Develop specifications for color and material selections once decided upon by client
- Prepare drawings and documents for construction of projects including, but not limited to, plans, elevations, sections, and perspectives
- Self-educate re: current and changing design technology and trends

Administrative
- Write and track purchase orders for clients; update clients bimonthly re: project progression and merchandise location
- Write and update work plans independently or with a Senior Designer, dependent on size of project
- For each project, refer frequently to own copy of the Letter of Agreement to remain on track
- Keep track of own time spent on project and inform Senior Designer of time spent, or learn to track small projects by updating the fee watch
- Keep track of travel time for client
- Assemble and maintain project correspondence binders in orderly fashion

Billing and Time Sheets
- Enter own time daily in Studio IT
- Return billing to Director of Sales and Project Management within 24 hours of reception
- Attempt resolution of client billing issues independently; if unable to resolve, seek assistance from Director of Sales and Project Management and Director of Design

Professional Practice and Marketing
- Present consistently professional manner in office, at client meetings, and within design community
- Be accountable for quality of work performed, client services, and profitability

Figure 5-1
Sechrist job description—Junior Designer.

Authority
- No direct supervisory authority

Other Responsibilities:
- Increase skills and knowledge pertinent to the position via onsite training and offsite classes; increase skills and knowledge pertinent to other positions, subject to supervisor approval
- Perform other tasks as assigned

Minimum Knowledge for Candidate to Have or Acquire:
- Min. three- or four-year interior design degree required
- Knowledge of basic design principles and concepts and methodology of interior design
- Drafting: knowledge of drafting techniques including labeling drawings, line weights, typical dimensions needed on drawings; ability to hand draft and letter architecturally
- Demonstrated proficiency in AutoCad R2000 to 2006
- Ability to understand and prepare interior design drawings including floor plans, reflected ceiling plans, and specifications to support Midlevel and Senior Designers
- Facility with software programs including MS Word, Outlook, Excel, and Photoshop
- General knowledge of Residential and Contract furniture and fabrics
- Ability to research and develop project solutions with direction from senior staff
- Ability to learn Studio Designer for input of purchase orders and proposals and time/billing information
- Ability to organize and track projects in order to stay within the scope of work
- Ability to assemble color and material boards
- Ability to communicate effectively in writing, orally, and using graphic media
- Ability to develop and maintain relationships with new and current clients

Position Requirements:
- Design duties (85%)
- Billing/time sheets (10%)
- Special projects as assigned (5%)

Hours: This is a salaried position. As such, a Junior Designer is expected to maintain hours necessary to address all responsibilities. A Junior Designer is expected to be in the office from at least 8:00 AM to 5:00 PM [subject to change by management and company requirements].

Figure 5-1
(Continued)

Job Title: Midlevel Designer

Overview: A Midlevel Designer (designer with 3 to 6 years experience) will work with other team members to develop conceptual designs, plan interior spaces and furnishings, produce sketches and construction drawings, and provide details as needed to implement overall design concepts. This position will select color and materials pallettes to complement the overall design concept. A Midlevel Designer will also develop specifications and color boards. They will begin to manage larger projects and have more client contact. A three- or four-year interior design degree is required.

This position is critical to project completion, process, profitability, and client satisfaction. Responsibilities may include planning, scheduling, and directing daily activities of Junior Designer personnel.

Figure 5-2
Sechrist job description—Midlevel Designer.

Reports to: Director of Project Management and Senior Designers

Employment/Pay Status & Pay Range: Salaried regular full-time employee. Base salary range is $_____ per year.

Key Responsibilities:
Design
- Programming: attend client meetings with or without Junior Designer; take notes and gather information to use in developing concept; write up and distribute meeting notes
- Develop concepts independently or as a leader of a design team, dependent on size of project
- Develop preliminary design using sketches and drawings as needed to communicate concept
- Develop color and material options for review by Director of Designer, Principle, or client
- Develop specifications for color and material selections once decided upon by client
- Prepare or over see drawings and documents for construction of projects including, but not limited to, plans, elevations, sections, and perspectives
- Self-educate re: current and changing design technology and trends

All of the above plus:

Administrative
- Write and track purchase orders for clients; update clients bimonthly re: project progression and merchandise location
- Write and update work plans independently or with a Senior Designer, dependent on size of project
- For each project, refer frequently to own copy of the Letter of Agreement to remain on track
- Keep track of own time spent on project and inform Senior Designer of time spent, or learn to track small projects by updating the fee watch
- Keep track of travel time for client

Billing and Time Sheets
- Enter own time daily in Studio IT
- Return billing to Director of Project Management within 24 hours of reception
- Attempt resolution of client billing issues independently; if unable to resolve, seek assistance from Director of Sales and Project Management and Director of Design

Professional Practice and Marketing
- Present consistently professional manner in office, at client meetings, and within design community
- Introduce client to Sechrist Design Associates at new client sales meetings; present company's work experience and capabilities; report back to Director of Sales and Project Management and together determine if client and project are a fit with company
- Be accountable for quality of work performed, client services, and profitability

Authority
- Dependant on type of project and who is working under you.

Other Responsibilities:
- Increase skills and knowledge pertinent to the position via onsite training and offsite classes; increase skills and knowledge pertinent to other positions, subject to supervisor approval
- Perform other tasks as assigned

Figure 5-2
(Continued)

Minimum Knowledge for Candidate to Have or Acquire:

- Min. three- or four-year interior design degree required.
- Knowledge of basic design principles and concepts and methodology of interior design
- Drafting: knowledge of drafting techniques including labeling drawings, line weights, typical dimensions needed on drawings
- Demonstrated proficiency in AutoCAD R2000 to 2006
- Ability to understand and prepare interior design drawings including floor plans, reflected ceiling plans, and specifications to support Midlevel and Senior Designers
- Facility with software programs including MS Word, Outlook, Excel, and Photoshop
- General knowledge of Residential and Contract furniture and fabrics
- Ability to research and develop project solutions with direction from senior staff
- Ability to learn Studio Designer for input of purchase orders and proposals and time/billing information.
- Ability to organize and track projects in order to stay within the scope of work
- Ability to assemble color and material boards
- Ability to communicate effectively in writing, orally, and using graphic media
- Ability to develop and maintain relationships with new and current clients

All of the above plus

- Effectively manage project schedules and budgets
- Some local/regional code knowledge
- Construction knowledge and understanding of construction trades/processes
- Excellent interpersonal skills
- Developing project management skills
- Strong design presentation skills
- Ability to supervise entry Junior Level Designers and interns as required
- Space planning experience
- Ability to handle several projects at one time and take project through to completion.

Position Requirements:

- Design duties (85%)
- Billing/time sheets (10%)
- Special projects as assigned (5%)

Hours: This is a salaried position. As such, a Midlevel Designer is expected to maintain hours necessary to address all responsibilities. A Midlevel Designer is expected to be in the office from at least 8:00 AM to 5:00 PM [subject to change by management and company requirements].

Figure 5-2
(Continued)

As many business owners come to learn, instituting change is always a challenge, and training is a crucial tool for getting everyone on the same page in order to successfully move to a standardized system. In Sechrist's case, all policies and procedures were analyzed, adjusted, and documented to assure that present and future employees will easily fit into the refined corporate structure. In addition, employee policies, AutoCAD drawing standards, proposals, and project paperwork

and procedures have all been documented, and detailed job descriptions have been developed for all employees.

Sechrist's biggest challenge—finding time to work on the business while working in the business—is one shared by many entrepreneurs wanting to expand and grow. Recalling her experiences, Sechrist notes that she wishes she had found the book *The E-Myth* years ago, as it would have helped her understand how to set up a structure for growth earlier in the process. Procedures could have been set from the beginning to ensure all projects would run the same way. Standards could have been set for all of their project drawings and forms, with projects documented in such a way that new designers would be taught the same procedures. "I wish I had known there was actually a business model I could have been following from the start," Sechrist laments. If she had it all to do over, she vows, "I would read all the books on business and management that I could at the very beginning. Then I would read them again every couple of years."

Still in the exploratory stage for additional planning and changes, Sechrist is considering changing the company name and developing a sales culture where designers are involved in lead generation and are responsible for generating set revenue levels. Sechrist plans to continue distancing herself from personal involvement in all projects in order to devote more time to CEO issues and allow for future management changes. She is also investigating exit strategies to provide the firm with the opportunity to increase its value so that it can be sold, acquire additional partners, or let Sechrist work less in the future.

Growth also remains on Sechrist's mind, and the firm is looking to expand to thirty professionals. However, learning from past experience, Sechrist doesn't plan to stop there. When each milestone is reached, another, higher goal is usually set. Will the future hold more dramatic growth, or a redirection of the firm's talents and resources? "Only time will tell," says Sechrist.

Part III:
The End Game

Chapter 6:

Planning for the Future

As we've seen from the case studies compiled in previous chapters, by this point firm owners have put their hearts and souls into building a successful practice over years and, for many, decades. They've struggled and triumphed, facing a multitude of challenges—and some wonderful opportunities—along the way. After all this hard work and effort, it is hard to think about letting go, but that's exactly what owners need to do. In fact, waiting until a firm is fully established and reaping the rewards of years of investment is too late to start thinking about the end. Planning for the end of a business should be considered from the beginning.

Learning from Experience:

KSA Interiors

KSA Interiors, an award-winning design firm, offers creative solutions for interior design and space planning, environmental graphics, and facility services. By embracing user-centered research techniques, understanding workflow sequencing, and utilizing knowledge of culture, KSA aims to design dynamic spaces for corporations (both private and public sector), colleges and universities, healthcare organizations, and continuing care retirement communities (CCRC). The business is a certified women-owned small business and one of the largest interior design firms in Virginia, with offices in Richmond, Hampton Roads, and Charlottesville. Kim Schoenadel, CID, ASID, KSA's president and CEO, has over thirty years of experience in space planning and

interior design. She earned a B.S. in interior design from Virginia Polytechnic Institute and State University (Virginia Tech), serves on Virginia Tech's advisory board for its School of Architecture + Design, and has taught interior design business procedures to the interior design department. She is past president for the Virginia Chapter of ASID and received the ASID Medalist award.

Her recognition of an unoccupied niche between interior design services provided through architectural firms and office furniture dealerships drove Kim Schoenadel to start a design firm of her own twenty-five years ago. Having previously worked at an architectural firm where the focus, as in many cases, was on finishes rather than furnishings or their placement, she felt there was a need for a design firm that better represented clients' needs.

Starting KSA Interiors on her own in Richmond, Virginia, under a full C corporation structure, Schoenadel hired a support person to help with the phones, paperwork, and typing of specifications. Six months into the venture another designer was added to help handle the growing design workload. As the support person was not working out, Schoenadel decided she and the other designer could handle those aspects just as well themselves, and let the support person go.

Early on, KSA outsourced work as its project load grew, but Schoenadel soon realized that having dedicated employees was the business's best option. Over the next twenty-two years, KSA grew by about 10 percent annually to a staff size of twenty, with annual revenues in the $1.5 million range. Its interior design services spanned corporate, healthcare, and college/university customers throughout Virginia.

Early in 2006 a colleague from a firm in Chesapeake, Virginia, approached Schoenadel. The owner of the colleague's firm had unexpectedly passed away, and the practice's designers encouraged Schoenadel to buy out the business. Intrigued by the idea of expanding her business into another area of Virginia, she contacted the deceased owner's husband to discuss the potential acquisition.

During her period of due diligence, it became evident that the firm was heavily in debt, something Schoenadel was not interested in being burdened with in her efforts to grow KSA. Being fortunate enough to have a husband in the banking industry and a number of colleagues with strong business backgrounds, she had no need to bring in outside consultants for advice and direction. An offer was made to buy out only the assets of the firm, taking on three existing employees and paying a percentage of profits from existing projects to the previous owner's estate. Had the previous owner created a succession plan to pass her business on after her retirement or death, there might well have been a more valuable business to sell at a higher cost to either employees or outsiders.

With Schoenadel's offer accepted, in 2006 KSA became a two-location design firm with three

additional experienced employees and the potential to grow and expand into other regions of the state. The acquisition also brought in experience in the tenant improvement sector. Shortly after this first business expansion, an opportunity arose for Schoenadel to acquire a second interior design practice in another region of the state, adding one more experienced interior designer to her staff. With a vision of becoming a nationally recognized interior design firm, Schoenadel is now working on a third deal, this one to acquire yet another design firm in another region of Virginia, and hoping to add still one more acquisition in the future to expand KSA's operations to cover the entire state.

Ten years ago, facing health issues, Schoenadel entertained ideas of succession planning or selling her firm and taking out the hard-earned profits from her years of work. Although the methods she reviewed and attempted at that time did not work out in terms of her ability to recoup the revenues she felt she had earned, or to do so in a timely manner, the need for a succession plan is still a top-of-mind issue for this entrepreneur. With three locations and a fourth on the horizon, retirement and succession planning have become even more important. For now, the firm has purchased key person insurance for Schoenadel, two design principals who oversee operations, and three design associates who oversee project management for the firm.

In her early fifties, Schoenadel, on the advice of her close group of business advisor colleagues, is beginning to investigate the potential of an employee stock ownership program (ESOP) to transfer some of the corporate stock and ownership to her employees. Schoenadel currently owns all KSA's stock, but it is important to her to keep the company she worked so hard to build alive long after she leaves. She is hopeful that an ESOP will do just that. With three locations and the potential for a fourth in the near future, plus a desire to become a national organization, Schoenadel's plans for the future appear to embrace growth even as she positions the company for her own retirement.

KSA Design Approach

KSA strives to be a leader in our industry. We believe in working together in a collaborative approach with our clients and architectural partners. We are committed to using thorough and well documented research to provide our clients with the best creative design solutions.

Our design team uses a mentoring system of training to leading our designers forward in education and skills development. We have a history of providing our clients with high quality design services in the areas of interior design, space planning, environmental graphics and facilities services.

KSA Vision

KSA will lead our industry through creative design solutions inspired by our clients' individual needs, our collaborative approach, our fun, family-oriented culture, and the drive to do what is right

KSA Mission

It is the KSA mission to be proactive, respectful, profitable innovators leading the design industry with knowledge, creativity, and exceptional service in a positive team environment.

KSA Core Values

Creativity & Ingenuity

Family & Friendship

Challenge & Service

Enjoyment & Well-being

Team & Loyalty

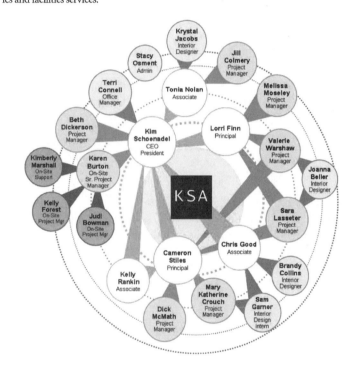

Figure 6-1
KSA Interiors organizational chart.

Thinking Ahead

KSA's experiences reiterate the importance of planning for the future from the beginning. As much as a designer may love his or her work, there are a number of factors that at some point may necessitate stepping away from the business that has been so lovingly nurtured to success.

The Value of Planning

Steve Simmons, Capital Business Brokers and CME Appraisals LLC

Steve Simmons, CBB, CMEA, CSBA, is a certified business broker at Capital Business Brokers and senior appraiser at CME Appraisals LLC in Charleston, South Carolina. Simmons also is a volunteer counselor for Service Corps of Retired Executives (SCORE) and a certified new venture and growth venture facilitator for FastTrac. Simmons has owned and operated a number of businesses for over twenty years, most recently in the business brokerage and appraisal industries. He has helped broker more than one hundred successful business transitions during his career.

Generally, any business owner should begin thinking about exit strategy from the first day of business. How you plan to leave your business is as important as how you start it up. Keeping good financial records and organizing the corporate papers, such as operating agreements, leases, and articles of incorporation, are all essential. In addition, managing profit trends and filing sales tax reports and income taxes in a timely fashion is not just good business; it also affects the desirability of a company and ease of transfer when selling a business. Over time, this data can help establish and defend fair market value for your business.

Everyone thinks—if only in the back of their mind—that their business will be valuable one day, and that it will pass on to family or be sold to fund their retirement, even if they do not have an active role in planning for the transfer of the business assets. The reality is that all businesses transfer ownership at some point. Market changes, illness, death, or sale are all considerations in managing any business for eventual transition.

With this in mind, it is a good idea, in addition to planning for the sale of a business, to also carry key person insurance. This is a term policy with enough value to pay for loss of the owner and maintain expenses and transition costs. It can be a simple and reasonably affordable alternative to more complex policies. The purpose of such a policy is to ensure a clean transfer of the business to partners and heirs in the event of tragedy. This may not seem relevant to the sale of a business, but often businesses come on the market because of the loss of a key owner and subsequent ownership transfer to heirs who do not have the financial means or desire to continue operation of the business. The exigent nature of this kind of sale can and usually does affect sales price negatively.

What is My Business Worth?

Keep in mind that potential buyers will ultimately want to see income statements, as well as any leases held by the firm, tax returns, and even your business's checkbooks. Reviewing all of this information is a part of performing due diligence on your company at the time of sale. But even before getting to the point of due diligence, in order to set an asking price an owner will need to have an idea of the value of his business.

The valuation process is the best way to establish a defendable fair market value of the business. The primary reasons for initiating a valuation are to present solid third-party data to potential buyers, and to place value on the tangible and intangible assets of a business. Often, a business with a good and recent valuation will sell at a higher price and with a smaller margin of negotiation between buyer and seller.

There are different types of values, and a number of myths surround value in a small business. Values are based on a number of specifics. Different types of industries, such as service or manufacturing, have different multiples for calculating value. Factors such as reasons for sale, comparable businesses on the market, profit trends in the industry, the specific business for sale, and the number of years a business has operated profitably can all be factors and play a role in the type of valuation needed.

A small business sold between an owner and a buyer will typically be handled as an asset sale—that is, the business will transfer only the assets of the business, both tangible and intangible. Any liabilities will be settled at the closing table, leaving the new buyer with only the assets of the business in the sale. With this type of sale, fair market value is established. Business trends, industry trends, profitability, and contracts are taken into consideration; intangibles like websites and goodwill are evaluated; and a price is set accordingly. Another type of valuation is liquidation, forced liquidation (such as auction) of assets, with the original business dissolving without changing hands to a new owner.

Valuation's Part in the Sales Process

Valuation is essential to the selling process. If a value cannot be placed and defended, there is no basis for sale and no market for the business. As a business broker I often see potential sellers—and, I am sad to say, other brokers—who gather the financials of the business and a few photos and present this as the package for sale. Having a qualified broker or other professional perform a proper evaluation of the business and properly gather and package necessary data for sale will greatly increase not just the final sales price but also the likelihood of a sale.

Does Size Matter?

As with most things bought and sold, there must be a buyer and a seller who ultimately agree on a price. Larger, more profitable businesses often involve more sophisticated and complex buyers and sources of funding. Larger size can also limit the number of people willing or able to purchase the business. In similar fashion, smaller businesses can be more accessible to a broader buyer base and may sell more

quickly and easily. But by the same token, smaller businesses may not produce sufficient earnings for the buyer to buy the business and also be able to meet his personal lifestyle needs.

More often than not, it is not the size of the business that dictates if it will sell, but rather how it is marketed and to whom it will sell. Bottom-line profits, the perception of a well-run and organized business, and a seller's willingness to offer some financing are most often the real influences on value and sale.

Building and Retaining Value in Your Business

Any owner should be prepared to provide three or more years of financial records for prospective buyers to review. Typically, tax returns, sales tax reports, and income statements are used. In addition, it will be necessary to provide a list of tangible assets, including furniture, fixtures, and equipment (FF&E), as well as inventory values at cost.

Having this data ready, organized, and available demonstrates that the seller is organized and prepared—often the basis for establishing, if not simply defending and getting, value for the business. Other factors to keep in mind are market trends. Is it a good time to sell? Is the business transferable? Specifically, if as a business owner you are the key component and without you the business cannot survive or maintain its profit trends, then the business is less likely to have value to a potential buyer. It may be easier for a potential buyer to simply start his or her own business.

One key element that is often overlooked is funding. Records show that less than 5 percent of baby boomers have $100,000 in cash. As a business broker, I see this reflected in the number of buyers that need financing to purchase a business. Nearly every business we sell requires some source of funding other than the buyer's checkbook. A seller who is willing to provide some financing is likely to get a better price and perhaps see a sale that would otherwise not happen. The seller should seriously consider the pros and cons of providing some level of financing. Typically, the seller carries 20 to 30 percent of the total sales price when seller financing is available.

Preparing to Sell

A little common sense can go a long way toward making your business appealing to potential buyers. Make the business presentable. Clean, well-organized businesses sell better than those that are not. Get documents together, and set realistic goals for price as well as for time necessary to sell the business. A business generally takes six to nine months to sell from the time it is listed until the seller receives payment. Factors contributing to time on the market and price are documentation, realistic sales price, presentation, and marketing to the proper buyers.

Getting Your Business Appraised and/or Valued

A business valuation generally establishes the value of both tangible and intangible assets. A common misconception is that an accountant or CPA can do this work. Accounting rules of thumb and book value are often not the primary contributing factors in performing a proper valuation or appraisal. Qualified business analysts and equipment appraisers are readily available. Their qualifications can vary greatly; it is a good idea to seek out those who belong to a professional organization that provides accrediting and a code of ethics for its members.

Businesses with significant tangible assets may require an equipment appraisal as part of the overall valuation of the business. Certified equipment appraisers are the best source for this service. Certified business analysts and certified machinery and equipment appraisers can typically work anywhere in the country. The Internet is a good source for finding qualified professionals. Remember to check references and ask for samples of work performed.

It is helpful to keep in mind that a valuation or appraisal is usually valid for about one year. Even that time frame can be affected by some specific event that alters the business and therefore its value. In addition to prospective sale, other situations when a valuation or appraisal might be desirable include establishing the basis for certain tax deductions, setting up exit strategies, or any time it is likely that some major transition in the company will occur; as well as in the event of partner buy-ins, divorces, insurance reassessments, or probate; or in order to establish value for accounting purposes.

Engaging the experts

For those who have never engaged in the sale of a business or who simply need to focus on running their business and spend less time marketing and selling the business, hiring a professional business broker and other necessary professionals is a sensible route to take (see Table 6-1). Using highly qualified professionals will ultimately yield a higher price for the business and probably cover any costs associated with hiring such professionals.

There are approximately 3,500 business brokers operating across the United States. A very small number of those brokers possess all the qualifications to both value and/or appraise your business and present it on the market for sale. Check brokers' credentials carefully before entering into a contract. Brokerage commission rates range between 10 and 12 percent of the sale price. By law, those commission rates are negotiable. Some firms have a set minimum fee for selling small businesses. Some may ask for a retainer or an upfront fee to cover advertising costs. Talk to several to find a firm or individual broker with whom you feel comfortable listing your business. Remember that a broker should be able to bring you prospective buyers that you would not be able to reach on your own.

Remember, time on the market, total price, and present value of cash earned with a quicker and more professional sale are all factors in the final profitability of the sale of a business. A good professional should positively influence each of these factors.

Legal and Financial Assistance

There are number of factors to consider when selling a business. Transactions can be complex and often require, at a minimum, consulting with outside experts. The right broker and qualified business attorney, experienced with business sales and transactions, are important players in the sale of your business. Your accountant or CPA can help get your financial records and reports in order.

Table 6-1
What Type of Sales Expert Do You Need?

Valuation: Valuation Expert
A business valuation is a method for placing value on the tangible and intangible assets of a business as a whole. Valuation is generally performed for an ongoing business. Valuation experts typically use book values and other general accounting principles for placing value on the tangible assets; often, this can "leave dollars on the table" in the overall valuation and total value of the business. Generally, a valuation expert can perform valuations anywhere in the country.

Equipment Appraisal: Certified Equipment Appraiser
An equipment appraisal (or certified machinery and equipment appraisal [CMEA]) is the method used for determining value of the tangible assets of a business. This can be done for ongoing businesses or for liquidation and auction purposes. CMEA experts generally do not place value on intangible assets. A CMEA expert can usually perform valuations anywhere in the country.

Real Estate Appraisal: Real Estate Appraiser
Most of us are familiar with real estate appraisals, which serve to place value on residential and commercial real estate and raw land, and are based on comparisons to similar properties within the local market. A real estate appraiser is generally best used within the geographic area where the real estate is located.

Business Sale: Business Broker
A business broker is an expert who lists and markets businesses for sale. Business brokers usually work with small business owners on what are generally classified as mergers and acquisitions. A broker working with small businesses, classified in the industry as a "main street business brokerage," is typically the best fit for most business owners. Note: Not all business brokers are certified. They are generally governed from state to state, and not all states regulate licensing or certification. It is best to find one with experience and with some certification or licensing. It is recommended that you find a business broker that understands and can carry out proper business evaluation work.

NOTE: The best results for many business owners may come from hiring an expert that specializes in multiple areas. Business owners should consider at least getting the proper valuation and appraisal work done before engaging in the listing and selling of their business. This will likely ensure better and quicker results.

In the event your business was structured as a corporation, a resolution just to engage in this process is required. Otherwise, the seller may pierce their corporate veil and surrender all liability protection. Understanding what type of legal entity is in place as well as the value of the business, and having access to financial records and professional assistance, are the best first steps to take in preparing your business for sale.

Challenges in the Valuation and Sale Process

Understanding the market, establishing a fair market value, and marketing the business are the biggest challenges to selling a business, but they are also some of the best assets for successfully selling a business. When establishing a reasonable and fair market value for any business sold, understanding the purpose of the valuation, preparing documentation, and providing the proper valuation methods are among the challenges faced.

Words to the Wise

Do your homework. Talk to professionals. Understand what they can and will do for you. Understand that this is your asset—and for many business owners, their business is the largest asset they have. Be prepared, present your business professionally, and set reasonable goals and expectations for the professionals you engage (see Table 6-2). These will be the best tools for the successful sale of your business.

Table 6-2
Twelve Questions to Ask a Broker

The first big decision you face after deciding to sell your business is whether or not to use a business broker. When interviewing potential brokers, it pays to ask some key questions before making your decision. Here, in no particular order, are twelve questions to ask when visiting with a business broker:

1. Can you please give me a little background on you and your firm?
2. Are you affiliated with any business brokerage associations or trade groups?
3. How much do you think I should ask for my business?
4. How will you market my business?
5. How will you show my business?
6. Will you display my business on any Internet sites?
7. Do you cooperate with other business brokers?
8. What is your commission/success fee?
9. How often will you contact me about progress and developments?
10. May I have a sample copy of your listing agreement?
11. Do you charge upfront fees?
12. Can you provide references from previous clients?

Obviously, you should ask any other questions that concern you. A business broker should be able to bring you prospective buyers that you would not be able to reach on your own.

Source: Steve Simmons, CBB, CMEA, CSBA

Next in Line: Succession Planning

Planning for the future also means addressing the issue of who will take the reins when the current leader steps down. Technically, succession planning is "the systematic steps or design that allows for one to follow another in time or place." In layman's terms, it means long-range planning to ensure that a business has programs and leadership in place to secure its continuity should a key player leave.

As mentioned numerous times before, it is never too early to start thinking about a firm's future, which means examining the firm from top to bottom. Succession planning may focus on ensuring that management positions are filled with suitable successors, but the planning, transition, and follow-through affect each and every firm employee. Succession planning is not just about preparing for the end of a firm; it's also about ensuring that the business has plans in place that both identify talented employees and provide a framework for promoting their development up the corporate ladder.

An Action Plan for Succession
Dorothy Russel, Essential Futures

In 2006 and 2007 Essential Futures, a Toronto, Ontario–based consultancy, conducted research on ownership and management succession in the design industry. Through in-depth interviews with founders and partners of more than thirty successful interior design, architecture, and engineering firms, Essential Futures founder Dorothy Russel found that succession transition often takes a generation. Many of the firm owners she interviewed had been in business several decades, and on average had been working on their firm's leadership transition for eight years. What's more, in many cases, it was expected that another eight years would elapse before the transition was complete. The following essay, written by Russel, draws from the study's findings to offer advice on ownership and management succession.

Start Early

Succession transition is a journey that involves not only you as firm founders or owners, but also your staff, clients, and prospective clients—the larger market. It's a process of building your firm for the future. It involves building new skills and capabilities, and transferring responsibility to new people. Throughout transition the firm will evolve from being owned and managed by the founder(s), to broader management control, and ultimately to the departure of the founders. It's a culture change that may take a generation to achieve.

Set a Vision for Future Ownership and Management: Think about What You Want the Firm to Become

The vision may be to sell the firm, build a firm that can continue without the founders, or close it down. The research showed that firms with a clear idea about how the firm will be owned and managed in the future are happier with the way their succession transition is going. People in the organization are in sync with the direction and steady progress is being made. In contrast, leaders without this clarity seem to be stalled in their transition.

Hire/Nurture Management Talent

Management talent is not the same as design talent. Management is about knowing what needs to be done, seeing how the pieces fit together, and bringing people together to achieve common goals. One firm owner likened the ideal leader to an orchestra conductor, able to get the best from each player and elicit a combined performance better than any individual could achieve alone. The first step is to identify the qualities the firm needs in its leaders—then look for those qualities in existing staff and new hires. A strong base of maturing management skill is a key component for successful transition.

Create an Ownership Transfer Mechanism

A business needs a certain amount of capital to operate. As owners think about withdrawing, they are likely to want to take their money with them. The firm needs a way to replace the money being paid out to departing owners, perhaps by selling shares in the business to new owners. An ideal mechanism will allow small investments over a long period of time. This will enable younger staff to buy in. It also ensures a gradual transition in ownership power rather than the sudden, perhaps disruptive, shift that would result from a large one-time investment.

Develop an Ownership Culture

Owners will do what's best for the business. One good way to encourage this is by creating a large pool of employee shareholders. Yes, it means you will need to share financial performance information more broadly. The result, though, is that staff will become more involved in the business. And as staff members understand their own business better, they will gain a deeper understanding of their clients' businesses and of how their work contributes to their clients' business success.

Transfer Contacts and Relationships

In a professional services firm, contacts, relationships, and connections are the foundation for new clients and projects. Typically, the founders and senior partners are the custodians of the firm's relationships and have primary responsibility for business

development. There may be a tendency among partners to hoard their contacts, keeping them to themselves. They might be enjoying the perks of relationships with powerful people at client organizations, such as social and sports invitations. Their relationships may have developed into personal friendships. But these relationships won't do the firm much good if the founder is on a long vacation in Europe or retired to the Virgin Islands. It's important to introduce the next generation in your firm to the people you know, and encourage new relationships to develop. That way, when you're ready to spend less time at the office, there will already be a strong connection to someone else who can keep building the business relationship.

Give Responsibility, Accountability, and Authority

People who are potential leaders need to learn and practice the skills of leadership. They need an opportunity to figure out what leadership approaches work for them, in real leadership situations. They need to be given responsibility for something, provided with the resources to carry it out, and be held accountable for results. Juniors with potential can be groomed and tested through a variety of assignments in different areas with progressively more responsibility and scope. Perhaps a special internal project needs a leader. Or there's an office move pending. Of course, managing and contributing to project work is a valuable learning ground, but it is fundamentally different from managing the firm. Creating temporary leadership assignments is an excellent way to see who your best emerging leaders are, and get some of the management work done as well.

Let Go

One of the hardest things for founders and entrepreneurs to do is to give up total control. The business is their creation and their responsibility. They have built the firm they want, the way they want—setting goals, deciding priorities, and allocating resources as they saw fit. Moving to a new generation of leaders requires a shift in control. When you give accountability and authority to others, things may not be done exactly the way you would have done them. Giving people responsibility and letting them try their own way is how they'll learn. And who knows, it might even be a better way. Once they're capable, you'll be free to pursue your other passions. Succession will be complete.

Setting Goals: Facilities Connection

Facilities Connection creates business environments that perform for manufacturing, healthcare, general office settings, education, and government. A one-stop source for facilities and furniture management services that was established by Patricia Holland-Branch, IIDA, in 1986 and incorporated in 1987 as HB/PZH, its offices and 16,000-sq.-ft. warehouse are headquartered in El Paso, Texas. A naturalized citizen of the United States born in Chihuahua, Mexico, Holland-Branch pursued studies at the University of Texas, El Paso and the University of Alaska at Anchorage, and graduated from El Paso Community College with an associate's degree in Interior Design Technology. She attends extensive professional interior design and business management courses annually to remain aware of new trends and technologies in interior and sustainable design for commercial, healthcare, and institutional industries.

Like many Americans following September 11, 2001, Patricia Holland-Branch awoke the next day to a new world. As some business owners went into survival mode just to keep their doors opens, Holland-Branch faced a serious decision of her own. The owner of Facilities Connection, a Haworth office furniture dealership in El Paso, Texas, Holland-Branch had to pick a future path. Would she close the business, significantly downsize, or put all her efforts into growing the practice?

Discovering that selling an office furniture dealership in a small market was unlikely, growth became the only viable option. It would not be easy: Facilities Connection needed to be recreated and reengineered, and only a seasoned executive team could do it. Holland-Branch also needed to continue planning for her own eventual exit from the business, hardly something she had in mind when first starting out.

An interior design professional registered in the state of Texas, Holland-Branch took a roundabout direction to arrive at ownership of Facilities Connection. An early job found her at a Herman Miller dealership, thrust into situations dealing with customers. She loved working with the customers, helping them create environments that supported their business goals. Capitalizing on this, Holland-Branch was soon bringing design projects into a dealership previously focused only on furniture sales. Finding the focus on design projects more rewarding than just selling furniture, Holland-Branch left the company to do freelance work in 1986. As more projects came her way and her reputation grew, she decided to incorporate Facilities Connection in 1987 as a home-based interior design business.

Being a business owner was something that had never entered Holland-Branch's realm of thought. No one in her family had a drop of entrepreneurial blood. Nonetheless, Holland-Branch threw herself into learning as much as she could about design and business. She researched design programs to find one that matched the kind of work she wanted to do. She had been unable to complete a design degree at one college, but managed to piece together the best programming available to come within a hair's breadth of her desired degree. She enrolled in business courses and searched for assistance through the Small Business Administration.

Holland-Branch was doing something right: Her twenty-year-old business grew from a startup staff of two other designers and an accountant to thirty employees. Of these employees, three are full-time interior designers, while other designers serve as account managers. The client base also grew, with business now coming in from Texas, southern New Mexico, and Mexico. Across the board, the firm now sustains annual revenues of $10 million.

Growth also required movement. In 1989, Holland-Branch left her home-based business model behind and advanced to a Haworth office furniture dealership. The next year, her husband, Dave, joined the business as a partner and president of Facilities Connection. In this role, he leads the strategic process for developing federal business opportunities. Certified by the Small Business Administration in 2006 as enrolled in the 8(a) program (designed to help socially and/or economically disadvantaged small business owners with marketing to the federal government), the company aggressively pursues federal government opportunities. It also leverages membership in the Minority Development Council and its status as a Texas HUB (Historically Underutilized Business) to expand opportunities with Fortune 100 companies and within the state of Texas.

Holland-Branch faced a number of challenges over the years, from economic upheaval or crashes beyond her control to finding employees that share her personal focus and passion for the business. But the biggest challenge, she says, is future-proofing the company. Looking back, Holland-Branch wishes someone had stressed the importance of future planning and strategic planning. A little more understanding about cash-flow issues wouldn't have hurt, either. Surviving crashes in the automotive and technology sectors, Holland-Branch learned that a business owner is ill advised if one client or industry dominates their cash flow. As a result, Facilities Connection—which is now a preferred Haworth dealer 100 percent owned by Holland-Branch—diversified, adding installation services, project management, and carpet and fabric maintenance to help buoy the firm through economic slumps.

Future planning also means planning for Holland-Branch's eventual exit. After five years of moving toward a succession plan, Holland-Branch admits she had no idea just how difficult the process would be. The first step involved calling on the expertise of an attorney and accountant familiar with family business, tax, and estate planning issues. Facilities Connection's insurance company's risk manager and estate specialists also got involved, and Haworth's dealer development team and the Solomon Coyle Dealer Enhancement Program provided

additional sources of help. Further, Holland-Branch talks regularly with other business owners both inside and outside of the industry, and has attended a number of Family Business Forum events hosted by the College of Business at the University of Texas, El Paso.

This team of consultants helped Holland-Branch and her husband structure the company and utilize available options to maximize their investment. It meant addressing a number of issues, including complexity with minority shareholders, capital investment capacity and requirements, funding vehicles, sweat equity, actual stock sale, and phantom stock. Time and effort has been spent defining growth objectives, an Employee Stock Ownership Program (ESOP), a company valuation process, emergency and contingency planning, disability planning, and a stock buy-back process.

All that time and effort is paying off, as Holland-Branch is now able to focus on hiring key staff at executive levels to grow and position the company for success at its goal levels. The Solomon Coyle and Haworth dealer development programs have been key in helping to define "best of class" benchmarks for the firm's accounting, sales, and operational processes, and the new executive team is positioned so that its performance, passion, and ability dictate actions based on very clear common goals.

An eye remains on the future: The business needs to be in good working order to assure a smooth transition when Holland-Branch moves to retirement. It is crucial that there be no loss of credibility for the company, and that new leadership can effortlessly continue with the customers and employees as well as significantly move the company to new success levels.

In 2007 a formal financial audit was conducted with the new controller in place alongside a new executive vice president who will eventually replace Holland-Branch as president. These key members of the succession team were selected for being proven and recognized within the business community. They have strong leadership qualities and previous successful business ownership. In addition, their education and intelligence, integrity, values, faith, passion, self-worth, and commitment, along with a

Dealership Process Model

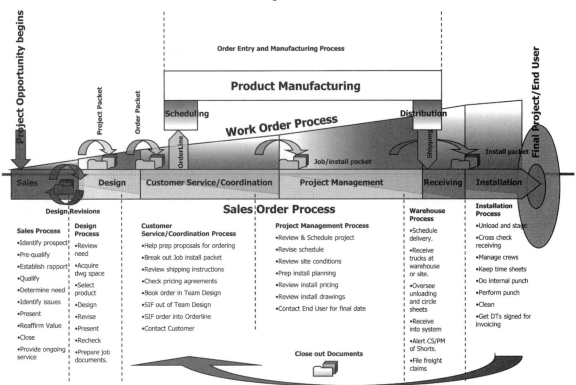

Order Entry and Manufacturing Process

Product Manufacturing

Scheduling

Project Packet

Order Packet

Work Order Process

Distribution

OrderLine

Shipping

Install packet

Job/install packet

Project Opportunity begins

Final Project/End User

| Sales | Design | Customer Service/Coordination | Project Management | Receiving | Installation |

Sales Order Process

Design Revisions

Close out Documents

Sales Process	**Design Process**	**Customer Service/Coordination Process**	**Project Management Process**	**Warehouse Process**	**Installation Process**
•Identify prospect	•Review need	•Help prep proposals for ordering	•Review & Schedule project	•Schedule delivery.	•Unload and stage
•Pre-qualify	•Acquire dwg space	•Break out Job install packet	•Revise schedule	•Receive trucks at warehouse or site.	•Cross check receiving
•Establish rapport	•Select product	•Review shipping instructions	•Review site conditions	•Oversee unloading and circle sheets	•Manage crews
•Qualify	•Design	•Check pricing agreements	•Prep install planning	•Receive into system	•Keep time sheets
•Determine need	•Revise	•Book order in Team Design	•Review install pricing	•Alert CS/PM of Shorts.	•Do internal punch
•Identify issues	•Present	•SIF out of Team Design	•Review install drawings	•File freight claims	•Perform punch
•Present	•Recheck	•SIF order into Orderline	•Contact End User for final date		•Clean
•Reaffirm Value	•Prepare job documents.	•Contact Customer			•Get DTs signed for invoicing
•Close					
•Provide ongoing service					

Figure 6-2

Facilities Connection work process flowcharts. Working with Haworth,
Facilities Connection developed these processes and work management practices.

---

healthy gut feeling on Holland-Branch's part, played into the decision.

The team is working closely with external accountants and business consultants to perfect accounting processes and cash management, improve A/R funding resources, and federal contracting compliance issues—all measures necessary to sustain profitable growth. The firm's long-time vice president of sales is also part of the succession plan, and plans are underway to add a registered interior designer, certified project manager, or architect to the team (who would ideally also be a LEED AP or CPM professional). Also high on Holland-Branch's list of issues are maintaining

fiscal control and implementing well-defined audit procedures.

Looking forward, Holland-Branch sees company revenues moving upward over the next ten years as the firm continues building federal business and continues to offer a comprehensive furniture and interiors practice. The first strategic goal is to not only reach that $10 million level, but to make that level sustainable and then move to $30 or $40 million.

Holland-Branch plans to spend more time working on the business rather than in the business for as long as she can be of value, providing vision and leadership to the organization. While her replacement will focus on

Simple Contract Furniture Value Chain

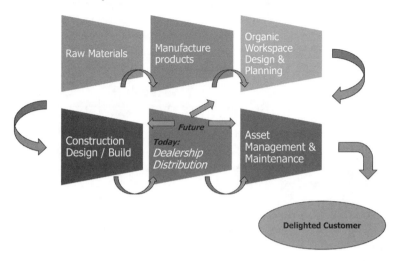

Figure 6-3
Facilities Connection work process flowcharts. Working with Haworth, Facilities Connection developed these processes and work management practices.

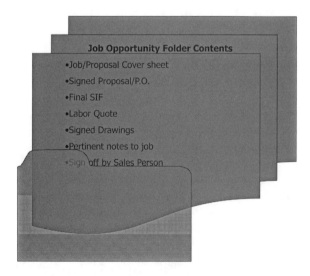

Figure 6-4
Facilities Connection job opportunity folder.

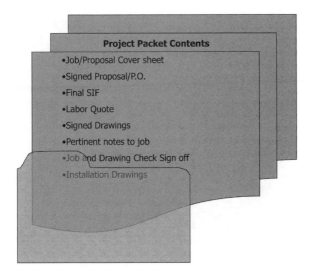

Figure 6-5
Facilities Connection project packet contents.

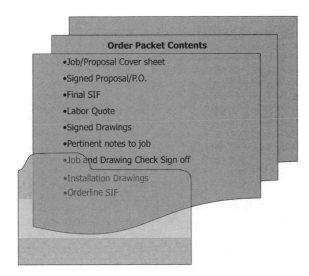

Figure 6-6
Facilities Connection order packet contents.

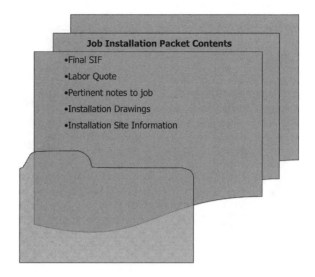

Figure 6-7
Facilities Connection job installation packet.

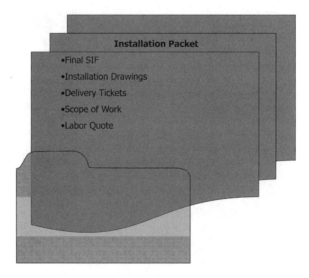

Figure 6-8
Facilities Connection installation packet.

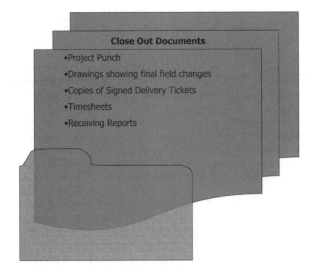

Figure 6-9
Facilities Connection close out documents.

Project Timeline Map

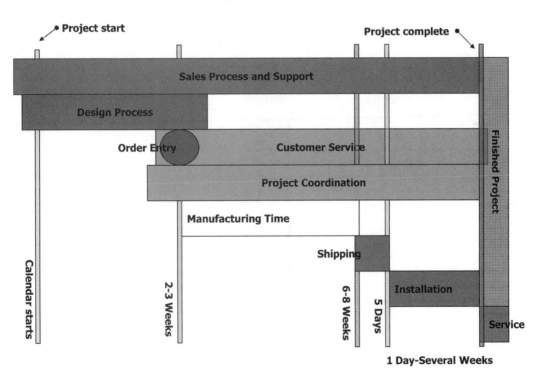

Figure 6-10
Facilities Connection project timeline map.

management, Holland-Branch will focus on leadership. Day-to-day operations are being turned over to the succession team members as they demonstrate their abilities, and Holland-Branch's executive VP is now teaching management and profit classes to ensure the entire company is passionate about profitability and performance.

The most useful thing Holland-Branch draws from her exit strategy planning? "Start early. Never stop looking for the right fit. Keep all doors open, and look outside the industry. Think big, act big. Be highly profitable, have high values, and never give up." Holland-Branch also advises: "Be sure to explore a number of options before making your decision about your exit strategy. Use the resources of business schools within your universities and other organizations within your industry to see what works and doesn't work. Ask others for help."

Successful Succession: TRIO Design Group and David-Michael Design Inc.

David-Michael Design Inc. is located in Santa Ana, California, and specializes in the design of high-end residences, model homes, sales centers, recreation centers, country clubs, hotels, corporate offices, and restaurants.

Throughout his design career, David-Michael Madigan has followed a mantra ingrained in him by his father: Always think ahead. After more than twenty years in the industry, he has found it to be the most valuable piece of advice he's been given, especially when operating in an industry that many people still consider a luxury expense. After all, when the purse strings start to tighten up, it's these expenses that go to the chopping block first.

Madigan, however, began on top. Shortly after graduating from the Fashion Institute of Design and Merchandising, the California native accepted the position of assistant to the director of design at Lusk Design, the in-house design division of The Lusk Company. Founded by John D. Lusk in the 1940s, The Lusk Company was a powerhouse developer that played a major role in transforming rural southern California into suburban developments, and in the late 1980s business was booming. Lusk Design had an ideal setup: it was operating in one of the nation's hottest markets, designing interiors for The Lusk Company's commercial developments, model homes, and other residential ventures.

But despite its storied history and ample success over the years, The Lusk Company and Lusk Design were not immune to the recession of the early 1990s. On the upside, although the practice mostly operated as an in-house design team, Nancy Lusk had also branched beyond company borders, taking on external clients as well, which gave the practice a bit of a cushion as the market slowed.

Change, however, was on its way. After more than thirty years in the business, the slowing economy gave Nancy Lusk the chance to consider retirement. Unlike the market dip, however, this was something more controllable and manageable, as she had already invested a number of years in developing the talent under her—namely Madigan and another senior designer at the company, Donna Gott.

As the firm's leader, Lusk had taken care to provide opportunities for junior designers to move through the ranks and learn the business. Throughout the firm, designers were given chances to build their skills while working on a range of commercial and residential project types, from high-end model homes and residential developments to more commercial ventures, including high rises, financial centers, medical centers, and shopping centers. With the firm working out of a corporate headquarters in Irvine, California, as well as branch divisions in Hawaii and San Diego and throughout northern California, designers were given chance to work in a number of offices, and project management duties exposed younger designers to the details of running not only a project but also a business. "We weren't micromanaged and told what to do," recalls Madigan. "We were given freedom and the ability to fly and develop ourselves. We were encouraged to develop our own design skill, which afforded people the chance to develop a signature style."

Capitalizing on the opportunities to dig into an array of projects, Madigan dove in with success. Within two years he was promoted to a project designer, and shortly thereafter rose to senior designer. As a result, when Lusk decided to retire in 1997, Madigan and Gott were positioned to take control.

The firm was considerably smaller than during its heyday, having shrunk from more than one hundred designers on more than twenty-five design teams in a number of divisions to fewer than five designers in the corporate office in Irvine, California. Despite its smaller size, the business still had clients, resources, and projects in the works, and Lusk, wanting to preserve these relationships, approached Madigan and Gott about taking over the firm's client roster and ongoing projects—essentially the heart of the company. Lusk Design would continue in theory but would further transition into a new name, TRIO Design Group, to recognize the duo's new leadership roles.

Lusk, Madigan, and Gott planned out the process over six months, allowing the soon-to-be-owners time to complete ongoing projects, brief clients on the upcoming transition, and lay the groundwork for new business opportunities as TRIO. Initially, the team worked from the home of one of their associates, before settling into an office space—coincidentally, about a quarter of a mile from Lusk Design's old offices.

Despite their experience, transitioning into the role of owner and business manager took some adjustment. They built their firm's internal structure around Lusk's templates, using the old brand's parameters as boilerplates for TRIO. "We felt it wasn't time to reinvent the wheel," Madigan says. The new principals informally divided up business responsibilities, with Gott taking on more back-end functions like finances and purchasing while Madigan oversaw more public functions like networking and marketing. The team also hired an outside accountant, who proved to be an essential team member. Not only did she help manage their finances, she also gave Madigan and Gott advice on the finer details of

running a business. Madigan also kept in close contact with Lusk, often turning to her for guidance and advice. It's a familial relationship that continues.

In transitioning to TRIO, Madigan and Gott had to think smaller, as the shaky economy could not guarantee that every client would continue to have work for the new brand. In addition, although the duo was joined by a third person acting in an associate capacity, three people could hardly do the work that more than one hundred once had. They carefully cut back their project load. Planning ahead, however, the team was careful to keep lines of conversation open with a range of clients and developers, recognizing that the market would eventually turn around.

As the economy began to pick up, this foresight paid off. Many developers who had closed up new properties during the slowdown were now putting developments back on the market. Seeking a fresh product, they began approaching TRIO about redesigning their model homes, and the design practice adopted this as its niche market.

Coming out of the recession, TRIO came into its own as a boutique firm, growing to a staff of ten and completing the transition from Lusk Design to TRIO. Gott and Madigan decided to cap their growth so that each principal could remain involved at the design level. As a result, the firm remained careful to turn down projects that may have necessitated a hiring spree or would have taxed the small staff. It was a management style that lasted for ten years.

Change, however, is a continual process, and in 2008 Madigan and Gott found themselves once again in transition. As TRIO grew, its partners, too, branched out into new directions. In 2004, flooring manufacturer Smith-Laredo asked Madigan to create a line of signature flooring products. It was Madigan's first foray into personal branding, and following the line's success he founded David-Michael Designs, a more personal brand. Madigan also began exploring design possibilities—both projects and products—in the burgeoning Asian markets. As he focused overseas, Gott continued to explore new opportunities stateside.

As the work evolved, the pair decided it would be better to close TRIO and start their own firms. With separate ventures, Gott could keep her local focus while Madigan could advance deeper into the Chinese marketplace.

To begin wrapping up TRIO, Madigan and Gott had a formal meeting to divide up clients. As both partners had remained involved in the design process, the client roster was essentially divided according to which partner had served as the project manager for each client. Madigan immediately purchased a live/work loft in an up-and-coming arts district in Santa Ana, California. His vision was vast, as his new company would absorb the entire staff from TRIO, while Gott retained one team member. Madigan's new firm, David-Michael Design Inc., would focus not only on his established China and U.S. markets, but also on his new brand of flooring products; "Design Forward," a design column he began writing for *The Orange County Register* and *Orange County HOME* magazine; and televised design segments he hosted on KTLA Warner Brothers, Los Angeles. Gott and Madigan's

new practices are collaborating under the TRIO name to complete projects in process.

Focusing on David-Michael Designs, Madigan hired additional employees: an office manager, purchasing manager, accounting manager, CPA, vice president of marketing, senior designer, project designer, assistant designers, a translations team, and two design interns. Madigan is the design principal. The firm, which draws nearly 75 percent of its clientele from overseas sectors, operates out of a three-story studio in Santa Ana, California, and actively pursues work overseas as the U.S. economy starts to dip once again.

Madigan is also thinking even farther into the future and sees the necessity of planning for retirement, or at least some sort of slowdown. "I think we'll have about a ten-year run," he says. "I want to work the rest of my life, but not at this speed," he explains, noting that despite his decades in the business and the many years of managerial experience under his belt, running a firm remains a full-time (and then some) job.

Conclusion

s evidenced in the array of perspectives compiled here, there are
as many different ways to approach running a successful interior design
business as there are professionals in the field. It should also be noted
that, like many other industries, the business of interior design is ever
evolving, as are the firms that have graciously lent their advice and
experience here. Economies tighten or boom, profits rise and fall, head counts
expand and contract, and business processes may adapt and change
accordingly. One thing that is certain, however, is that members of this
professional community can continually benefit from sharing their
experiences with one another. In this regard, *Interior Design in Practice: Case
Studies of Successful Business Models* is but a starting point to jumpstart the
discussion of how best to run *your* business—now and many successful years
into the future.

Appendix A:

ASID Sample Interior Design Services Agreements

ASID Document ID120

RESIDENTIAL INTERIOR DESIGN
SERVICES AGREEMENT

This **AGREEMENT** is

made this _____ day of _____ in the year of Two Thousand and _____

BETWEEN the **CLIENT**:
(name and address)

---

and the **DESIGNER**:
(name and address)

The **CLIENT** and the **DESIGNER** agree as follows:

The Project pertains to the following areas within Client's residence located at

_____:

(List areas below:)

---

1. **INTERIOR DESIGN SERVICES**

Designer shall perform the following interior design services:

(Describe the interior design services to be performed by Designer)

---

2. **DESIGNER'S COMPENSATION**

(Describe the methods of Designer's compensation and the services to which each compensation method applies if more than one compensation method is used)

ID120-1996   1

3. MISCELLANEOUS

3.1 Should Designer agree to perform any design service not described above, such "Additional Service" will be invoiced to Client at the following hourly rates:

Design Principal	$_____
Project Designer	$_____
Staff Designer	$_____
Draftsman	$_____
Other employees	$_____

Hourly charges will be invoiced to Client _____ and are payable upon receipt of invoice.

3.2 Disbursements incurred by Designer in the interest of the Project shall be reimbursed by Client to Designer upon receipt of Designer's invoices, which are rendered _____. Reimbursements shall include, among other things, costs of local and long distance travel, long distance telephone calls, duplication of plans, drawings and specifications, messenger services and the like.

3.3 Designer's drawings and specifications are conceptual in nature and intended to set forth design intent only. They are not to be used for architectural or engineering purposes. Designer does not provide architectural or engineering services.

3.4 Designer's services shall not include undertaking any responsibility for the design or modification of the design of any structural, heating, air-conditioning, plumbing, electrical, ventilation or other mechanical systems installed or to be installed at the Project.

3.5 Should the nature of Designer's design concepts require the services of any other design professional, such professional shall be engaged directly by Client pursuant to separate agreement as may be mutually acceptable to Client and such other design professional.

3.6 As Designer requires a record of Designer's design projects, Client will permit Designer or Designer's representatives to photograph the Project upon completion of the Project. Designer will be entitled to use photographs for Designer's business purposes but shall not disclose Project location or Client's name without Client's prior written consent.

3.7 All concepts, drawings and specifications prepared by Designer's firm ("Project Documents") and all copyrights and other proprietary rights applicable thereto remain at all times Designer's property. Project Documents may not be used by Client for any purpose other than completion of Project by Designer.

3.8 Designer cannot guarantee that actual prices for merchandise and/or interior installations or other costs or services as presented to Client will not vary either by item or in the aggregate from any Client proposed budget.

ID120-1996 2

3.9 This Agreement may be terminated by either party upon the other party's default in performance, provided that termination may not be effected unless written notice specifying nature and extent of default is given to the concerned party and such party fails to cure such default in performance within _____ (___) days from date of receipt of such notice. Termination shall be without prejudice to any and all other rights and remedies of Designer, and Client shall remain liable for all outstanding obligations owed by Client to Designer and for all items of merchandise, interior installations and other services on order as of the termination date.

3.10 In addition to all other legal rights, Designer shall be entitled to withhold delivery of any item of merchandise or the further performance of interior installations or any other services, should Client fail to timely make any payments due Designer.

3.11 Any controversy or claim arising out of or relating to this Agreement, or the breach thereof, shall be decided by arbitration only in the _____ in accordance with the Commercial Arbitration Rules of the American Arbitration Association then in effect, and judgment upon the award rendered by the arbitrator(s) may be entered in any court having jurisdiction thereof.

3.12 Client will provide Designer with access to the Project and all information Designer may need to complete the Project. It is Client's responsibility to obtain all approvals required by any governmental agency or otherwise in connection with this Project.

3.13 Any sales tax applicable to Design Fees, and/or merchandise purchased from Designer, and/or interior installations completed by Designer shall be the responsibility of Client.

3.14 Neither Client nor Designer may assign their respective interests in this Agreement without the written consent of the other.

3.15 The laws of the State of _____ shall govern this Agreement.

3.16 Any provision of this Agreement held to be void or unenforceable under any law shall be deemed stricken, and all remaining provisions shall continue to be valid and binding upon both Designer and Client.

3.17 This Agreement is a complete statement of Designer's and Client's understanding. No representations or agreements have been made other than those contained in this Agreement. This Agreement can be modified only by a writing signed by both Designer and Client.

ID120-1996 **3**

4. ADDITIONAL TERMS

CLIENT:

_____

_____

DESIGNER:

_____

_____

ID120-1996   4

ASID Document ID121

RESIDENTIAL INTERIOR DESIGN SERVICES AGREEMENT

<u>SPECIAL INSTRUCTIONS REGARDING PAGE 3</u>

Note that this Agreement contains two alternative paragraphs 2.3. Each alternative appears on a separate "Page 3." Except for Paragraph 2.3, the remaining language on each alternative "Page 3" is identical.

If Designer does not intend to charge a fee for Merchandise and Interior Installations purchased by Client through Designer, then (1) <u>carefully remove and discard the second "Page 3"</u>; and (2) <u>use the first "Page 3"</u> which contains the following language in Paragraph 2.3:

> *Merchandise and Interior Installations to be purchased through Designer will be specified in a written "Proposal" prepared by Designer and submitted in each instance for Client's written approval. Each Proposal will describe the item and its price to Client (F.O.B. point of origin). The price of each item shall be the amount charged to Designer by the supplier of such item ("Client Price").*

If Designer intends to charge a fee for Merchandise and Interior Installations purchased by Client through Designer, then (1) carefully <u>remove and discard the first "Page 3"</u>; and (2) <u>use the second "Page 3"</u> which contains the following language in Paragraph 2.3:

> *Merchandise and Interior Installations to be purchased through Designer will be specified in a written "Proposal" prepared by Designer and submitted in each instance for Client's written approval. Each Proposal will describe the item and its price to Client (F.O.B. point of origin). The price of each item to Client ("Client Price") shall be the amount charged to Designer by the supplier of such item ("Supplier Price"), plus Designer's purchase fee equal to _____ percent (____%) of the Supplier Price (exclusive of any freight, delivery or like charges or applicable tax). The fee is in addition to the hourly fees payable to Designer for its Interior Design Services.*

ID121-1996

ASID Document ID121

RESIDENTIAL INTERIOR DESIGN SERVICES AGREEMENT

This **AGREEMENT** is

made this _____ day of _____ in the year of Two Thousand and _____

BETWEEN the **CLIENT**:
(name and address)

and the **DESIGNER**:
(name and address)

The **CLIENT** and the **DESIGNER** agree as follows:

The Project pertains to the following areas within Client's residence located at

_____:

(List areas below:)

INTERIOR DESIGN SERVICES

1. Design Concept Services

1.1 In this phase of the Project, Designer shall, as and where appropriate, perform the following:

   A. Determine Client's design preferences and requirements.

   B. Conduct an initial design study.

ID121-1996   1

C. Prepare drawings and other materials to generally illustrate Designer's suggested interior design concepts, to include color schemes, interior finishes, wall coverings, floor coverings, ceiling treatments, lighting treatments and window treatments.

D. Prepare layout showing location of movable furniture and furnishings.

E. Prepare schematic plans for recommended cabinet work, interior built-ins and other interior decorative details ("Interior Installations").

1.2 Prior to commencing Design Concept Services, Designer shall receive an Initial Design Fee of _____ dollars ($_____). This non-refundable Design Fee is payable upon signing this Agreement and is in addition to all other compensation payable to Designer under this Agreement.

2. Interior Specifications and Purchasing Services

2.1 Upon Client's approval of the Design Concepts, Designer will, as and where appropriate:

A. Select and/or specially design required Interior Installations and all required items of movable furniture, furnishings, light fixtures, hardware, fixtures, accessories and the like ("Merchandise").

B. Prepare and submit for Client's approval Proposals for completion of Interior Installations and purchase of Merchandise.

2.2 Designer may, at times, request Client to engage others to provide Interior Installations, pursuant to the arrangements set forth in the Project Review services described in paragraph 3 of this Agreement.

2.3 Merchandise and Interior Installations to be purchased through Designer will be specified in a written "Proposal" prepared by Designer and submitted in each instance for Client's written approval. Each Proposal will describe the item and its price to Client (F.O.B. point of origin). The price of each item to Client ("Client Price") shall be the amount charged to Designer by the supplier of such item ("Supplier Price"), plus Designer's purchase fee equal to _____ percent (___%) of the Supplier Price (exclusive of any freight, delivery or like charges or applicable tax). The fee is in addition to the hourly fees payable to Designer for its Interior Design Services.

ID121-1996   2

2.4 No item can be ordered by Designer until the Proposal has been approved by Client, in writing, and returned to Designer with Designer's required initial payment equal to _____ percent (____%) of the Client Price. The balance of the Client Price, together with delivery, shipping, handling charges and applicable taxes, is payable when the item is ready for delivery to and/or installation at Client's residence, or to a subsequent supplier for further work upon rendition of Designer's invoice. Proposals for fabrics, wall coverings, accessories, antiques, and items purchased at auction or at retail stores require full payment at time of signed Proposal.

3. Project Review

3.1 If the nature of the Project requires engagement by Client of any contractors to perform work based upon Designer's concepts, drawings or interior design specifications not otherwise provided for in the Interior Specifications and Purchasing Services, Client will enter into contracts directly with the concerned contractor.

3.2 Designer will make periodic visits to the Project site as Designer may consider appropriate to observe the work of these contractors to determine whether the contractors' work is proceeding in general conformity with Designer's concepts. Constant observation of work at the Project site is not a part of Designer's duties. Designer is not responsible for the performance, quality, timely completion or delivery of any work, materials or equipment furnished by contractors pursuant to direct contracts with Client.

4. COMPENSATION

4.1 For all Interior Design Services provided by Designer pursuant to this Agreement, Designer shall be compensated by Design Fees computed on the following hourly basis:

Design Principal	$_____
Project Designer	$_____
Staff Designer	$_____
Draftsman	$_____
Other employees	$_____

4.2 Hourly charges will be invoiced to Client _____ and are payable upon receipt of invoice.

5. MISCELLANEOUS

5.1 Should Designer agree to perform any design service not described above, such "Additional Service" will be invoiced to Client at the following hourly rates:

Design Principal	$_____
Project Designer	$_____
Staff Designer	$_____
Draftsman	$_____
Other employees	$_____

Hourly charges will be invoiced to Client _____ and are payable upon receipt of invoice.

ID121-1996 **3**

5.2 Disbursements incurred by Designer in the interest of the Project shall be reimbursed by Client to Designer upon receipt of Designer's invoices, which are rendered _____. Reimbursements shall include, among other things, costs of local and long distance travel, long distance telephone calls, duplication of plans, drawings and specifications, messenger services and the like.

5.3 Designer's drawings and specifications are conceptual in nature and intended to set forth design intent only. They are not to be used for architectural or engineering purposes. Designer does not provide architectural or engineering services.

5.4 Designer's services shall not include undertaking any responsibility for the design or modification of the design of any structural, heating, air-conditioning, plumbing, electrical, ventilation or other mechanical systems installed or to be installed at the Project.

5.5 Should the nature of Designer's design concepts require the services of any other design professional, such professional shall be engaged directly by Client pursuant to separate agreement as may be mutually acceptable to Client and such other design professional.

5.6 As Designer requires a record of Designer's design projects, Client will permit Designer or Designer's representatives to photograph the Project upon completion of the Project. Designer will be entitled to use photographs for Designer's business purposes but shall not disclose Project location or Client's name without Client's prior written consent.

5.7 All concepts, drawings and specifications prepared by Designer's firm ("Project Documents") and all copyrights and other proprietary rights applicable thereto remain at all times Designer's property. Project Documents may not be used by Client for any purpose other than completion of Project by Designer.

5.8 Designer cannot guarantee that actual prices for Merchandise and/or Interior Installations or other costs or services as presented to Client will not vary either by item or in the aggregate from any Client proposed budget.

5.9 This Agreement may be terminated by either party upon the other party's default in performance, provided that termination may not be effected unless written notice specifying nature and extent of default is given to the concerned party and such party fails to cure such default in performance within _____ (____) days from date of receipt of such notice. Termination shall be without prejudice to any and all other rights and remedies of Designer, and Client shall remain liable for all outstanding obligations owed by Client to Designer and for all items of Merchandise, Interior Installations and other services on order as of the termination date.

5.10 In addition to all other legal rights, Designer shall be entitled to withhold delivery of any item of Merchandise or the further performance of Interior Installations or any other services, should Client fail to timely make any payments due Designer.

ID121-1996   4

5.11 Any controversy or claim arising out of or relating to this Agreement, or the breach thereof, shall be decided by arbitration only in the _____ in accordance with the Commercial Arbitration Rules of the American Arbitration Association then in effect, and judgment upon the award rendered by the arbitrator(s) may be entered in any court having jurisdiction thereof.

5.12 Client will provide Designer with access to the Project and all information Designer may need to complete the Project. It is Client's responsibility to obtain all approvals required by any governmental agency or otherwise in connection with this Project.

5.13 Any sales tax applicable to Design Fees, and/or Merchandise purchased from Designer, and/or Interior Installations completed by Designer shall be the responsibility of Client.

5.14 Neither Client nor Designer may assign their respective interests in this Agreement without the written consent of the other.

5.15 The laws of the State of _____ shall govern this Agreement.

5.16 Any provision of this Agreement held to be void or unenforceable under any law shall be deemed stricken, and all remaining provisions shall continue to be valid and binding upon both Designer and Client.

5.17 This Agreement is a complete statement of Designer's and Client's understanding. No representations or agreements have been made other than those contained in this Agreement. This Agreement can be modified only by a writing signed by both Designer and Client.

6. ADDITIONAL TERMS

CLIENT:

_____

_____

DESIGNER:

_____

_____

ID121-1996 5

ASID Document ID122

RESIDENTIAL INTERIOR DESIGN
SERVICES AGREEMENT

This **AGREEMENT** is

made this _____ day of _____ in the year of Two Thousand and _____

BETWEEN the **CLIENT**:
(name and address)

and the **DESIGNER**:
(name and address)

The **CLIENT** and the **DESIGNER** agree as follows:

The Project pertains to the following areas within Client's residence located at

_____ :

(List areas below:)

INTERIOR DESIGN SERVICES

1. **Design Concept Services**

1.1 In this phase of the Project, Designer shall, as and where appropriate, perform the following:

A. Determine Client's design preferences and requirements.

B. Conduct an initial design study.

ID122-1996   1

C. Prepare drawings and other materials to generally illustrate Designer's suggested interior design concepts, to include color schemes, interior finishes, wall coverings, floor coverings, ceiling treatments, lighting treatments and window treatments.

D. Prepare layout showing location of movable furniture and furnishings.

E. Prepare schematic plans for recommended cabinet work, interior built-ins and other interior decorative details ("Interior Installations").

1.2 Not more than _____ (_____) revisions to the Design Concept will be prepared by Designer without additional charges. Additional revisions will be billed to Client as Additional Services.

2. Interior Specifications and Purchasing Services

2.1 Upon Client's approval of the Design Concepts, Designer will, as and where appropriate:

A. Select and/or specially design required Interior Installations and all required items of movable furniture, furnishings, light fixtures, hardware, fixtures, accessories and the like ("Merchandise").

B. Prepare and submit for Client's approval Proposals for completion of Interior Installations and purchase of Merchandise.

2.2 Designer may, at times, request Client to engage others to provide Interior Installations, pursuant to the arrangements set forth in the Project Review services described in paragraph 3 of this Agreement.

2.3 Merchandise and Interior Installations to be purchased through Designer will be specified in a written "Proposal" prepared by Designer and submitted in each instance for Client's written approval. Each Proposal will describe the item and its price to Client (F.O.B. point of origin). The price of each item shall be the amount charged to Designer by the supplier of such item ("Client Price").

2.4 No item can be ordered by Designer until the Proposal has been approved by Client, in writing, and returned to Designer with Designer's required initial payment equal to _____ percent (____%) of the Client Price. The balance of the Client Price, together with delivery, shipping, handling charges and applicable taxes, is payable when the item is ready for delivery to and/or installation at Client's residence, or to a subsequent supplier for further work upon rendition of Designer's invoice. Proposals for fabrics, wall coverings, accessories, antiques, and items purchased at auction or at retail stores require full payment at time of signed Proposal.

ID122-1996   2

3. Project Review

3.1 If the nature of the Project requires engagement by Client of any contractors to perform work based upon Designer's concepts, drawings or interior design specifications not otherwise provided for in the Interior Specifications and Purchasing Services, Client will enter into contracts directly with the concerned contractor.

3.2 Designer will make periodic visits to the Project site as Designer may consider appropriate to observe the work of these contractors to determine whether the contractors' work is proceeding in general conformity with Designer's concepts. Constant observation of work at the Project site is not a part of Designer's duties. Designer is not responsible for the performance, quality, timely completion or delivery of any work, materials or equipment furnished by contractors pursuant to direct contracts with Client.

4. COMPENSATION

4.1 Designer's compensation for the Interior Design Services described above shall be a fixed fee of _____ dollars ($_____) payable as follows:

4.2 Designer's compensation shall be subject to renegotiation if:

A. The scope of the Project changes materially; or

B. Through no fault of Designer, its Interior Design Services are not substantially completed within _____ (___) months of the date of signing this Agreement.

5. MISCELLANEOUS

5.1 Should Designer agree to perform any design service not described above, such "Additional Service" will be invoiced to Client at the following hourly rates:

Design Principal	$_____
Project Designer	$_____
Staff Designer	$_____
Draftsman	$_____
Other employees	$_____

Hourly charges will be invoiced to Client _____ and are payable upon receipt of invoice.

5.2 Disbursements incurred by Designer in the interest of the Project shall be reimbursed by Client to Designer upon receipt of Designer's invoices, which are rendered _____. Reimbursements shall include, among other things, costs of local and long distance travel, long distance telephone calls, duplication of plans, drawings and specifications, messenger services and the like.

ID122-1996 **3**

5.3 Designer's drawings and specifications are conceptual in nature and intended to set forth design intent only. They are not to be used for architectural or engineering purposes. Designer does not provide architectural or engineering services.

5.4 Designer's services shall not include undertaking any responsibility for the design or modification of the design of any structural, heating, air-conditioning, plumbing, electrical, ventilation or other mechanical systems installed or to be installed at the Project.

5.5 Should the nature of Designer's design concepts require the services of any other design professional, such professional shall be engaged directly by Client pursuant to separate agreement as may be mutually acceptable to Client and such other design professional.

5.6 As Designer requires a record of Designer's design projects, Client will permit Designer or Designer's representatives to photograph the Project upon completion of the Project. Designer will be entitled to use photographs for Designer's business purposes but shall not disclose Project location or Client's name without Client's prior written consent.

5.7 All concepts, drawings and specifications prepared by Designer's firm ("Project Documents") and all copyrights and other proprietary rights applicable thereto remain at all times Designer's property. Project Documents may not be used by Client for any purpose other than completion of Project by Designer.

5.8 Designer cannot guarantee that actual prices for Merchandise and/or Interior Installations or other costs or services as presented to Client will not vary either by item or in the aggregate from any Client proposed budget.

5.9 This Agreement may be terminated by either party upon the other party's default in performance, provided that termination may not be effected unless written notice specifying nature and extent of default is given to the concerned party and such party fails to cure such default in performance within _____ (____) days from date of receipt of such notice. Termination shall be without prejudice to any and all other rights and remedies of Designer, and Client shall remain liable for all outstanding obligations owed by Client to Designer and for all items of Merchandise, Interior Installations and other services on order as of the termination date.

5.10 In addition to all other legal rights, Designer shall be entitled to withhold delivery of any item of Merchandise or the further performance of Interior Installations or any other services, should Client fail to timely make any payments due Designer.

5.11 Any controversy or claim arising out of or relating to this Agreement, or the breach thereof, shall be decided by arbitration only in the _____ in accordance with the Commercial Arbitration Rules of the American Arbitration Association then in effect, and judgment upon the award rendered by the arbitrator(s) may be entered in any court having jurisdiction thereof.

ID122-1996   4

5.12   Client will provide Designer with access to the Project and all information Designer may need to complete the Project. It is Client's responsibility to obtain all approvals required by any governmental agency or otherwise in connection with this Project.

5.13   Any sales tax applicable to Design Fees, and/or Merchandise purchased from Designer, and/or Interior Installations completed by Designer shall be the responsibility of Client.

5.14   Neither Client nor Designer may assign their respective interests in this Agreement without the written consent of the other.

5.15   The laws of the State of _____ shall govern this Agreement.

5.16   Any provision of this Agreement held to be void or unenforceable under any law shall be deemed stricken, and all remaining provisions shall continue to be valid and binding upon both Designer and Client.

5.17   This Agreement is a complete statement of Designer's and Client's understanding. No representations or agreements have been made other than those contained in this Agreement. This Agreement can be modified only by a writing signed by both Designer and Client.

6. ADDITIONAL TERMS

CLIENT:

_____

_____

DESIGNER:

_____

_____

ID122-1996   5

RESIDENTIAL INTERIOR DESIGN
SERVICES AGREEMENT

SPECIAL INSTRUCTIONS REGARDING PAGE 2

Note that this Agreement contains two alternative paragraphs 1.2. Each alternative appears on a separate "Page 2." Except for Paragraph 1.2, the remaining language on each alternative "Page 2" is identical.

If Designer intends to charge a fixed fee for Design Concept Services, then (1) carefully remove and discard the second "Page 2"; and (2) use the first "Page 2" which contains the following language in Paragraph 1.2:

> *Prior to commencing Design Concept Services, Designer shall receive an Initial Design Fee of _____ dollars ($_____). This non-refundable Design Fee is payable upon signing this Agreement and is in addition to all other compensation payable to Designer under this Agreement. Not more than _____(____) revisions to the Design Concept will be prepared by Designer without additional charges. Additional revisions will be billed to Client as Additional Services.*

If Designer intends to charge hourly fees for Design Concept Services, then (1) carefully remove and discard the first "Page 2"; and (2) use the second "Page 2" which contains the following language in Paragraph 1.2:

> *Designer shall be compensated for its Design Concept Services on an hourly basis at the rates set forth in paragraph 4.1 of this Agreement. Hourly charges will be invoiced to Client _____ and are payable by Client upon receipt of invoice. Upon signing this Agreement, Designer shall receive a non-refundable initial advance of _____ dollars ($_____), which constitutes the minimum fee due Designer for Design Concept Services. This advance will be credited against hourly charges otherwise payable by Client to Designer for Design Concept Services.*

COPYRIGHT©1996 THE AMERICAN SOCIETY OF INTERIOR DESIGNERS. ALL RIGHTS RESERVED.
608 MASSACHUSETTS AVENUE, N.E., WASHINGTON, DC 20002-6006.

ID123-1996

188   Appendix A: ASID Sample Interior Design Services Agreements

ASID Document ID123

RESIDENTIAL INTERIOR DESIGN SERVICES AGREEMENT

This **AGREEMENT** is

made this _____day of_____ in the year of Two Thousand and _____

BETWEEN the CLIENT:
(name and address)

---

and the DESIGNER:
(name and address)

The **CLIENT** and the **DESIGNER** agree as follows:

The Project pertains to the following areas within Client's residence located at

_____:

(List areas below:)

INTERIOR DESIGN SERVICES

1. <u>**Design Concept Services**</u>

1.1 In this phase of the Project, Designer shall, as and where appropriate, perform the following:

    A. Determine Client's design preferences and requirements.

    B. Conduct an initial design study.

ID123-1996   **1**

C. Prepare drawings and other materials to generally illustrate
   Designer's suggested interior design concepts, to include color
   schemes, interior finishes, wall coverings, floor coverings, ceiling
   treatments, lighting treatments and window treatments.

D. Prepare layout showing location of movable furniture and
   furnishings.

E. Prepare schematic plans for recommended cabinet work, interior
   built-ins and other interior decorative details ("Interior Installations").

1.2 Prior to commencing Design Concept Services, Designer shall receive an Initial Design
     Fee of _____ dollars ($_____). This non-refundable
     Design Fee is payable upon signing this Agreement and is in addition to all other
     compensation payable to Designer under this Agreement. Not more than_____
     (____) revisions to the Design Concept will be prepared by Designer without
     additional charges. Additional revisions will be billed to Client as Additional Services.

2. Interior Specifications and Purchasing Services

2.1 Upon Client's approval of the Design Concepts, Designer will, as and
     where appropriate:

A. Select and/or specially design required Interior Installations and
   all required items of movable furniture, furnishings, light fixtures,
   hardware, fixtures, accessories and the like ("Merchandise").

B. Prepare and submit for Client's approval Proposals for completion
   of Interior Installations and purchase of Merchandise.

2.2 Merchandise and Interior Installations specified by Designer shall, if Client wishes to
     purchase them, be purchased solely through Designer. Designer may, at times,
     request Client to engage others to provide Interior Installations, pursuant to the
     arrangements set forth in the Project Review services described in paragraph 3 of this
     Agreement.

2.3 Merchandise and Interior Installations to be purchased through Designer will be
     specified in a written "Proposal" prepared by Designer and submitted in each
     instance for Client's written approval. Each Proposal will describe the item and its
     price to Client (F.O.B. point of origin). The price of each item to Client ("Client
     Price") shall be the amount charged to Designer by the supplier of such item
     ("Supplier Price"), plus Designer's fee equal to _____ percent (____%) of the
     Supplier Price (exclusive of any freight, delivery or like charges or applicable tax).

ID123-1996   **2**

2.4 No item can be ordered by Designer until the Proposal has been approved by Client, in writing, and returned to Designer with Designer's required initial payment equal to _____ percent (___%) of the Client Price. The balance of the Client Price, together with delivery, shipping, handling charges and applicable taxes, is payable when the item is ready for delivery to and/or installation at Client's residence, or to a subsequent supplier for further work upon rendition of Designer's invoice. Proposals for fabrics, wall coverings, accessories, antiques, and items purchased at auction or at retail stores require full payment at time of signed Proposal.

3. Project Review

3.1 If the nature of the Project requires engagement by Client of any contractors to perform work based upon Designer's concepts, drawings or interior design specifications not otherwise provided for in the Interior Specifications and Purchasing Services, Client will enter into contracts directly with the concerned contractor. Client shall provide Designer with copies of all contracts and invoices submitted to Client by the contractors.

3.2 Designer will make periodic visits to the Project site as Designer may consider appropriate to observe the work of these contractors to determine whether the contractors' work is proceeding in general conformity with Designer's concepts. Constant observation of work at the Project site is not a part of Designer's duties. Designer is not responsible for the performance, quality, timely completion or delivery of any work, materials or equipment furnished by contractors pursuant to direct contracts with Client.

3.3 Designer shall be entitled to receive a fee equal to _____ percent (___%) of the amount to be paid by Client to each contractor performing any work based upon Designer's concepts, drawings, specifications ("Project Review Fees").

3.4 The Project Review Fees shall be payable by Client to Designer as follows:

4. MISCELLANEOUS

4.1 Should Designer agree to perform any design service not described above, such "Additional Service" will be invoiced to Client at the following hourly rates:

Design Principal	$_____
Project Designer	$_____
Staff Designer	$_____
Draftsman	$_____
Other employees	$_____

Hourly charges will be invoiced to Client _____ and are payable upon receipt of invoice.

ID123-1996   3

4.2   Disbursements incurred by Designer in the interest of the Project shall be reimbursed by Client to Designer upon receipt of Designer's invoices, which are rendered _____. Reimbursements shall include, among other things, costs of local and long distance travel, long distance telephone calls, duplication of plans, drawings and specifications, messenger services and the like.

4.3   Designer's drawings and specifications are conceptual in nature and intended to set forth design intent only. They are not to be used for architectural or engineering purposes. Designer does not provide architectural or engineering services.

4.4   Designer's services shall not include undertaking any responsibility for the design or modification of the design of any structural, heating, air-conditioning, plumbing, electrical, ventilation or other mechanical systems installed or to be installed at the Project.

4.5   Should the nature of Designer's design concepts require the services of any other design professional, such professional shall be engaged directly by Client pursuant to separate agreement as may be mutually acceptable to Client and such other design professional.

4.6   As Designer requires a record of Designer's design projects, Client will permit Designer or Designer's representatives to photograph the Project upon completion of the Project. Designer will be entitled to use photographs for Designer's business purposes but shall not disclose Project location or Client's name without Client's prior written consent.

4.7   All concepts, drawings and specifications prepared by Designer's firm ("Project Documents") and all copyrights and other proprietary rights applicable thereto remain at all times Designer's property. Project Documents may not be used by Client for any purpose other than completion of Project by Designer.

4.8   Designer cannot guarantee that actual prices for Merchandise and/or Interior Installations or other costs or services as presented to Client will not vary either by item or in the aggregate from any Client proposed budget.

4.9   This Agreement may be terminated by either party upon the other party's default in performance, provided that termination may not be effected unless written notice specifying nature and extent of default is given to the concerned party and such party fails to cure such default in performance within _____ (____) days from date of receipt of such notice. Termination shall be without prejudice to any and all other rights and remedies of Designer, and Client shall remain liable for all outstanding obligations owed by Client to Designer and for all items of Merchandise, Interior Installations and other services on order as of the termination date.

4.10   In addition to all other legal rights, Designer shall be entitled to withhold delivery of any item of Merchandise or the further performance of Interior Installations or any other services, should Client fail to timely make any payments due Designer.

ID123-1996   4

4.11 Any controversy or claim arising out of or relating to this Agreement, or the breach thereof, shall be decided by arbitration only in the _____ in accordance with the Commercial Arbitration Rules of the American Arbitration Association then in effect, and judgment upon the award rendered by the arbitrator(s) may be entered in any court having jurisdiction thereof.

4.12 Client will provide Designer with access to the Project and all information Designer may need to complete the Project. It is Client's responsibility to obtain all approvals required by any governmental agency or otherwise in connection with this Project.

4.13 Any sales tax applicable to Design Fees, and/or Merchandise purchased from Designer, and/or Interior Installations completed by Designer shall be the responsibility of Client.

4.14 Neither Client nor Designer may assign their respective interests in this Agreement without the written consent of the other.

4.15 The laws of the State of _____ shall govern this Agreement.

4.16 Any provision of this Agreement held to be void or unenforceable under any law shall be deemed stricken, and all remaining provisions shall continue to be valid and binding upon both Designer and Client.

4.17 This Agreement is a complete statement of Designer's and Client's understanding. No representations or agreements have been made other than those contained in this Agreement. This Agreement can be modified only by a writing signed by both Designer and Client.

5. ADDITIONAL TERMS

CLIENT:

_____

_____

DESIGNER:

_____

_____

ID123-1996 5

ASID Document ID124

RESIDENTIAL INTERIOR DESIGN
SERVICES AGREEMENT

SPECIAL INSTRUCTIONS REGARDING PAGE 2

Note that this Agreement contains two alternative paragraphs 1.2. Each alternative appears on a separate "Page 2." Except for Paragraph 1.2, the remaining language on each alternative "Page 2" is identical.

If Designer intends to charge a fixed fee for Design Concept Services, then (1) <u>carefully remove and discard the second "Page 2"</u>; and (2) <u>use the first "Page 2"</u> which contains the following language in Paragraph 1.2:

> *Prior to commencing Design Concept Services, Designer shall receive an Initial Design Fee of _____ dollars ($_____). This non-refundable Design Fee is payable upon signing this Agreement and is in addition to all other compensation payable to Designer under this Agreement. Not more than _____(____) revisions to the Design Concept will be prepared by Designer without additional charges. Additional revisions will be billed to Client as Additional Services.*

If Designer intends to charge hourly fees for Design Concept Services, then (1) <u>carefully remove and discard the first "Page 2"</u>; and (2) <u>use the second "Page 2"</u> which contains the following language in Paragraph 1.2:

> *Designer shall be compensated for its Design Concept Services on an hourly basis at the rates set forth in paragraph 4.1 of this Agreement. Hourly charges will be invoiced to Client _____ and are payable by Client upon receipt of invoice. Upon signing this Agreement, Designer shall receive a non-refundable initial advance of _____ dollars ($_____), which constitutes the minimum fee due Designer for Design Concept Services. This advance will be credited against hourly charges otherwise payable by Client to Designer for Design Concept Services.*

ID124-1996

ASID Document ID124

RESIDENTIAL INTERIOR DESIGN
SERVICES AGREEMENT

This **AGREEMENT** is

made this _____ day of_____ in the year of Two Thousand and _____

BETWEEN the **CLIENT**:
(name and address)

and the **DESIGNER**:
(name and address)

The **CLIENT** and the **DESIGNER** agree as follows:

The Project pertains to the following areas within Client's residence located at

_____:

(List areas below:)

INTERIOR DESIGN SERVICES

1. Design Concept Services

1.1 In this phase of the Project, Designer shall, as and where appropriate, perform the following:

A. Determine Client's design preferences and requirements.

B. Conduct an initial design study.

ID124-1996 1

C. Prepare drawings and other materials to generally illustrate Designer's suggested interior design concepts, to include color schemes, interior finishes, wall coverings, floor coverings, ceiling treatments, lighting treatments and window treatments.

D. Prepare layout showing location of movable furniture and furnishings.

E. Prepare schematic plans for recommended cabinet work, interior built-ins and other interior decorative details ("Interior Installations").

1.2 Prior to commencing Design Concept Services, Designer shall receive an Initial Design Fee of _____ dollars ($_____). This non-refundable Design Fee is payable upon signing this Agreement and is in addition to all other compensation payable to Designer under this Agreement. Not more than_____ (____) revisions to the Design Concept will be prepared by Designer without additional charges. Additional revisions will be billed to Client as Additional Services.

2. Interior Specifications and Purchasing Services

2.1 Upon Client's approval of the Design Concepts, Designer will, as and where appropriate:

A. Select and/or specially design required Interior Installations and all required items of movable furniture, furnishings, light fixtures, hardware, fixtures, accessories and the like ("Merchandise").

B. Prepare and submit for Client's approval Proposals for completion of Interior Installations and purchase of Merchandise.

2.2 Merchandise and Interior Installations specified by Designer shall, if Client wishes to purchase them, be purchased solely through Designer. Designer may, at times, request Client to engage others to provide Interior Installations, pursuant to the arrangements set forth in the Project Review services described in paragraph 3 of this Agreement.

2.3 Merchandise and Interior Installations to be purchased through Designer will be specified in a written "Proposal" prepared by Designer and submitted in each instance for Client's written approval. Each Proposal will describe the item and its price to Client (F.O.B. point of origin). The price of each item to Client ("Client Price") shall be the amount charged to Designer by the supplier of such item ("Supplier Price"), plus Designer's fee equal to _____ percent (____%) of the Supplier Price (exclusive of any freight, delivery or like charges or applicable tax).

2.4 No item can be ordered by Designer until the Proposal has been approved by Client, in writing, and returned to Designer with Designer's required initial payment equal to _____ percent (____%) of the Client Price. The balance of the Client Price, together with delivery, shipping, handling charges and applicable taxes, is payable when the item is ready for delivery to and/or installation at Client's residence, or to a subsequent supplier for further work upon rendition of Designer's invoice. Proposals for fabrics, wall coverings, accessories, antiques, and items purchased at auction or at retail stores require full payment at time of signed Proposal.

3. Project Review

3.1 If the nature of the Project requires engagement by Client of any contractors to perform work based upon Designer's concepts, drawings or interior design specifications not otherwise provided for in the Interior Specifications and Purchasing Services, Client will enter into contracts directly with the concerned contractor.

3.2 Designer will make periodic visits to the Project site as Designer may consider appropriate to observe the work of these contractors to determine whether the contractors' work is proceeding in general conformity with Designer's concepts. Constant observation of work at the Project site is not a part of Designer's duties. Designer is not responsible for the performance, quality, timely completion or delivery of any work, materials or equipment furnished by contractors pursuant to direct contracts with Client.

3.3 Time expended by Designer for all Project Review services will be charged to Client on an hourly basis at the rates set forth in paragraph 4.1 of the Agreement.

4. MISCELLANEOUS

4.1 Should Designer agree to perform any design service not described above, such "Additional Service" will be invoiced to Client at the following hourly rates:

Design Principal	$_____
Project Designer	$_____
Staff Designer	$_____
Draftsman	$_____
Other employees	$_____

Hourly charges will be invoiced to Client _____ and are payable upon receipt of invoice.

4.2 Disbursements incurred by Designer in the interest of the Project shall be reimbursed by Client to Designer upon receipt of Designer's invoices, which are rendered _____. Reimbursements shall include, among other things, costs of local and long distance travel, long distance telephone calls, duplication of plans, drawings and specifications, messenger services and the like.

ID124-1996   **3**

4.3 Designer's drawings and specifications are conceptual in nature and intended to set forth design intent only. They are not to be used for architectural or engineering purposes. Designer does not provide architectural or engineering services.

4.4 Designer's services shall not include undertaking any responsibility for the design or modification of the design of any structural, heating, air-conditioning, plumbing, electrical, ventilation or other mechanical systems installed or to be installed at the Project.

4.5 Should the nature of Designer's design concepts require the services of any other design professional, such professional shall be engaged directly by Client pursuant to separate agreement as may be mutually acceptable to Client and such other design professional.

4.6 As Designer requires a record of Designer's design projects, Client will permit Designer or Designer's representatives to photograph the Project upon completion of the Project. Designer will be entitled to use photographs for Designer's business purposes but shall not disclose Project location or Client's name without Client's prior written consent.

4.7 All concepts, drawings and specifications prepared by Designer's firm ("Project Documents") and all copyrights and other proprietary rights applicable thereto remain at all times Designer's property. Project Documents may not be used by Client for any purpose other than completion of Project by Designer.

4.8 Designer cannot guarantee that actual prices for Merchandise and/or Interior Installations or other costs or services as presented to Client will not vary either by item or in the aggregate from any Client proposed budget.

4.9 This Agreement may be terminated by either party upon the other party's default in performance, provided that termination may not be effected unless written notice specifying nature and extent of default is given to the concerned party and such party fails to cure such default in performance within _____ (____) days from date of receipt of such notice. Termination shall be without prejudice to any and all other rights and remedies of Designer, and Client shall remain liable for all outstanding obligations owed by Client to Designer and for all items of Merchandise, Interior Installations and other services on order as of the termination date.

4.10 In addition to all other legal rights, Designer shall be entitled to withhold delivery of any item of Merchandise or the further performance of Interior Installations or any other services, should Client fail to timely make any payments due Designer.

4.11 Any controversy or claim arising out of or relating to this Agreement, or the breach thereof, shall be decided by arbitration only in the _____ in accordance with the Commercial Arbitration Rules of the American Arbitration Association then in effect, and judgment upon the award rendered by the arbitrator(s) may be entered in any court having jurisdiction thereof.

ID124-1996 4

4.12 Client will provide Designer with access to the Project and all information Designer may need to complete the Project. It is Client's responsibility to obtain all approvals required by any governmental agency or otherwise in connection with this Project.

4.13 Any sales tax applicable to Design Fees, and/or Merchandise purchased from Designer, and/or Interior Installations completed by Designer shall be the responsibility of Client.

4.14 Neither Client nor Designer may assign their respective interests in this Agreement without the written consent of the other.

4.15 The laws of the State of _____ shall govern this Agreement.

4.16 Any provision of this Agreement held to be void or unenforceable under any law shall be deemed stricken, and all remaining provisions shall continue to be valid and binding upon both Designer and Client.

4.17 This Agreement is a complete statement of Designer's and Client's understanding. No representations or agreements have been made other than those contained in this Agreement. This Agreement can be modified only by a writing signed by both Designer and Client.

5. ADDITIONAL TERMS

CLIENT:

_____

_____

DESIGNER:

_____

_____

ID124-1996 5

ASID Document ID125

RESIDENTIAL INTERIOR DESIGN
SERVICES AGREEMENT

SPECIAL INSTRUCTIONS REGARDING PAGE 2

Note that this Agreement contains two alternative paragraphs 1.2. Each alternative appears on a separate "Page 2." Except for Paragraph 1.2, the remaining language on each alternative "Page 2" is identical.

If Designer intends to charge a fixed fee for Design Concept Services, then (1) <u>carefully remove and discard the second "Page 2"</u>; and (2) <u>use the first "Page 2"</u> which contains the following language in Paragraph 1.2:

> *Prior to commencing Design Concept Services, Designer shall receive an Initial Design Fee of _____ dollars ($_____). This non-refundable Design Fee is payable upon signing this Agreement and is in addition to all other compensation payable to Designer under this Agreement. Not more than _____(___) revisions to the Design Concept will be prepared by Designer without additional charges. Additional revisions will be billed to Client as Additional Services.*

If Designer intends to charge hourly fees for Design Concept Services, then (1) <u>carefully remove and discard the first "Page 2"</u>; and (2) <u>use the second "Page 2"</u> which contains the following language in Paragraph 1.2:

> *Designer shall be compensated for its Design Concept Services on an hourly basis at the rates set forth in paragraph 4.1 of this Agreement. Hourly charges will be invoiced to Client _____ and are payable by Client upon receipt of invoice. Upon signing this Agreement, Designer shall receive a non-refundable initial advance of _____ dollars ($_____), which constitutes the minimum fee due Designer for Design Concept Services. This advance will be credited against hourly charges otherwise payable by Client to Designer for Design Concept Services.*

ID125-1996

Appendix A: ASID Sample Interior Design Services Agreements

ASID Document ID125

RESIDENTIAL INTERIOR DESIGN SERVICES AGREEMENT

This **AGREEMENT** is

made this _____ day of _____ in the year of Two Thousand and _____

BETWEEN the **CLIENT**:
(name and address)

---

and the **DESIGNER**:
(name and address)

The **CLIENT** and the **DESIGNER** agree as follows:

The Project pertains to the following areas within Client's residence located at

_____ :

(List areas below:)

INTERIOR DESIGN SERVICES

1. Design Concept Services

1.1 In this phase of the Project, Designer shall, as and where appropriate, perform the following:

   A. Determine Client's design preferences and requirements.

   B. Conduct an initial design study.

ID125-1996   1

C. Prepare drawings and other materials to generally illustrate Designer's suggested interior design concepts, to include color schemes, interior finishes, wall coverings, floor coverings, ceiling treatments, lighting treatments and window treatments.

D. Prepare layout showing location of movable furniture and furnishings.

E. Prepare schematic plans for recommended cabinet work, interior built-ins and other interior decorative details ("Interior Installations").

1.2 Prior to commencing Design Concept Services, Designer shall receive an Initial Design Fee of _____ dollars ($_____). This non-refundable Design Fee is payable upon signing this Agreement and is in addition to all other compensation payable to Designer under this Agreement. Not more than_____ (____) revisions to the Design Concept will be prepared by Designer without additional charges. Additional revisions will be billed to Client as Additional Services.

2. Interior Specifications and Purchasing Services

2.1 Upon Client's approval of the Design Concepts, Designer will, as and where appropriate:

A. Select and/or specially design required Interior Installations and all required items of movable furniture, furnishings, light fixtures, hardware, fixtures, accessories and the like ("Merchandise").

B. Prepare and submit for Client's approval Proposals for completion of Interior Installations and purchase of Merchandise.

2.2 Merchandise and Interior Installations specified by Designer shall, if Client wishes to purchase them, be purchased solely through Designer. Designer may, at times, request Client to engage others to provide Interior Installations, pursuant to the arrangements set forth in the Project Review services described in paragraph 3 of this Agreement.

2.3 Merchandise and Interior Installations to be purchased through Designer will be specified in a written "Proposal" prepared by Designer and submitted in each instance for Client's written approval. Each Proposal will describe the item and its price to Client (F.O.B. point of origin) ("Client Price"). The Client Price for each item of Merchandise and Interior Installations includes a fee for services rendered in this phase of the Project.

2.4 No item can be ordered by Designer until the Proposal has been approved by Client, in writing, and returned to Designer with Designer's required initial payment equal to _____ percent (____%) of the Client Price. The balance of the Client Price, together with delivery, shipping, handling charges and applicable taxes, is payable when the item is ready for delivery to and/or installation at Client's residence, or to a subsequent supplier for further work upon rendition of Designer's invoice. Proposals for fabrics, wall coverings, accessories, antiques, and items purchased at auction or at retail stores require full payment at time of signed Proposal.

ID125-1996   2

3. Project Review

3.1 If the nature of the Project requires engagement by Client of any contractors to perform work based upon Designer's concepts, drawings or interior design specifications not otherwise provided for in the Interior Specifications and Purchasing Services, Client will enter into contracts directly with the concerned contractor. Client shall provide Designer with copies of all contracts and invoices submitted to Client by the contractors.

3.2 Designer will make periodic visits to the Project site as Designer may consider appropriate to observe the work of these contractors to determine whether the contractors' work is proceeding in general conformity with Designer's concepts. Constant observation of work at the Project site is not a part of Designer's duties. Designer is not responsible for the performance, quality, timely completion or delivery of any work, materials or equipment furnished by contractors pursuant to direct contracts with Client.

3.3 Designer shall be entitled to receive a fee equal to _____ percent (___%) of the amount to be paid by Client to each contractor performing any work based upon Designer's concepts, drawings or specifications ("Project Review Fees").

4. MISCELLANEOUS

4.1 Should Designer agree to perform any design service not described above, such "Additional Service" will be invoiced to Client at the following hourly rates:

Design Principal	$_____
Project Designer	$_____
Staff Designer	$_____
Draftsman	$_____
Other employees	$_____

Hourly charges will be invoiced to Client _____ and are payable upon receipt of invoice.

4.2 Disbursements incurred by Designer in the interest of the Project shall be reimbursed by Client to Designer upon receipt of Designer's invoices, which are rendered _____. Reimbursements shall include, among other things, costs of local and long distance travel, long distance telephone calls, duplication of plans, drawings and specifications, messenger services and the like.

4.3 Designer's drawings and specifications are conceptual in nature and intended to set forth design intent only. They are not to be used for architectural or engineering purposes. Designer does not provide architectural or engineering services.

4.4 Designer's services shall not include undertaking any responsibility for the design or modification of the design of any structural, heating, air-conditioning, plumbing, electrical, ventilation or other mechanical systems installed or to be installed at the Project.

ID125-1996 **3**

4.5 Should the nature of Designer's design concepts require the services of any other design professional, such professional shall be engaged directly by Client pursuant to separate agreement as may be mutually acceptable to Client and such other design professional.

4.6 As Designer requires a record of Designer's design projects, Client will permit Designer or Designer's representatives to photograph the Project upon completion of the Project. Designer will be entitled to use photographs for Designer's business purposes but shall not disclose Project location or Client's name without Client's prior written consent.

4.7 All concepts, drawings and specifications prepared by Designer's firm ("Project Documents") and all copyrights and other proprietary rights applicable thereto remain at all times Designer's property. Project Documents may not be used by Client for any purpose other than completion of Project by Designer.

4.8 Designer cannot guarantee that actual prices for Merchandise and/or Interior Installations or other costs or services as presented to Client will not vary either by item or in the aggregate from any Client proposed budget.

4.9 This Agreement may be terminated by either party upon the other party's default in performance, provided that termination may not be effected unless written notice specifying nature and extent of default is given to the concerned party and such party fails to cure such default in performance within _____ (____) days from date of receipt of such notice. Termination shall be without prejudice to any and all other rights and remedies of Designer, and Client shall remain liable for all outstanding obligations owed by Client to Designer and for all items of Merchandise, Interior Installations and other services on order as of the termination date.

4.10 In addition to all other legal rights, Designer shall be entitled to withhold delivery of any item of Merchandise or the further performance of Interior Installations or any other services, should Client fail to timely make any payments due Designer.

4.11 Any controversy or claim arising out of or relating to this Agreement, or the breach thereof, shall be decided by arbitration only in the _____ in accordance with the Commercial Arbitration Rules of the American Arbitration Association then in effect, and judgment upon the award rendered by the arbitrator(s) may be entered in any court having jurisdiction thereof.

4.12 Client will provide Designer with access to the Project and all information Designer may need to complete the Project. It is Client's responsibility to obtain all approvals required by any governmental agency or otherwise in connection with this Project.

4.13 Any sales tax applicable to Design Fees, and/or Merchandise purchased from Designer, and/or Interior Installations completed by Designer shall be the responsibility of Client.

4.14 Neither Client nor Designer may assign their respective interests in this Agreement without the written consent of the other.

4.15 The laws of the State of _____ shall govern this Agreement.

ID125-1996 4

4.16 Any provision of this Agreement held to be void or unenforceable under any law shall be deemed stricken, and all remaining provisions shall continue to be valid and binding upon both Designer and Client.

4.17 This Agreement is a complete statement of Designer's and Client's understanding. No representations or agreements have been made other than those contained in this Agreement. This Agreement can be modified only by a writing signed by both Designer and Client.

5. ADDITIONAL TERMS

CLIENT:

_____

_____

DESIGNER:

_____

_____

ID125-1996 5

ASID Document ID126

RESIDENTIAL INTERIOR DESIGN
SERVICES AGREEMENT

SPECIAL INSTRUCTIONS REGARDING PAGE 2

Note that this Agreement contains two alternative paragraphs 1.2. Each alternative appears on a separate "Page 2." Except for Paragraph 1.2, the remaining language on each alternative "Page 2" is identical.

If Designer intends to charge a fixed fee for Design Concept Services, then (1) <u>carefully remove and discard the second "Page 2"</u>; and (2) <u>use the first "Page 2"</u> which contains the following language in Paragraph 1.2:

> *Prior to commencing Design Concept Services, Designer shall receive an Initial Design Fee of _____ dollars ($_____). This non-refundable Design Fee is payable upon signing this Agreement and is in addition to all other compensation payable to Designer under this Agreement. Not more than _____(____) revisions to the Design Concept will be prepared by Designer without additional charges. Additional revisions will be billed to Client as Additional Services.*

If Designer intends to charge hourly fees for Design Concept Services, then (1) <u>carefully remove and discard the first "Page 2"</u>; and (2) <u>use the second "Page 2"</u> which contains the following language in Paragraph 1.2:

> *Designer shall be compensated for its Design Concept Services on an hourly basis at the rates set forth in paragraph 4.1 of this Agreement. Hourly charges will be invoiced to Client _____ and are payable by Client upon receipt of invoice. Upon signing this Agreement, Designer shall receive a non-refundable initial advance of _____ dollars ($_____), which constitutes the minimum fee due Designer for Design Concept Services. This advance will be credited against hourly charges otherwise payable by Client to Designer for Design Concept Services.*

ID126-1996

ASID Document ID126

RESIDENTIAL INTERIOR DESIGN SERVICES AGREEMENT

This **AGREEMENT** is

made this _____ day of_____ in the year of Two Thousand and _____

BETWEEN the CLIENT:
(name and address)

and the DESIGNER:
(name and address)

The **CLIENT** and the **DESIGNER** agree as follows:

The Project pertains to the following areas within Client's residence located at

_____ :

(List areas below:)

INTERIOR DESIGN SERVICES

1. Design Concept Services

1.1 In this phase of the Project, Designer shall, as and where appropriate, perform the
following:

    A. Determine Client's design preferences and requirements.

    B. Conduct an initial design study.

ID126-1996   **1**

C. Prepare drawings and other materials to generally illustrate
   Designer's suggested interior design concepts, to include color
   schemes, interior finishes, wall coverings, floor coverings, ceiling
   treatments, lighting treatments and window treatments.

D. Prepare layout showing location of movable furniture and
   furnishings.

E. Prepare schematic plans for recommended cabinet work, interior
   built-ins and other interior decorative details ("Interior Installations").

1.2 Prior to commencing Design Concept Services, Designer shall receive an Initial Design
Fee of _____ dollars (\$_____). This non-refundable
Design Fee is payable upon signing this Agreement and is in addition to all other
compensation payable to Designer under this Agreement. Not more than_____
(____) revisions to the Design Concept will be prepared by Designer without
additional charges. Additional revisions will be billed to Client as Additional Services.

2. Interior Specifications and Purchasing Services

2.1 Upon Client's approval of the Design Concepts, Designer will, as and
where appropriate:

A. Select and/or specially design required Interior Installations and
   all required items of movable furniture, furnishings, light fixtures,
   hardware, fixtures, accessories and the like ("Merchandise").

B. Prepare and submit for Client's approval Proposals for completion
   of Interior Installations and purchase of Merchandise.

2.2 Merchandise and Interior Installations specified by Designer shall, if Client wishes to
purchase them, be purchased solely through Designer. Designer may, at times,
request Client to engage others to provide Interior Installations, pursuant to the
arrangements set forth in the Project Review services described in paragraph 3 of this
Agreement.

INTERIOR DESIGN SERVICES

1. Design Concept Services

1.1 In this phase of the Project, Designer shall, as and where appropriate, perform the
following:

A. Determine Client's design preferences and requirements.

B. Conduct an initial design study.

ID126-1996 2

Appendix A: ASID Sample Interior Design Services Agreements

C. Prepare drawings and other materials to generally illustrate Designer's suggested interior design concepts, to include color schemes, interior finishes, wall coverings, floor coverings, ceiling treatments, lighting treatments and window treatments.

D. Prepare layout showing location of movable furniture and furnishings.

E. Prepare schematic plans for recommended cabinet work, interior built-ins and other interior decorative details ("Interior Installations").

1.2 Designer shall be compensated for its Design Concept Services on an hourly basis at the rates set forth in paragraph 4.1 of this Agreement. Hourly charges will be invoiced to Client _____ and are payable by Client upon receipt of invoice. Upon signing this Agreement, Designer shall receive a non-refundable initial advance of _____ dollars ($_____), which constitutes the minimum fee due Designer for Design Concept Services. This advance will be credited against hourly charges otherwise payable by Client to Designer for Design Concept Services.

2. Interior Specifications and Purchasing Services

2.1 Upon Client's approval of the Design Concepts, Designer will, as and where appropriate:

A. Select and/or specially design required Interior Installations and all required items of movable furniture, furnishings, light fixtures, hardware, fixtures, accessories and the like ("Merchandise").

B. Prepare and submit for Client's approval Proposals for completion of Interior Installations and purchase of Merchandise.

2.2 Merchandise and Interior Installations specified by Designer shall, if Client wishes to purchase them, be purchased solely through Designer. Designer may, at times, request Client to engage others to provide Interior Installations, pursuant to the arrangements set forth in the Project Review services described in paragraph 3 of this Agreement.

2.3 Merchandise and Interior Installations to be purchased through Designer will be specified in a written "Proposal" prepared by Designer and submitted in each instance for Client's written approval. Each Proposal will describe the item and its price to Client (F.O.B. point of origin) ("Client Price"). The Client price for each item of Merchandise and Interior Installations includes a fee for services rendered in this phase of the Project.

2.4 No item can be ordered by Designer until the Proposal has been approved by Client, in writing, and returned to Designer with Designer's required initial payment equal to _____ percent (____%) of the Client Price. The balance of the Client Price, together with delivery, shipping, handling charges and applicable taxes, is payable when the item is ready for delivery to and/or installation at Client's residence, or to a subsequent supplier for further work upon rendition of Designer's invoice. Proposals for fabrics, wall coverings, accessories, antiques, and items purchased at auction or at retail stores require full payment at time of signed Proposal.

ID126-1996 2

3. Project Review

3.1 If the nature of the Project requires engagement by Client of any contractors to perform work based upon Designer's concepts, drawings or interior design specifications not otherwise provided for in the Interior Specifications and Purchasing Services, Client will enter into contracts directly with the concerned contractor.

3.2 Designer will make periodic visits to the Project site as Designer may consider appropriate to observe the work of these contractors to determine whether the contractors' work is proceeding in general conformity with Designer's concepts. Constant observation of work at the Project site is not a part of Designer's duties. Designer is not responsible for the performance, quality, timely completion or delivery of any work, materials or equipment furnished by contractors pursuant to direct contracts with Client.

3.3 Time expended by Designer for all Project Review services will be charged to Client on an hourly basis at the rates set forth in paragraph 4.1 of the Agreement.

4. MISCELLANEOUS

4.1 Should Designer agree to perform any design service not described above, such "Additional Service" will be invoiced to Client at the following hourly rates:

Design Principal	$_____
Project Designer	$_____
Staff Designer	$_____
Draftsman	$_____
Other employees	$_____

Hourly charges will be invoiced to Client _____ and are payable upon receipt of invoice.

4.2 Disbursements incurred by Designer in the interest of the Project shall be reimbursed by Client to Designer upon receipt of Designer's invoices, which are rendered _____. Reimbursements shall include, among other things, costs of local and long distance travel, long distance telephone calls, duplication of plans, drawings and specifications, messenger services and the like.

4.3 Designer's drawings and specifications are conceptual in nature and intended to set forth design intent only. They are not to be used for architectural or engineering purposes. Designer does not provide architectural or engineering services.

4.4 Designer's services shall not include undertaking any responsibility for the design or modification of the design of any structural, heating, air-conditioning, plumbing, electrical, ventilation or other mechanical systems installed or to be installed at the Project.

ID126-1996 3

4.5 Should the nature of Designer's design concepts require the services of any other design professional, such professional shall be engaged directly by Client pursuant to separate agreement as may be mutually acceptable to Client and such other design professional.

4.6 As Designer requires a record of Designer's design projects, Client will permit Designer or Designer's representatives to photograph the Project upon completion of the Project. Designer will be entitled to use photographs for Designer's business purposes but shall not disclose Project location or Client's name without Client's prior written consent.

4.7 All concepts, drawings and specifications prepared by Designer's firm ("Project Documents") and all copyrights and other proprietary rights applicable thereto remain at all times Designer's property. Project Documents may not be used by Client for any purpose other than completion of Project by Designer.

4.8 Designer cannot guarantee that actual prices for Merchandise and/or Interior Installations or other costs or services as presented to Client will not vary either by item or in the aggregate from any Client proposed budget.

4.9 This Agreement may be terminated by either party upon the other party's default in performance, provided that termination may not be effected unless written notice specifying nature and extent of default is given to the concerned party and such party fails to cure such default in performance within _____ (___) days from date of receipt of such notice. Termination shall be without prejudice to any and all other rights and remedies of Designer, and Client shall remain liable for all outstanding obligations owed by Client to Designer and for all items of Merchandise, Interior Installations and other services on order as of the termination date.

4.10 In addition to all other legal rights, Designer shall be entitled to withhold delivery of any item of Merchandise or the further performance of Interior Installations or any other services, should Client fail to timely make any payments due Designer.

4.11 Any controversy or claim arising out of or relating to this Agreement, or the breach thereof, shall be decided by arbitration only in the _____ in accordance with the Commercial Arbitration Rules of the American Arbitration Association then in effect, and judgment upon the award rendered by the arbitrator(s) may be entered in any court having jurisdiction thereof.

4.12 Client will provide Designer with access to the Project and all information Designer may need to complete the Project. It is Client's responsibility to obtain all approvals required by any governmental agency or otherwise in connection with this Project.

4.13 Any sales tax applicable to Design Fees, and/or Merchandise purchased from Designer, and/or Interior Installations completed by Designer shall be the responsibility of Client.

4.14 Neither Client nor Designer may assign their respective interests in this Agreement without the written consent of the other.

4.15 The laws of the State of _____ shall govern this Agreement.

ID126-1996   4

4.16 Any provision of this Agreement held to be void or unenforceable under any law shall be deemed stricken, and all remaining provisions shall continue to be valid and binding upon both Designer and Client.

4.17 This Agreement is a complete statement of Designer's and Client's understanding. No representations or agreements have been made other than those contained in this Agreement. This Agreement can be modified only by a writing signed by both Designer and Client.

5. ADDITIONAL TERMS

CLIENT:

_____

_____

DESIGNER:

_____

_____

ID126-1996 5

Appendix B:

ASID Code of Ethics and Professional Conduct

1.0 Preamble

Members of the American Society of Interior Designers are required to conduct their professional practice in a manner that will inspire the respect of clients, suppliers of goods and services to the profession and fellow professional designers, as well as the general public. It is the individual responsibility of every member of ASID to uphold this code and bylaws of the Society.

2.0 Responsibility to the Public

2.1 Members shall comply with all existing laws, regulations and codes governing business procedures and the practice of interior design as established by the state or other jurisdiction in which they practice.

2.2 Members shall not seal or sign drawings, specifications or other interior design documents except where the member or the member's firm has prepared, supervised or professionally reviewed and approved such documents, as allowed by applicable laws, rules and regulations.

2.3 Members shall at all times consider the health, safety and welfare of the public in spaces they design. Members agree, whenever possible, to notify property managers, landlords, and/or public officials of conditions within a built environment that endanger the health, safety and/or welfare of occupants. If, during the course of a project, a Member becomes aware of an action to be taken by, or on behalf of the Member's client, which in the Member's reasonable opinion is likely to result in a material adverse effect on the health, safety and welfare of persons occupying or using the space, the Member shall refuse to consent to, or participate in that action, and if required by law and/or under circumstances the Member deems reasonably prudent to do so, the Member shall report such action to the governmental agency having jurisdiction over the project.

2.4 Members shall not engage in any form of false or misleading advertising or promotional activities.

2.5 Members shall neither offer, nor make any payments or gifts to any public official, nor take any other action, with the intent of unduly influencing the official's judgment in connection with an existing or prospective project in which the members are interested.

2.6 Members shall not assist or abet improper or illegal conduct of anyone in connection with any project.

3.0 Responsibility to the Client

3.1 Members' contracts with clients shall clearly set forth the scope and nature of the projects involved, the services to be performed and the methods of compensation for those services.

3.2 Members shall not undertake any professional responsibility unless they are, by training and experience, competent to adequately perform the work required.

3.3 Members shall fully disclose to a client all compensation that the member shall receive in connection with the project and shall not accept any form of undisclosed compensation from any person or firm with whom the member deals in connection with the project.

3.4 Members shall not divulge any confidential information about the client or the client's project, or utilize photographs of the client's project, without the permission of the client.

3.5 Members shall be candid and truthful in all their professional communications.

3.6 Members shall act with fiscal responsibility in the best interest of their clients and shall maintain sound business relationships with suppliers, industry and trades.

4.0 Responsibility to Other Interior Designers and Colleagues

4.1 Members shall not interfere with the performance of another interior designer's contractual or professional relationship with a client.

4.2 Members shall not initiate, or participate in, any discussion or activity that might result in an unjust injury to another interior designer's reputation or business relationships.

4.3 Members may, when requested and it does not present a conflict of interest, render a second opinion to a client or serve as an expert witness in a judicial or arbitration proceeding.

4.4 Members shall not endorse the application for ASID membership and/or certification, registration or licensing of an individual known to be unqualified with respect to education, training, experience or character, nor shall a member knowingly misrepresent the experience, professional expertise of that individual.

4.5 Members shall only take credit for work that has actually been created by that member or the member's firm, and under the member's supervision.

4.6 Members should respect the confidentiality of sensitive information obtained in the course of their professional activities.

5.0 Responsibility to the Profession

5.1 Members agree to maintain standards of professional and personal conduct that will reflect in a responsible manner on the Society and the profession.

5.2 Members shall seek to continually upgrade their professional knowledge and competency with respect to the interior design profession.

5.3 Members agree, whenever possible, to encourage and contribute to the sharing of knowledge and information between interior designers and other allied professional disciplines, industry and the public.

6.0 Responsibility to the Employer

6.1 Members leaving an employer's service shall not take drawings, designs, data, reports, notes, client lists or other materials relating to work performed in the employer's service except with permission of the employer.

6.2 A member shall not unreasonably withhold permission from departing employees to take copies of material relating to their work while employed at the member's firm, which are not proprietary and confidential in nature.

6.3 Members shall not divulge any confidential information obtained during the course of their employment about the client or the client's project or utilize photographs of the project, without the permission of both client and employer.

7.0 Enforcement

7.1 The Society shall follow standard procedures for the enforcement of this code as approved by the ASID Board of Directors.

7.2 Members having a reasonable belief, based upon substantial information, that another member has acted in violation of this code, shall report such information in accordance with accepted procedures.

7.3 Any violation of this code, or any action taken by a member which is detrimental to the Society and the profession as a whole, shall be deemed unprofessional conduct subject to discipline by the ASID Board of Directors.

7.4 If the Disciplinary Committee decides the concerned Member did not violate the Society's Code of Ethics and Professional Conduct, it shall dismiss the complaint and at the concerned Member's request, a notice of exoneration from the complaint shall be made public. If the Disciplinary Committee decides that the concerned Member violated one or more provisions of the Society's Code of Ethics and Professional Conduct, it shall discipline the concerned Member by reprimand, censure, suspension or termination of membership. The Disciplinary Committee may, in its discretion, make public its decision and the penalty imposed. The Disciplinary Committee does not impose any other form of penalty. The Disciplinary Committee cannot require payment of any monies or mandate certain action to be taken by the concerned Member.

Notes

Chapter 1

1. National Federation of Independent Business (NFIB): The Voice of Small Business. http://www.411sbfacts.com/speeches.html#q1

2. U.S. Small Business Administration. FAQs: Frequently Asked Questions. Advocacy Small Business Statistics and Research.

3. U.S. Small Business Administration. FAQs: Frequently Asked Questions. Advocacy Small Business Statistics and Research.

4. National Federation of Independent Business (NFIB). Small business facts. http://www.nfib.com/object/smallBusinessFacts

5. National Federation of Independent Business (NFIB). Small business facts. http://www.nfib.com/object/smallBusinessFacts

6. U.S. Small Business Administration. FAQs: Frequently Asked Questions. Advocacy Small Business Statistics and Research.

7. U.S. Small Business Administration. http://www.sba.gov/smallbusinessplanner/plan/getready/SERV_ SBPLANNER_ISENTFORU.html

Chapter 2

American Society of Interior Designers. 2007. "The interior design profession: Facts and figures."

Chapter 3

Adam Lerner. "Marketing your design firm: How to brand yourselves as well as you brand your clients."
http://www.core77.com/reactor/0506_lerner.asp

Bibliography

For those readers interested in further exploration of the subjects discussed in this book, the following books may be of help.

Business Planning

Abrams, Rhonda. *The Successful Business Plan: Secrets and Strategies.* The Planning Shop, 2003.

Bangs, David H. *Business Plans Made Easy.* Entrepreneur Press, 2005.

Hendricks, Mark. *Business Plans Made Easy.* Entrepreneur Press, 2002.

Friend, Graham, and Stefan Zehle. *Guide to Business Planning.* Entrepreneur Press, 2005.

McKeever, Mike. *How to Write a Business Plan.* NOLO, 2008.

Stutely, Richard. *The Definitive Business Plan: The Fast Track to Intelligent Business Planning for Executives and Entrepreneurs.* FT Press, 2007.

Strategic Planning

Barksdale, Susan, and Teri Lund. *10 Steps to Successful Strategic Planning.* ASTD Press, 2006.

Bradford, Robert W., and J. Peter Duncan. *Simplified Strategic Planning: The No-Nonsense Guide for Busy People Who Want Results Fast.* Chandler House Press, 2000.

Johnson, John E., and Smith, Anne Marie. *60 Minute Strategic Plan.* 2006

Olsen, Erica. *Strategic Planning for Dummies.* For Dummies, 2006.

Financial Planning

Alderman, Robert L. *How to Prosper as an Interior Designer: A Business and Legal Guide.* Wiley, 1997.

Alderman, Robert L. *How to Make Money at Interior Design.* Van Nostrand Reinhold Publishing, 1982.

Williams, Theo Stephan. *The Interior Designer's Guide to Pricing, Estimating and Budgeting.* Allworth Press, 2005.

Starting a Business

Harper, Stephen C. *The McGraw-Hill Guide to Starting Your Own Business: A Step-By-Step Blueprint for the First-Time Entrepreneur.* McGraw-Hill, 2003.

Kennedy, Joe. *The Small Business Owner's Manual: Everything You Need to Know to Start Up and Run Your Business.* Career Press, 2005.

Norman, Jan. *What No One Ever Tells You about Starting Your Own Business: Real-Life Start-Up Advice from 101 Successful Entrepreneurs.* Kaplan Business, 2004.

Pakroo, Peri. *Small Business Start-Up Kit.* NOLO, 2008.

Steingold, Fred. *Legal Guide for Starting & Running a Small Business.* NOLO, 2008.

Turner, Marcia Layton. *The Unofficial Guide to Starting a Small Business.* Wiley, 2004.

Human Resources and Employee Relations

Duane, Michael J. *Customized Human Resource Planning: Different Practices for Different Organizations.* Quorum Books, 1996.

Falcone, Paul. *96 Great Interview Questions to Ask Before You Hire.* AMACON, 2008.

Fyock, Cathy. *The Truth About Hiring the Best.* FT Press, 2007.

Hiring and Keeping the Best People. Harvard Business School Press, 2003.

Hoevermeyer, Victoria A. *High-Impact Interview Questions: 701 Behavior-Based Questions to Find the Right Person for Every Job.* AMACON, 2005.

Snider, Marvin. *Human Relations Management in Young, Growing Companies: A Manual for Entrepreneurs and Executives.* Quorum Books, 2001.

Marketing

Goldstein, Beth. *The Ultimate Small Business Marketing Toolkit: All the Tips, Forms, and Strategies You'll Ever Need.* McGraw-Hill, 2007.

Gordon, Kim T. *Maximum Marketing, Minimum Dollars: The Top 50 Ways to Grow Your Small Business.* Kaplan Business, 2006.

Jantsch, John. *Duct Tape Marketing: The World's Most Practical Small Business Marketing Guide.* Thomas Nelson, 2008.

McMurty, Jeanette Maw. *Big Business Marketing For Small Business Budgets.* McGraw-Hill, 2003.

Stephenson, James. *Entrepreneur Magazine's Ultimate Small Business Marketing Guide: 1500 Great Marketing Tricks That Will Drive Your Business Through the Roof.* Entrepreneur Press, 2003.

Branding

Beals, Jeff. *Self Marketing Power: Branding Yourself as a Business of One.* Keynote Publishing, 2008.

Beckwith, Harry, and Christine Clifford Beckwith. *You, Inc.: The Art of Selling Yourself.* Business Plus, 2007.

Hammond, James. *Branding Your Business: Promoting Your Business, Attracting Customers and Standing Out in the Market Place.* Kogan Page, 2008.

Montoya, Peter, and Tim Vandehey. *The Brand Called You: The Ultimate Brand-Building and Business Development Handbook to Transform Anyone into an Indispensable Personal Brand.* Personal Branding Press, 2003.

Sartain, Libby, and Mark Schumann. *Brand From the Inside: Eight Essentials to Emotionally Connect your Employees to Your Business.* Jossey-Bass, 2006.

Wheeler, Alina. *Designing Brand Identity: A Complete Guide to Creating, Building, and Maintaining Strong Brands.* Wiley, 2006.

Internet Marketing and Websites

Antion, Tom. *The Ultimate Guide to Electronic Marketing for Small Business: Low-Cost/High Return Tools and Techniques that Really Work.* Wiley, 2005.

Claxton, Lena, and Alison Woo. *How to Say It: Marketing with New Media. A Guide to Promoting Your Small Business Using Websites, E-zines, Blogs and Podcasts.* Prentice Hall Press, 2008.

Hise, Phaedra. *Growing Your Business Online: Small-Business Strategies for Working the World Wide Web.* Owl Books, 1996.

Growing and Managing Your Business

Drucker, Peter F. *Managing for the Future*. Elsevier Limited, 1993.

Drucker, Peter F. *Management Challenges for the 21st Century*. Collins Business, 2001.

Flamholtz, Eric G., and Yvonne Randle. *Growing Pains: Transitioning from an entrepreneurship to a professionally managed firm*. Jossey-Bass, 2007.

Hawken, Paul. *Grow a Business*. Simon and Schuster, 1988.

Henricks, Mark. *Grow Your Business*. Entrepreneur Press, 2001.

Henricks, Mark. *Entrepreneur Magazine's Growing Your Business: A Step-by-Step Guide to Success*. Entrepreneur Media, 2001.

LeBlanc, Mark. *Growing Your Business!* Expert Publishing, Inc., 2003.

Sherman, Andrew. *Complete Guide to Running and Growing Your Business*. Crown Business, 1997.

Succession and Exit Planning

Atwood, Christee Gabour. *Succession Planning Basics*. ASTD Press, 2007.

Hawkey, John. *Exit Strategy Planning: Grooming Your Business for Sale or Succession*. Gower Publishing, 2002.

Leonetti, John M. *Exiting Your Business, Protecting Your Wealth: A Strategic Guide for Owners and Their Advisors*. Wiley, 2008.

Pokras, Sandy. *Crisp: Systematic Succession Planning: Building Leadership from Within*. Crisp Learning, 1996.

Rothwell, William J. *Effective Succession Planning: Ensuring Leadership Continuity and Building Talent From Within*. AMACON, 2005.

Rothwell, William J., Robert D. Jackson, Shaun C. Knight, and John E. Lindholm. *Career Planning and Succession Management: Developing Your Organization's Talent—for Today and Tomorrow*. Praeger Publishers, 2005.

Selling a Business

Heslop, Andrew. *How to Value and Sell Your Business: The Essential Guide to Preparing, Valuing and Selling a Company for Maximum Profit*. Kogan Page, 2008.

Laabs, James. *The Business Sale System: Insider Secrets to Selling Any Small Business*. First American Publishing, 2006.

Lipman, Frederick. *Valuing Your Business: Strategies to Maximize the Sale Price*. Wiley, 2005.

Steingold, Fred S. *The Complete Guide to Selling a Business*. NOLO, 2007.

Index

Accounting and accountants, 16,
    29–30, 109, 131, 156
    finding an, 29–30
Adesso Design Inc., 53–54
Advertising, 85, 88
Alvarado, Leonard and Sue, 114–115
American & International Designs,
    Inc., 14
American Institute of Architects
    (AIA), 123
American Society of Interior Designers
    (ASID), ix, x, 4, 8–9, 17, 20–22,
    31, 33–34, 36, 38, 45–46, 49–50,
    53, 94–97, 103, 105, 117–118, 125,
    129, 132–135, 142, 151, 173–179,
    181, 184
    Code of Ethics, 91–92, 181–184
    Document ID123: Residential
        Interior Design Services
        Agreement, 173–179
Ames, Michael, 4
Anderson, Stephanie, 134–136
Angel investor, 130
Appraisers, business, 154–158
Arann, Susan Huckvale, 14–18
Arce, Hugo, 8–9
Association of Registered Interior
    Designers of Ontario (ARIDO),
    46, 49
Attorneys, 29–30, 109, 119, 120, 131
    finding, 29–30

Baker Tilley Virchow Krause (formerly
    Virchow Krause & Company), 131

Barbara Goodman Designs, Inc.,
    115–117
Bautista, Bob, 68, 71
Beaton, Tom, 39
Benefits, 139–140
Berle, Gustav, 5
Bill Behrle Associates, 129
Billing, 13–18
Boyer, Diane, 129–131
Branding, 59–73, 123
    competitive impact, 61
    parts of a brand, 62
    what is a brand, 60
Brigham, Bruce J., 81–83
Brokers, 157–158
    12 questions to ask, 158
Brown, Bunyan, Moon & More
    (BBM&M), 67–71
Browne, Debra, 20–22
Bruck, Eva Doman, 21
Bruss, Stephanie, 109–110
Bullock Associates Design Consultants,
    Inc., 46–48
Bullock, Doug, 46–48
Bureau of Labor Statistics, 4
Business managers, 93, 105
Business planning, 5–6, 68, 113, 127,
    151
    evaluating strengths and weaknesses,
        5
    vs. strategic planning, 5–6
Business structure, 40, 113, 130, 153
    organizational chart, 113, 130, 153
Buying a business, 151–152

Carpenter, Charles C., 23–25
Carson Guest Interior Design Services, Inc., 9–10
Catlin Design, Inc., 105–107
Catlin, Juliana, 105–107
Chute Gerdeman Retail, 41–43
Chute, Elle, 41–43
Cini, Lisa, 103–105
Clients and customers, 50–57, 80, 106
   communicating with, 50–56, 80
   customer service, 106
   fundamentals for effective relationships, 50–51
   long–term relationships, 53–57
CME Appraisals, 50
Cole Martinez Curtis and Associates (CMCA), 121–123
Cole, Jill I., 121–123
Collaboration, 12, 43–46, 119, 122
Compensation:
   for interior designers, by state, 133–135
   in contracts, 22
   payroll and benefits, 39, 104–105, 136, 139
Competitive research, 72
Computers, see Technology, computers
Consultants 9, 12, 39, 72, 93, 105, 116, 119, 120, 143, 162–163
Contract magazine, 132
Contract Office Group (COG), 114–115
Contracts, 16–18, 20–22, 160, 174–179
   ASID Document ID123: Residential Interior Design Services Agreement, 22, 173–179
   assigning responsibility, 22
   compensation arrangements, 22
   describing the project, 21
   identifying parties, 21
   listing specific services, 21
   specifications, purchasing, budget and schedule, 22
Cooper, Craig, 48–50
Council for Interior Design Accreditation (CIDA), ix, 75
Crawford, Tad, 21
Creative Business Interiors, 134–136
Culture, corporate, 123–124
Curtis, Kati, 14–17

D SCALE, 51
Daroff Design Inc. + DDI Architects PC, 11–12
Daroff, Karen, 11–12

David–Michael Design Inc., 167–170
Dealerships, 111–117, 134–136
Designers Furniture Gallery, 91–93
Designs of the Interior (DOTI), 109–110
Diamond, Jack, 118
Diane Boyer Interiors LLC, 129–131, 136
Domus Design Group, 78–81
Drexel Heritage, 116
Duffy Design Group, 51–52
Duffy, Dennis, 51–52
Duncan, Kim, 111–113

Ecoworks Studio, 45–46
EHS Design (formerly Emick Howard & Seibert, Inc.), 140–142
Elements IV Interiors, 111–113
Emick, Jack, 140–142
Employee handbooks, 92, 137
Employee stock ownership program (ESOP), 152, 162
E–newsletters, 73, 84–85, 88
Entrepreneurship, 5
Environmental scanning, 8–9
Essential Futures, 159–161
Ethics, 37, 91–93, 181–184
   ASID Code of Ethics and Professional Conduct, 181–184
Exit strategies, 7–8, 148, 161–167

Facilities Connection, 161–167
Falk, JJ, 63–67
Fees, 13–18, 109
Financial planning, 10–12, 14–17, 120
Firm structure, 10–11, 38–40
Franchises, 102–103, 107–110
   becoming a franchisee, 107
   becoming a franchisor, 107
   evaluating a package, 109
   selecting a, 108–109
Frank, Dina, 123–124
Furniture Services Unlimited, 116

Gerdeman, Dennis, 41–43
Gilman, Richard, 131–132
Gianotti, Wayne, 114
Goff, Bruce, 78–81
Goodman, Barbara Cresswell, 115–117
Gott, Donna, 168–190
Grigsby, Mary Jane, 53–54
Growth, 7, 101–148
   acquisitive, 102–103
   deciding to, 101
   how to, 102

kinds of, 102–103, 107
organic, 102–103
planning, 7, 101, 124
sustaining, 121–127
transitions, 129–148
Guest, Rita Carson, 9–10

Hansen, Marilyn Schooley, 91–93
Harrison Browne Interior Design, Ltd.,
    20
Harrison, Barry, 83–86
Haworth, Inc., 111–112, 114–115,
    161–167
HEDGE Design Collective, 43–44
Heilborn, Jim, 30–31
Hiring, 26, 30–36, 39, 93, 102–104,
    106–107, 112–116, 124, 126, 136,
    159–160, 170
  finding candidates, 32–33
  mistakes, 43–44
  narrowing candidates, 35
  process, six steps, 30–31
  questions, 30–31
Hirsch, John, 43–44
Holland–Branch, Patricia, 161–163,
    167
Home Grown Store, The, 8
Horner, Martin, 39–40
Howard, Mindy, 140
Human resources, 77, 132, 136–140
  consultants, 132, 136–137
  management software, 77
Hurowitz, Bruce, 85–87

Insurance, 18–20, 139–140, 152
  buying, 18–20
  coverage types, 18–20
Insurance Exchange, The, 18
Interior design business statistics, ix, 4
Interior design registration laws, 94–96
International Facility Management
    Association (IFMA), 23, 103
International Franchise Association,
    108
International Interior Design
    Association (IIDA), 31, 51, 63, 75,
    84, 103, 105, 117, 123
Internet, see Web sites
Interviewing, 30–31

JJ Falk Design LLC, 63–67
Jim Heilborn Associates, 30
Joan Lloyd & Associates, 35–36
Job descriptions, 34, 145–147
Johnson Consulting Services, 5–6

Johnson, Jill, 5–6
Jones, Carlie Bullock, 45–46

Kathryn Scott Design Studio, 14
King, Jack, 112
Knacksteadt, Mary V., 21
Knoll, 134
KSA Interiors, 151–154

Larry Wilson Design Associates,
    117–119
LEED, 34, 45–46
Letter of intent, 121
Licensing, certification and registration,
    9, 37, 93–97
  state laws, 94–96
Limited Liability Corporation (LLC),
    10, 63, 131
Location, office:
  choosing a, 23–25
  leasing strategies, 24
  multiple offices, 80, 102–013
  rent calculation, 23
Lonsway Consulting, 40
Lonsway, Kris, 40
Lloyd, Joan, 35–36
Lusk, Nancy, 168–169

Madigan, David–Michael, 167–170
Management systems, 40, 143
Mancini Duffy, 123–124
Marketing, 26, 28, 71–74
  e–newsletters, 73, 84–85, 88
  online, 80, 82–91
McCabe John, 114
Mergers and acquisitions, 102–103, 107,
    117–121, 142, 152
  preparing for, 118–121
Merlino Design Partnership, 85–87
Miles & Stockbridge, PC., 119–121
Miller, Steven, 54–55
Milton I. Swimmer Planning and
    Design, Inc./Swimmer Cole
    Martinez Curtis and Associates,
    122
Minority–owned business programs,
    162
Mirza, Romana, 60–63
Mission statement, 64, 66
Mosaic Design Studio, 103–105

Name recognition, 73
National Council for Interior Design
    Qualifications (NCIDQ), ix, 75,
    94, 124

National Foundation for Independent Business (NFIB), 4
Networking, 74–76, 85
Next Step LLC, 39
Nirmada Interior Architecture and Design, 14–17
Norfolk, John, 135

Office Furniture USA, 112
Outsourcing, 33, 112
Ownership transition, 114–115, 160

Palladeo, 67–71
Partnerships 26, 111–112, 117, 123
Patterson House Design Group, 36–38
    Distinctive Decors, 37
Patterson, Diana L., 36–38
Personnel:
    management, 136–140
    manuals, 137–139
Peterson–Arce Design Group, 8–9
Peterson, B.J., 8–9
Planning:
    business, 6–7
    financial, 10–12, 14–17, 120
    market, 6
    strategic, 6–10, 39, 124, 143, 162
Processes/standardization, 39–42, 47, 143–144, 163–167
Policies and guidelines, 92, 137–139
Professional employer organizations, 136
Professional organizations, 74–76
Project management, 12, 38–43, 168
Public relations, 12, 38–43, 71–74, 168

Rabaut Design Associates, 31–32
Rabaut, Jo, 31–32
Rappoport, Jim, 12
Rainho, Tony, 47–48
Renwall Interiors Limited, 47–48
Resolve Digital, 83–86
Retail Clarity Consulting, 81–83
Retainer, 15
Retirement planning, 8
RINK Design Partnership Inc. (Rink Reynolds Diamond Fisher), 117–119
Risk, 18–20
Rottler, Paul, 67–68, 71
Russel, Dorothy, 159–161

S Corporation, 10
Schelberg, Charles B., 119–121
Schirippa, Anthony, 123–124
Schoenadel, Kim, 151–154

Schoessler Lynn, Rachelle, 33–34
SCORE, 127–128
Scott, Kathryn, 14–17
Seibert, Paul, 142
Sechrist Design Associates, 142–148
Sechrist, Melinda and T. Michael, 142–148
Seigel, Alan M., 21, 91
Seigel, Harry, 21
Selling a business, 154–158
    preparing to sell, 156
Sheridan Interiors, Inc., 4
Sheridan, Judy, 4
Simmons, Steve, 154–158
SJvD Design, 55–57
Slifer Designs, 87–91
Slifer, Beth, 87–91
Small business statistics, 4
Society for Human Resource Management (SHRM), 136, 140
Sole proprietorship, 36–38
Soucie Horner Ltd., 39–40
Soucie, Shea, 39–40
Space International, 43–44
Starting a design business, 1–127
Steven Miller Design Studio (SMDS), 54–55
Strategic alliances, 102, 122
Strategic planning, 5–10
Studio 2030, 33–34
Studio Pinpoint Consulting, 60–63
Succession planning, 152, 159–160, 170
Suppliers, 46–50, 128
Sustainable design, 33–34, 87–88, 115
Swimmer, Milton I., 121

Team building, 29–33, 119
Technology:
    computers, 76–80, 83
    integrating in the workplace, 59, 76–97
    internet, 76–80, 83. See also Web sites
    office equipment, 76–80, 82
Thomas, Michael, 91
TRIO Design Group, 167–170

U.S. Bureau of Labor Statistics, 132
U.S. Census Bureau, 4
U.S. Department of Commerce, 107
U.S. Small Business Administration, 4, 5, 108

Valuation, 120, 154–158
van Dijs, Sybil, 55–57

Vendors, 46–50, 128
Visioning, 71
Volunteerism, 32, 74–75, 143

Web sites, 38, 48, 65–66, 72–73, 76,
    80–87, 125–127, 157
  blogs, 73, 84, 89–90
  branding, 65–66, 87–80
  e–newsletters, 73, 84–85, 88
  online retail, 91
  search engine optimization, 84–85
Welsh, Jeremy, 18
West, Lena L., 76–78

Williams, Mark, 112
Wilson Associates, 125–127
Wilson, John, 8
Wilson, Larry and Laurie, 117–119
Wilson, Trisha, 125–127
Women's Business Enterprise (WBE),
    11, 112

xyno Media, 76–78

Zimmerman, Jr., Gary, 134
Zweig White, 27
Zweig, Mark, 25–27